Auto Brand

Auto Brand

Building successful car brands for the future

Anders Parment

LONDON PHILADELPHIA NEW DELHI

First published in Great Britain and the United States in 2014 by Kogan Page Limited

2nd Floor, 45 Gee Street	1518 Walnut Street, Suite 1100	4737/23 Ansari Road
London EC1V 3RS	Philadelphia PA 19102	Daryaganj
United Kingdom	USA	New Delhi 110002
www.koganpage.com		India

© Anders Parment, 2014

ISBN   978 0 7494 6929 0
E-ISBN   978 0 7494 6930 6

British Library Cataloguing-in-Publication Data

A CIP record for this book is available from the British Library.

Library of Congress Cataloging-in-Publication Data

Parment, Anders, 1972-
  Auto brand : building successful car brands for the future / Anders Parment
    pages cm
  Includes bibliographical references
  ISBN 978-0-7494-6929-0 – ISBN 978-0-7494-6930-6 (ebk)   1. Automobiles–Marketing.   2. Automobile industry and trade.   I. Title.
    HD9710.A2P256 2014
    629.222068'8–dc23

                                                                              2013043356

Typeset by Graphicraft Limited, Hong Kong
Print production managed by Jellyfish
Printed and bound in the UK by CPI Group (UK), Croydon, CR0 4YY

CONTENTS

PREFACE

I've been dealing with the automotive industry on a professional basis since I started writing my doctoral dissertation in 1999 ('Car distribution organization', Linköping University, 2005). I had the privilege to travel and carry out extensive case studies on automobile marketing in Germany, the United Kingdom, Spain, Australia and Sweden. Since 2002 I've been working more intensively as a consultant for automobile companies and related businesses – insurance, finance, inspection and repairs, industry organizations, etc. As author, speaker and columnist I've also had the opportunity to hear from others in the industry. And there are many opinions out there!

My experience is that the car industry, like many other industries, is hardworking and multi-faceted with some inherent difficulties when it comes to adapting to new circumstances. Recently, I worked with an international insurance company that still hadn't understood the meaning of value-based pricing – using excellent risk calculations, the insurance company set prices with no regard to competitors' prices and buyers' willingness to pay. Limited competition and, maybe the most important explanation, low buyer purchase involvement makes the insurance company very profitable and customer loyalty is, given the high transparency these days, surprisingly high. Why would a car or house owner change insurance company? Insurance is not something people think about every day. Cars, on the other hand, are typical high-involvement products. And car companies know very well how to build strong brands, how to charge premium prices, how to keep residual values high, and how to keep customers happy. The main problems are very tough competition, overcapacity and low marginal production costs – all car companies have strong incentives to increase sales.

How can an auto brand be successful and stay competitive in this very tough industry? This book emphasizes the business aspects of the key challenges the car industry is facing while taking the broader picture into account, something that should make the book appealing to the general business reader. The book is well-founded in research and best practice and, of course, particularly appealing to the car company manager. I hope this book will give some understanding of key market characteristics and the interplay between supply and demand along with an understanding of the mechanisms that create strong brands and make them successful.

In summer 1999 I visited Konstanz in the very southern part of Germany to see some friends in the International Business Programme. I spent an entire day in the extensive library, but surprisingly (or maybe not) among the hundreds of books on the automotive industry, there weren't any that dealt with the problems mentioned above. Even worse, more recent research and industry reports have shown a lack of understanding of the problems that go back to the supply-demand imbalance: industry reports that show the benefits and problems of pull strategies are nice to read, but not very useful for managers who have to deal with the tough competition in the industry on a daily basis.

In writing this book, I've interviewed and talked to hundreds of people in Australia, Germany, the United States (New York and California), Austria, Switzerland, Norway, Finland, Denmark, the United Kingdom, Spain, France and Brazil – the international dimension has made it mostly inspiring, but also a little frustrating, to write this book.

I hope you'll enjoy reading the book. If you have any questions or points to make, don't hesitate to contact me at info@andersparment.com

Introduction

The car – once everybody's dream and a key status symbol – has been subject to intense scrutiny, in particular in recent years. Urbanization, traffic congestion, pollution problems, heavy reliance on scarce oil supplies, safety issues and lack of parking space, have provided challenges for politicians, urban planners, car makers, pedestrians, consumers and companies in their efforts to organize transport, logistics and healthy living. There is little doubt that the car has been a key target in discussions on these matters. At the same time, consumers, inspired by developments in other industries, have increased their demands in terms of quality, safety, design and environmental-friendliness in cars, and strong consumer protection and easy access to up-to-date information on products and offers have placed extra power in the hands of consumers.

Authorities are forcing car makers to produce cars that are more environmentally friendly and the tax burden on car use is getting heavier – in many countries public opinion now favours heavy taxes on car ownership and use, in contrast to strong criticism of car taxation in the 1960s and 1970s. Consumer movements have made the public's voice crucial in many decisions related to the car, along with other significant stakeholders such as political policy-makers, city planners and those concerned with safety and environmental issues.

Popular culture is slowly moving away from cars as symbols of affluent living, a common theme in movies and television programmes that appeal to younger people particularly. Young consumers show a declining interest in cars and the percentage of people with a driving licence is going down in Western countries.

But what about the future? Extensive changes in consumer behaviour, product characteristics and public policy-making may be a huge opportunity for proactive companies that understand what is going on and have the courage to apply new approaches that make sense in the emerging competitive landscape. While the future of the car seems to be in some doubt, there are nevertheless many reasons to have high hopes for its future. First, although urbanization across the world is likely to continue, many people – even in bigger cities – need a car to organize their lives, get to work, and see clients, family and friends. Second, an increasing portion of world-wide economic activity is taking place in non-Western economies where the problems mentioned above certainly are substantial, but the overall desire for, and acceptance of, cars is considerably higher, at least so far. Third, most car makers are taking environmental issues seriously. The fuel efficiency of cars is getting better while safety improves, not least thanks to the integration of new technologies in cars. Many countries and cities are developing sustainable strategies for traffic to make sure there will be a balance between public and private transport in the future. In addition, cars are increasingly being developed to meet customers' desire for fuel-efficiency, safety and quality – attractive design and an emotional appeal alone do not make sales any more.

The lack of a genuine interest in cars among young car buyers in many countries has forced some car makers to fundamentally rethink their design and marketing approaches in an attempt to regain acceptance. Mercedes-Benz is running a fashion week in key markets, and by hiring celebrities and attractive locations the company hopes to regain a strong position in popular culture. Citroën is introducing numerous new models in the colourful DS series, BMW has launched innovative i3 and i8 models and all car makers are focusing on design to make sure their cars appeal to today's customers. That being said, many challenges remain. There are numerous elements of the car industry that could take advantage of new technologies, adapt to emerging trends in consumer behaviour and improve profitability.

This book takes a closer look at a number of issues related to how companies in the car industry – manufacturers, dealers, importers, finance companies, emerging types of brokers, car pools, etc – can take advantage of what is going on. Companies that contribute to making sure that the car retains a strong functional role in society and develops a great emotional appeal will benefit from the insights on consumer behaviour, market channel effectiveness, product packaging and competitive advantage presented in the book. The book also deals with issues such as how the automotive industry can be a great place to work for young people when other opportunities appear to be more attractive – empirical evidence suggests that few companies in the sector are seen as attractive by employees. Also, issues related to how the transition towards new, more environmentally-friendly alternative fuels can be forced through in the face of political and public resistance will be dealt with. With all the criticism that the car has been subject to it is very important to take seriously the issues to which car companies have paid scant attention in developing an agenda for future competitiveness.

The answers to the problems faced by the industry largely lie in its own hands, or at least those of the more proactive companies. Success will depend on the market and how car makers, dealers and others adjust their business models and ways of thinking to new realities. One thing is certain: there will be more than one way to achieve success, and a broad sweep of inspiration, from within and outside the industry, will contribute to great solutions. Open-minded managers will raise tough questions and think about clever solutions. For instance: will car makers and their marketing channel partners continue to spend 20 per cent of a car's retail price on marketing and advertising, or go for value for money and superior product performance that could have greater market potential? Increased consumer awareness and market transparency give less room for overcharging consumers – so how can attractive consumer offers be created under these circumstances? How will cars be sold in the future? Will the complex car purchase (trading-in, preparation, maintenance, etc) strengthen the proactive dealer's advantage, or will other marketing channels take over?

Ten challenges for the car industry

Before we begin, here is a brief look at 10 key challenges facing the car industry.

1. Dealing with overcapacity

Extensive manufacturing overcapacity – estimated to be between 50 and 60 per cent – puts strong pressure on car makers to sell lots of cars. Over time, the cost of developing new cars has increased while the marginal cost of producing an extra unit has gone down; hence car makers have strong incentives to achieve high sales figures. This is a key factor in understanding the very intense competition in the car industry.

Many new ideas for automobile retailing have been put forward, and while some of them are great, others have little likelihood of success. One new idea is the move from push to pull systems. In the 1990s and the beginning of the new millennium car makers announced that a transition to a pure order-to-delivery system would save a lot of money: estimates suggested about €1,000 per car (Ciferri, 2002; Parment, 2009). Selling cars on the internet or at IKEA, Bauhaus or Carrefour was also discussed. Extensive cost calculations proved that the elimination of the dealer, often called 'lean distribution', would save enormous amounts of money. However, this line of reasoning did not take into account the competitive situation or manufacturing overcapacity: it was based on a restricted analysis that looked at push vs pull as if it were purely a choice of selling either pre-produced cars from stock or cars produced to order.

2. Finding the balance between marketing and branding and short-term sales volume

The enormous pressure to strengthen the brand and at the same time maintain high sales volumes is a key challenge for all players in the industry. The larger a brand is in terms of market share, the more difficult it is to grow – hence numerous car makers have introduced new brands (Lexus, Infinity, Smart, Dacia) or taken over or merged with companies that make it possible to use brands with a strong tradition (Rolls Royce, Skoda, Mini). In this way, benefits from economies of scale can be combined with offering a broad range of attractive brands, reaching many segments in a competitive market.

Profitability in competitive markets during a crisis

It's common sense in business overall and in the car industry in particular that strong brands lay the foundation of successful sales. At the same time, car makers struggle with high sales targets. Unless there is a boom in the market – which means there may be a reasonable balance between supply and demand – even strong brands with attractive products and offers struggle to reach those targets.

Assume a car maker has a global market share of 3 per cent and aims at 3.5 for the upcoming year: 1.7 million cars are to be produced and marketing programmes are designed to reflect that goal. For a specific market area with 20 million inhabitants and an estimated sales level of 500,000 cars, the national sales company has, under heavy pressure from the factory, decided to increase market share from 7 to 9 per cent – an increase from 35,000 to 45,000 cars; not a problem with a strong brand and an attractive product portfolio, it is argued. Sales managers often overstate the market potential for the brand they're representing, something that has several explanations: the personality of sales managers; the pressure put upon them – from senior managers but also the social environment – to perform; and a myopic attitude that fails to see any weaknesses in their brands and the strengths of competitors. The year starts with a financial crisis, real economic problems and increasing unemployment rates. Competitors are desperate to fight for market share, something that can't compensate for the 25 per cent loss in overall market sales volume, ie 375,000 cars sold. A rebate war starts and even premium brands are available at 15 to 20 per cent discount on the price list. Nobody can win this war, so margins erode while only a few small players manage to keep their market share. The goal of 45,000 cars would translate into 33,750 if the market share of 9 per cent is going to be kept. However, assuming the attractiveness of the brand and product portfolio are maintained compared to the competition, only 26,250 units could be expected to be sold – 7 per cent of the 375,000 units. Heavy discounts lower the value of new and used cars in stock, and so residual values go down, something that annoys individual buyers and fleet car companies. This all contributes to reducing the attractiveness and price premium of the brand.

3. Becoming sustainable – from image to substance

Given the trend for the car to lose its role as a status symbol in many parts of the world, it is likely that it will undergo a transition from image to substance – the car must deliver not only on emotional content but also upon promises and expectations related to its functional characteristics and the environment.

Over time, manufacturers of 'emotional' cars have experienced increased demands from buyers to deliver on functional characteristics. Of course, there will always be a substantial part of any offer that appeals on either functional or emotional criteria, but in general terms, car buyers are demanding and require a degree of both. If at one time a Jaguar or Porsche were forgiven for being delivered with poor head lights, an inefficient heating system or other functional or quality-related limitations, buyers now won't accept that. Luckily, both Jaguar and Porsche now offer great products, and even niche, low volume brands such as Maserati can deliver high quality cars that deliver performance, design and reliability at an acceptable cost over the lifecycle.

We've seen many industries undergo a transition from something exclusive and glamorous to commodities: white goods, mobile phones and air travel to mention a few. When a product loses its role as a status symbol, an increasing number of buyers see it as a low- rather than high-involvement product. The former are characterized by lower consumer interest, less perceived differences between brands and buyers not spending a lot of time researching before they make the purchase decision – and they are less likely to engage heavily after the purchase to get confirmation of having made the right choice (see Holmes and Crocker, 1987; Kotler *et al*, 2011, 2013; Rotschild, 1979). Younger buyers have a lower involvement in the car purchase than older buyers (Parment, 2013a). Traditional wisdom suggests that car makers, particularly those with upmarket ambitions, want buyers to see the car as a high-involvement item. Such a purchase is characterized by buyers spending a lot of time and effort on finding the right product, and that social and other risks, financial in the case of a car, are considered before the purchase decision is made. The high-involvement product is often important for the buyer's image, making it very important for the seller to emphasize the emotional qualities of the product.

There are many signs of commoditization in the car industry, particularly so in the Western world, while the situation in emerging countries is more multifaceted. Commoditization gives room for companies that offer functional products with a limited emotional appeal. A fast purchase decision and fewer concerns over not having made the right decision give opportunities for sellers that offer high availability, fast delivery and affordable prices (Parment and Söderlund, 2010). The movement of people to metropolitan areas, increased competition from other products in terms of time, money and attention, and fewer young people having a driving licence speak for a continued commoditization.

To reach genuine sustainability, cars must deliver not only on functional and emotional purchase criteria, but also reflect a higher awareness of the environmental and social consequences of extensive car use. The latter will be crucial since an increasing number of car buyers are taking the environmental implications of car use into account in making purchase decisions.

4. Dealing with simultaneous pressure to be efficient, customer-oriented and build strong brands

Cost efficiency on the one hand and the communication of brand values on the other constitute two fundamental demands on automobile companies in dealing with markets – and they are in many cases conflicting. The tension between branding and a cost focus affects almost any decision in the car industry. For instance, demands on branding speak for dedicated, solus franchising dealer networks while cost minimization may be more easily accomplished in a multi-franchise dealer network. However, it's not really that easy: multi-franchising may incur higher costs than solus franchising and multi-franchising may give advantages in reaching new customers, as displaying one car brand with others gives access to customers the first brand would not reach in a solus franchising setting.

Another instance of this tension is car makers announcing a new model but not advertising a price – the traditional wisdom of premium brands. But stiff competition forces them to advertise prices and soon they are part of a never-ending discount war. It's happening increasingly often.

Pricing in the service department, direct marketing activities, the profile of sales people, the brands of lubricants and tyres provided in the dealership – all these decisions have brand and cost implications. Tensions don't always have to be solved – and in many cases they can't be – and they can be productive.

Tensions between roles and departments may be constructive

The business literature often focuses on eliminating or reducing conflicts and finding solutions to problems. But in the real world, tensions across departments and organizational layers are commonplace and may even be useful. Common tensions exist between top management and middle managers (although not always explicit), between product design and sales, and between metro and rural areas, in addition to the type of tensions this book deals with: that between car makers and dealers, and between marketing and sales.

Wileman and Jary propose a creative balance between branding and cost focus as a solution to the dominance of the trading philosophy in retailing:

> *The trading philosophy focuses on the short-term maximisation of sales and profits. The brand management philosophy focuses on building long-term customer loyalty and customer preference, and thereby on the long-term maximisation of brand and business value. The two philosophies need to be in balance – or in a state of constant creative tension.*

> (Wileman and Jary, 1997: 1)

The fact is that tensions may result in great compromises – and it's unlikely that a sales manager or a marketing manager without knowing about the influence of the other would create better decisions than when tension exists.

A reactive dealer will have a tough job in dealing with the simultaneous pressure to implement the car manufacturer's corporate identity and branding programmes and dealing with the competition and trying to make the business viable. A dealer that doesn't have the upper hand with the car maker or customers has a tough time and has to balance branding and attempts to sell cars.

There is a way out and larger dealers with access to resources can regain strength by taking a proactive attitude and seeing the tension as an opportunity. At the end of the day, all companies in the industry have to deal with difficult branding vs sales trade-offs. Proactive companies and individuals have the chance to change existing ideas about who is in power by taking the lead, eg proactive car dealers that use their market and negotiating power in relation to car makers. A Swedish car dealer, Holmgrens Bil, once sold two brands, Saab and Opel, but realized that these two brands wouldn't secure a viable retail business in the future. By building one of Scandinavia's largest automobile dealerships along the heavily used E4 road in Jönköping (most traffic between Sweden's largest cities Stockholm and Gothenburg goes that way) and taking on several new brands, a very strong position was created when the dealership was launched in 2004. It was a very proactive stance given that Jönköping has 130,000 inhabitants. Holmgrens Bil is selling 10 brands in a multi-franchised environment, which focuses on finding the right car for the customer rather than fulfilling manufacturer requirements. Now, Holmgrens Bil has the upper hand in discussions with car makers. Once a year or so, Holmgrens Bil hands back franchise contracts that don't make sense in terms of profitability and makes room for new, more attractive franchise contracts.

This proactive strategy is turning conventional ideas about who has the upper hand upside-down. Instead of seeing the dealer as having to agree to what car makers and customers want, Holmgrens Bil, like many other dealer groups, runs tough negotiations with car makers and doesn't hesitate to close down relationships that prove unprofitable – but always in a pleasant, professional way, since it knows car makers may come back when they realize what they're missing in terms of market presence and sales.

While many car manufacturers and some of the downstream actors are busy with brand-building programmes and similar, sales volume appears to be the overriding logic, in particular when there is a downturn in the economy. People all the way from the car maker CEO to salespeople are focused on sales volume. Hence it appears to be more important to reach high sales targets than to be profitable.

5. Urbanization

More than half the world's population lives in big cities and the percentage increases day by day. In bigger cities, people rely less on the car and more on public transport for getting to work, seeing relatives and friends, and leisure activities. This doesn't mean the car is not a necessary means of transport, but for many individuals public transport is more useful and the disadvantages of having a personal car in terms of cost and inconvenience are significantly higher than in towns and rural areas.

Fewer individuals have a driver's licence – there is no absolute need to have one and the social pressure to do so is limited. Car ownership is more expensive – insurance premiums, parking, servicing and inspections are all more expensive and car tolls are increasingly used. Lobbyists and organizations critical of cars are often located in metro areas.

New-build apartments (2012) at Lindhagen in Stockholm offer double-park slots in the building's garage for SEK 1,800 (c €200) a month – the resident shares a parking spot with a neighbour not of the resident's choosing, meaning that when one needs the car it may be blocked by the neighbour's car. This is a small but very interesting sign of the car losing its role as a symbol of freedom, in metro areas in particular: who wants to move the neighbour's car every time they want to use their own car?

While a couple of decades ago middle and senior managers were in general expected to live in a suburb, it's now common sense to live in city centres. The Upper East Side in Manhattan, New York or Kensington, London have for centuries been seen as attractive city locations, desired by many and affordable to the happy few. This way of living has recently become widespread in metro and city areas. Data from Germany prove that senior managers – in the job market or retired – increasingly want to live in downtown districts, something that is boosting prices for apartments (Stocker, 2012). A similar development is found in many other countries too.

Urbanization is likely to contribute to reducing the image and emotional appeal of the car in general, so car makers and car dealers have strong reasons to reconsider their strategies and see how they can contribute to mobility in the future.

6. Understanding mobility and car culture in the future

Key to understanding the future is going beyond the current state of thinking and knowing more about future trends, what is going on in the market and likely developments than one's competitors. Apple founder Steve Jobs has been both praised and criticized for his management style – it has been widely argued that his style was not always in line with his stated ambitions of creating a better world (eg the well-known episodes of chasing staff in bare feet with a fire extinguisher). Nonetheless, it remains clear that Steve Jobs was very good at understanding customers, the market and future opportunities – in most cases before anybody else did.

Integration with other modes of transport is a crucial part of the car industry's future. In recent years, car pools have gained a strong foothold in many larger cities, but integration with other modes of transport is very limited. Car-pooling shares the financial and ownership logic of other modes of transport – although there may be a membership fee for the car pool, it's basically free to use the service to the extent one wants to, and it can, like rental cars which normally can be hired one way, be combined with other modes of transport. Somebody living in Zürich could go by train to Paris, rent a car in central Paris, leave it in Marseilles, fly back to Zürich Airport, and then drive a pool car home (or take a taxi). It's not like a private (or company) car where the owner takes on many obligations and high fixed costs.

The increased interest in car pools and other creative mobility solutions has a number of driving forces: improved technologies for sharing cars, less status in having a car, and increased costs of driving (rising tax, car tolls), parking and taking care of a car in a city centre – these are all indications of lower interest in cars, something that gives a reactive dealer strong reasons to scale down the business. Proactive companies – dealers or other sellers – see the changes as a huge opportunity to gain a market foothold, develop competitive advantage, build a loyal customer base, and earn money.

7. Learning from and cooperating with other industries

Once upon a time car makers could survive on their own by building a strong position in the market. In the best case a company became successful by protecting itself from the competition, hence making its market position difficult to target for competitors. With high market transparency, fast communication and aware buyers it is increasingly difficult to create passive protection from competition; rather, it's recognized that strong competition improves a company and makes the industry overall more attractive to a variety of stakeholders. So, what can the car industry learn from other industries? A lot, probably. And it has learnt a lot over the years – while other industries have learnt from the car industry. If the industry itself doesn't learn a lot from other industries, buyers will bring expectations founded on experiences from other industries, hence infusing the industry with new demands and inputs.

Industry boundaries are ever-changing and, over time, increasingly overlap. Banks start insurance companies, companies in the insurance sector start banks, and car finance companies have begun selling cars. New industries emerge while old ones struggle to stay competitive. The car industry will increasingly have to work with other industries to make sure connectivity, safety and environmental issues are dealt with – but also to make sure that users can enjoy the benefits of immediate traffic information, listening to podcasts while driving, downloading new software for improved functionality of the car, or gaining the benefits of integrating different modes of transport.

In addition to the extensive cooperation that takes place among car makers, there is a lot of evidence that cooperation with other players downstream and upstream is beneficial. The view on competition has changed in recent years, something that has gained companies' attention as well as attention from researchers. It's now seen as a natural part of a well-functioning industry to have demanding buyers, competitors, authorities and other stakeholders. Car makers are all deeply involved in cooperation with competitors in a way nobody would have thought of a few decades ago. Who would imagine that Mercedes-Benz and BMW would start cooperating on hybrid technology to stay competitive with Toyota/Lexus? Who would imagine that most of the engines in the Volvo V40 are from Ford (petrol) or Ford/Peugeot/Citroën (diesel)[1], or that BMW delivers diesel engines for Europe-produced Toyotas?

8. Applying a modern view on competition

Car buyers are increasingly aware, enlightened individuals who know how to take advantage of the opportunities that today's society gives them: they know when and how to shop around, compare deals and prices, and the opportunities and risks associated with different choices. And they evince flexible purchase patterns – it gets increasingly difficult to forecast purchases based on the demographic profile of a buyer.

There are many great German expressions such as *'Erfahrung is nur eine Spielerei der Nostalgie'* (meaning that referring to experience is nostalgic instead of dealing with the future), *'Ja-sager brauche ich keine'* (I don't want people who don't question my decisions) and *'Die Konkurrenz schläft nicht'* (competitors aren't sleeping) – all of them apply to the car industry and its lack of ability to adapt to changes. The latter is particularly interesting since many people working in the industry still have an arrogant attitude towards competitors and their products. This approach has two rules: 1) never confess that a competitor is doing better than you except when it's obvious; 2) always strive to be more 'premium' if you can.

Why are these problems severe? They reduce the attractiveness of the industry and effectively hinder development and innovations. Regarding the first rule, an Audi boss said, 'We don't compete with Volvo' in reply to a question from a journalist. Although Audi is considered more premium than Volvo in general, the Audi Q5 and Volvo XC60 are close competitors in some markets, and in 2008, the Volvo V70 T6 beat the Audi A6 3.2 in a test in the German *auto motor & sport* magazine. Exception or not, qualified people found the Volvo better than the Audi. 'Skoda is not our competitor' is a typical Volvo dealer statement – however, with heavy discounts, a Volvo V70 may be cheaper than a comparable Skoda Superb in some markets and it's a fact that a substantial number of potential Volvo buyers are looking around, in many cases taking Skodas into consideration.

The second rule drives costs and turns buyers off. It sometimes seems like the marketing department is happier with the premium profile than many of the customers. A 38-year-old engineer, and Audi owner for 14 years, says: 'I can't buy an Audi again; obviously they don't want me as a customer. Their customer magazine is overloaded with €10,000 watches and Guide Michelin dinners. Inspections are overpriced. I'm a family father of three children and I want to live a normal life' – and this person certainly has a higher income than the average Audi buyer.

Premium marques have worked consistently with their brands, and everything that is visible is thought through. They are profitable and successful.

However, this doesn't mean every brand benefits from presenting itself as 'having an aggressive strategy to become premium'. At the end of the day, that's a race not everybody could win. The only recent example of a volume brand becoming a genuine premium brand is Audi. That's a solid performance but it took as least 25 years to get there (it started around 1980). Toyota is certainly slightly 'more premium' than 30 years ago, and Mercedes has gone for the mass markets and lost a bit of its premium feel.

Volvo's position is unclear but remains somewhere between volume and premium; the same holds for Volkswagen. In both cases the brands are 'less premium' in their home markets. Brands go up and down, and increasingly broad model ranges emphasize the difficulties in categorizing brands. Peugeot and Renault compete on price in many countries with the Clio, Megane, 208, 308, etc, but also offer more exclusive products such as the RCZ and the diesel hybrid 508 RHX. Fiat has gained strength recently and while Mercedes obviously has lost a large part of its price premium (and quality-performance advantage) for the lower spec A, B, C and E cars, its strong premium position in the higher segments is unchallenged. The number of competitors may have increased but Mercedes' core values remain. The 2014 new S Class inherits traditional Mercedes values in terms of design, safety and comfort.

In fact, a new Toyota, Holden, Cadillac or Nissan may not only compete with other new cars – which may be more or less premium – but also with just about any other product, at least when consumers buy cars. A two-week trip to China, a new kitchen, 10 days in the Alps, summer studies at a great university for the kids – or just keeping the old car and saving the money – there are many options. The less interest individuals show in cars, the less likely they will change cars just for the sake of showing off. Urbanization contributes to this too, as described earlier.

In fact, new car buyers dislike salespeople who give little or no help apart from promoting their company's own products. Studies show that buyers dislike salespeople being pushy, late, deceitful, and unprepared or disorganized. The qualities they value most include good listening skills, empathy, honesty, dependability, thoroughness and follow-through.[2] This should include an understanding of buyers and why they make the choices they make – including going for competitors' products. Multi-franchised dealers may reduce the influence of one-brand salespeople and result in more balanced consumer recommendations. However, while product specialization becomes less significant and advice may appear more balanced, the salesperson still bases recommendations on margins and bonuses.

Michael Porter's (1980) best-selling book on competitive strategy was very influential. He examines a number of methods for limiting competition by building entry barriers to the market (advantages of scale, patents, raw materials, etc) and by establishing a unique market position. The main message of the book – which contains well-known models such as the five forces model that describes competition in a typical industry, and the generic strategies of cost leadership, differentiation or niche focus – is that companies that protect themselves from competition are successful.

One decade later, Porter published *The Competitive Advantage of Nations*, which provides a fundamentally different view on competition. The interplay between the company and its environment, including competitors, creates clusters, and demanding customers contribute to strengthening competitiveness. The Swedish heavy trucks industry is used as an example. Subcontractors, infrastructure and support businesses have made the development of competitive heavy trucks possible. The situation with two equal players – Scania and Volvo – resulted in tough negotiations, such as when a bus company invited a tender for 80 buses from Scania and Volvo and the manufacturers were forced to make particularly strong efforts to acquire the order. Porter's view of the benefit of clusters underlines the value of an interplay between demanding customers and competitors. In reality, this interplay is exercised by the organization's employees, on occasion via contacts with partner companies.

There is no doubt the view on competition has changed over time, largely from keeping a position and protecting it from competition to an understanding of the benefits of cooperating with companies within or outside the industry in which the company is operating.

9. Making money in transparent, commoditized markets

For many years the new car market has been subject to intense competition – and it has become more intense recently. A decade ago or so, competition in services related to car ownership such as servicing, inspection and repairs was limited in many markets, except in the United States where a mass market has existed for some time. Increasing competition is largely driven by aware and well-informed customers as well as increased transparency. Buyers now shop around to get a good deal for new brake pads, an inspection or a new catalytic converter. An attitude change has taken place, driven by a complex set of factors: more information, more legal rights, television programmes that emphasize consumer rights, sellers more open with pricing, internet price comparison sites, and last but not least, a change from being loyal to the local dealer to finding the best deal. Dealerships are discussed and ranked on internet forums, so there is little room for convincing buyers unless a genuinely great offer is available.

Finance and insurance have for a long time provided opportunities for profitable business, but they're also challenged by increased transparency and a tendency among customers to shop around. For insurance, laws restricting commission have been introduced in many countries, removing a rather insignificant contribution to dealer incomes.

There are at least four things a dealership can do to maintain or strengthen its competitive position under the present circumstances:

a Be faster and more flexible than competitors in responding to buyers' requests for products, prices and time slots.

b Offer a greater range and higher quality of services than competitors. The former may only be provided by actors of a significant size.

c Be cheaper: lower prices and a satisfactory service performance will always work, particularly in the car industry with aware customers, high market transparency and intensive competition in all aspects of the business.

d Through bundling: by tying different parts of the car business to each other, a lock-in effect is created. It may certainly be an effective way of keeping customers, but if it's taken too far it will irritate them and be seen as abusing market power. Examples of bundling are discounts on finance or insurance when bringing the car to the authorized repair shop for inspection; free breakdown assistance if the service schedule is followed and the car brought to the dealer for servicing; free software upgrades if the car maker/dealer's insurance product is bought, and combinations of the above. Bundling may be a very effective way of keeping customers loyal – additional services may be cheap to offer but valuable to customers and in addition increase dealer showroom traffic.

10. Attracting key talent

As the car is losing its attractiveness among young people, the car industry will find it harder to recruit great talent. There is a strong correlation between the attractiveness of a company as a corporate brand and how it is seen from an employer brand perspective (Parment and Dyhre, 2009). Overall, being attractive to different stakeholders will become increasingly important in the future as society is getting more transparent and ideas, customer feedback, offers and other important inputs to profitable businesses will spread faster across customers, industries and cultures.

The car industry has some generic disadvantages compared to other industries. First, workplace location is an important criteria for young people when looking for a job: 39 per cent say workplace location is a very important ideal employer criterion (Schewe *et al*, 2013) (see Figure 0.1), and dealers like car NSCs (national sales companies) and car makers are often located in areas at a distance from city centres, where qualified workers increasingly want to live (Parment and Dyhre, 2009). Second, flexibility is limited: workers' attempts to combine work life with a family and children may be difficult with increasing pressure on dealerships to be open late at night and during weekends. This is a very general problem in retailing – opening hours tend to get longer overall. Car dealers may have to consider long opening hours but without all services being available. Third, the reputation of the car industry is certainly better than some other industries, but it doesn't automatically add to a person's image and a key criterion for young individuals is being proud to say for whom they work – personal branding is increasingly important (Parment, 2011a). The brand, too, brings certain standards to the job so selling a premium brand in an area with high socio-economic standards is likely to give a higher status than working for a weaker brand.

FIGURE 0.1 'Very important' in describing an ideal employer according to individuals born in the late 1980s; sample from the United States, New Zealand and Sweden

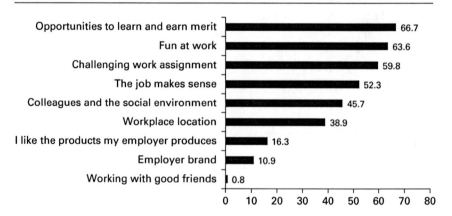

There are several elements in building the brand of an employer: the car brand or brands it represents, the position in the marketing channel (car maker, NSC, manufacturer-owned dealership, franchised dealer), and the context – working for Ford in Australia, Brazil, Poland or Canada may be perceived differently. In addition, dealers may have reputations based on what they did in the past, eg a very strong connection to a brand or a geographic area. All in all, actors in the car industry have to make sure they are attractive to key talent by identifying their strengths and weaknesses and attempting to present themselves in a way that attracts and retains the right talent.

Car companies tend to attract people who love cars, while they need people with a broad mindset. Positions as marketing managers, sales managers and brand managers are often occupied by individuals with a great interest in cars. However, sometimes their understanding of society and how it develops, the economy in general, popular culture, how people live and what the car means for an average customer of their brand/product range is very limited. What the industry needs is people with a broader outlook, interested in redefining the role of the car in society, not keeping to the status quo since that is unlikely to work.

In Germany, car companies are seen as great places to work. In the 2013 Universum Communications survey, BMW and Audi were the most liked employers among business and engineering students; Porsche third for the former and fourth for the latter; and Volkswagen sixth for both student groups.[3] As in most countries, a limited set of professions are subject to employer attractiveness rankings, while car makers and dealers need to recruit key talents in a broad range of professional fields; nonetheless, ideal employer rankings are good indications of how the attraction develops. There is a strong connection between consumer brand and employer brand. This applies in almost any market. The reason Google, BMW, Apple and IKEA are seen as 'great places to work' in many countries[4] is partly to do with the qualities of these employers, but also to a large extent the strong consumer brands they represent. The stronger an employer's presence in consumer markets, the more likely it will be seen as an attractive employer (Parment, 2009, 2013b).

A note on methods and the selection of material

This book, by its very nature, does not cover every aspect of auto brands, the car and its future. Although the book is rich with examples, there are many markets, auto brands and competitive dimensions that are not dealt with in detail. The car, the most significant technological artefact of the 20th century, has a range of meanings and implications, socially, economically, culturally and for society and sustainability. But there is a limit to the extent of material, references, research and text that this book can provide – the primary purpose of the book is to give numerous rich examples, illustrations and insights to the general business reader.

Despite efforts to create as logical a structure to the book as possible, there is an unavoidable arbitrariness to the organization of the ideas and insights presented. Making auto brands, car makers and dealers fit for the future is a complex venture, and the limited dynamic of a book can't provide insights and understanding in an order that will appeal to all readers. To avoid duplication and redundancy, the ambition has been to follow a simple structure and not take in every interrelated aspect in dealing with different themes – that would make the book much longer and less reader-friendly. In sum, reading through all the chapters should give the reader a good understanding of all the themes this book wants to present.

Data and material used

This book builds on a number of different data sources. First, there are research experiences ranging from theoretical and abstract reasoning on competitiveness, market structures and supply-demand mechanisms (which facilitates the understanding of how the car industry works and has been evolving) to more concrete studies on purchase behaviour, cost calculations and price-setting. Second, there are historical studies of the car industry, market structures and car cultures. Third, 118 interviews with managers in the car industry, ranging from manufacturer CEOs to small dealerships, are included. In addition, interviews have been carried out with managers in insurance companies, free-standing workshops, car finance companies and representatives of rental car businesses. Hence, this research takes a top-down perspective rather than a grassroots perspective on the management of car companies – but managers at all levels have been interviewed. Fourth, there are consultancy experiences from projects with car makers, importers, dealers, insurance companies, car finance and workshop chains. Fifth, data on car buyer preferences and behaviour collected in the United States (1,014 complete surveys collected), China (1,040), Germany (1,623) and Sweden (1,030) are presented.

A survey sample may not accurately portray the greater population studied due to over- or underrepresented demographics, so responses have been weighted to make sure the results scale responses according to population statistics. The questionnaire was sent to three generational cohorts: 20–23 years old (1,492 responses), 30–33 (1,461) and 50-plus (1,754), representing the 1990s cohort, the Generation Y/Millennials cohort, and the Baby Boomer cohort that represents the hitherto strongest segment of car buyers in major markets. Age categories are hence representations of specific generational cohorts, based on cohort marketing assumptions.[5] In addition, the results are categorized based on market area, dividing respondents into metro areas (areas with 800,000+ inhabitants; 1,545 respondents), city areas (80,000–800,000 inhabitants; 1,441 respondents) and rural areas (less than 80,000 inhabitants; 1,692 respondents). This categorization builds on earlier research that suggests significant differences among the three types of areas (Parment, 2009a).

Survey results are referred to as 'The Car Buyer 2013 Survey' throughout the book. Data were collected in June and July 2013. The extensive database could be used for more detailed analysis, also for specific auto brands since there are brand-specific data that can't be described in detail in this book as that would make it very lengthy. The ambition is, hence, to provide knowledge and interpretations about general patterns such as differences in buyer behaviour across generational cohorts and market areas – although these differences may be different in different countries. To an extent, such variations are commented on in the text.

Although the analysis will take as a starting point the four countries in the car buyer survey, and additional countries where interviews have been performed (Spain, Austria, Italy, the United Kingdom and Australia), the insights and arguments will largely be applicable to any medium to highly developed country. Earlier studies suggest differences across markets are limited: issues and problems are different but the basic mechanisms of competitiveness and competitive strategies for car companies appear to be rather similar (Parment, 2009).[6] In purchase behaviour, differences appear to be stronger, and this book will provide some further insights into that area.

Notes

1 In early 2014, Volvo will offer their own engines in the new VEA (Volvo Engine Architecture) line, thus step-by-step replacing Ford and Peugeot/Citroën engines in all model ranges.

2 Betsy Cummings, 'Listening for deals', *Sales and Marketing Management*, August 2005, p 8. Also see Michele Marchetti, 'Listen to me!', *Sales and Marketing Management*, April 2007, p 12.

3 Universum Communications survey 2012, presented in *Wirtschaftswoche*, 49, 3 December 2012, p 82.

4 See surveys from, for example, A Great Place to Work, www.agreatplacetowork.com and Universum Communications, universumglobal.com.

5 This has been extensively researched over the years, eg by Meredith and Schewe, 1994; Ryder, 1985 [1959]; Mannheim, 1927; Cutler, 1977; Parment, 2011; Rentz *et al*, 1983; Rogler, 2002; Hill, 1970; Rogler and Cooney, 1984; Schewe *et al*, 2013); and Parment, 2013a. Shared experiences during the highly impressionable coming-of-age years (17 to 23) embed values, or cohort effects. This stream of research suggests that these values remain relatively unchanged throughout life. 'Defining moments' during one's coming-of-age influence one's values, preferences, attitudes and buying behaviour in ways that remain for an entire lifetime. This provides the foundation of a generational cohorts perspective.

6 This is also supported by confidential consultancy reports and anecdotal evidence from a variety of companies in the car industry.

The car – fashion item or out of fashion?

01

For many decades, starting in the 1930s and with a golden era in the 1950s and 1960s, the car had a central role in society as a means of transport and as a symbol of status, affluence and personal freedom. Popular culture and public policies, with relatively few exceptions, supported the car and its strong role in society. In recent years, however, the car has been questioned for a number of reasons including its impact on the environment, and increasing traffic which results in traffic agglomerations and jams, particularly in bigger cities. Consumers have turned their interest to other products and have accordingly transferred their purchasing power to other areas: cheap travel abroad, housing and hobbies, to name a few examples.

That cars may cause problems is not a new phenomenon. It has been extensively dealt with in modern history (Lutz and Fernandez, 2010). In 1914, the mayor of Cali, Colombia, decided to regulate the impact of cars since they were – even though only in the hands of rich people – causing a lot of problems. According to the mayor:

> unfortunately, it is an evident fact that quite a few young men and persons
> of notoriety use the automobile at night to associate with women of ill repute,
> sometimes accompanied by minors, and they drive about town, especially in
> the rougher neighbourhoods, singing lewd songs, drinking heavily, making
> a racket, and disturbing citizens, who cannot sleep, while these people are
> involved in all manner of racy behaviour.
>
> (Giucci, 2012)

The 'branded society' and an increase in promoting the brand experience throughout the entire customer purchase process have also gained more attention in recent years. This chapter will discuss the impact of brand focus and aestheticization on the car industry and how companies can deal with this.

How the car lost its advantage – emotional and functional rationales

Companies in the car industry must understand the move towards a branded society and the transition of the car from having a place in popular culture to the current situation in many markets where a decreasing percentage of young people have a driving licence and there is a strong lobby against the car. The internet has contributed to the fundamental change in consumers' attitudes (particularly amongst the young) to transport, where and how to live their lives, and what constitutes a status symbol. This change would be hard to reverse. Proactive car companies can take advantage of the situation by gaining key insights into how actors in the car industry and in other sectors have benefited from the changes in the market and launched new concepts that delight customers, improve industry reputation and create sustainable competitive advantages.

In big markets such as China, India and some countries in South America and the Middle East, the car still has a strong role as a symbol of freedom, status and affluence. But there may be an opportunity to regain a strong position for the car in people's everyday lives where it has been diminishing recently. When the car is being questioned by different stakeholder groups, calculations on the costs of cars for society are made – a very complex task, often strongly influenced by the interests at hand. It's hard to imagine a society without cars, so it's difficult to calculate the implications of cars from a pure cost-benefit perspective. It has been suggested that fuel taxes in the United States cover about two-thirds of highway construction and repair costs, but little of the cost to construct or repair local roads. But cars also take up space that could be used for other applications, and traffic police enforcement, pollution and road maintenance are all costs that should be considered against all the benefits that car driving generates in terms of social mobility, economic growth and individualized welfare for the masses.

Cars have always been expensive to own and drive. Although many people hark back to the period before the oil crisis in the early 1970s, or the Gulf war in 1990–91, when fuel was cheaper, the fact remains: even if fuel was cheaper then, there have always been high costs involved in owning and driving cars. Cars are highly depreciating items, insurance is expensive, taxes are significant, inspections/servicing is expensive and there are significant costs involved in finance, maintenance and parking. These high costs contribute to the car's role as status symbol. Another key explanation is the car's promise of freedom, something that has been extensively restricted over the years.

In Europe, 15 million cars were sold in 2007; in 2013 it will be fewer than 12 million, and 2014 is expected to be even lower (LMC Automotive's). It's easy, like many automotive managers do, to blame a recession, the end of scrappage bonuses to stimulate new cars sales, high taxes and high unemployment rates. But the future is more complicated. Consumers have many more choices when it comes to spending their money and the car has largely lost its role as a status symbol. Cars are increasingly associated with problems and costs – and less with freedom, status and dreams.

Urbanization contributes to the problems. According to OECD, 86 per cent of the rich people in the world will live in big cities in 2050, compared to 77 per cent in 2010. The number of households without a car will increase, and car pools will expand at the cost of individuals having their own cars.

If successful, progressive families back in the 1950s and 1960s were portrayed with and around the car: it's now more likely to be a picture without a car in sight – but maybe a newly renovated kitchen, a man cooking, a woman working in an architect-designed garden, or children playing. When the car's status goes down, brands like Dacia, Skoda and Kia are likely to benefit: there is no shame in driving these brands any more. It rather reflects buyers being modern and balanced in the way they related to cars.

BMW is one of the few auto brands that have been extensively involved in understanding changes in society and the business environment. It has started an organization that works with mobility of the future and through acquisitions has access to the latest developments; for instance, New York-based 'My City Way', a company that provides real-time traffic updates.

Changes in societal values and the role of the car

The car has always been strongly related to individualistic ideologies. While right-wing politicians have emphasized the freedom aspect of car use and the importance of the car for economic growth and business development, left-wing politicians have emphasized the functional qualities of the car, but also the environmental and social problems it causes: cars may even create social isolation in a society built around cars when socio-economic groups that can't afford a car have limited opportunities to take part in different societal activities. Without a car, visiting a DIY store, travelling to Yosemite National Park or seeing friends in their summer homes may be very difficult.

Every generational cohort is programmed from birth. The coming-of-age assumption holds that early years shape a generation's values and behavioural traits, but with particular influence during the years from 17 to 23 (Parment, 2011a; 2013, Schewe *et al*, 2013). This means that individuals born in the 1980s and 1990s grew up in a society that in many respects is different from the one that earlier generations grew up in. Although societies differ substantially across nations and continents, there are some general patterns that describe the development from a global perspective, or at least from the perspective of developed countries. Some of the changes are rather obvious, eg that the young generational cohort grew up surrounded by the internet and new tools to communicate and make friends: mobile phones and a multitude of TV channels became available to just about everybody. This change laid the foundation of the emergence of social media, a key tool in setting up a marketing communications mix that appeals to young individuals in particular. But there are other more fundamental shifts in society that may be derived from less obvious events and trends.

As with other vehicles, automobiles have been incorporated into artworks including music, books and movies. Between 1905 and 1908, more than 120 songs were written in which the automobile was the subject (Jackson, 1985). Until the 1980s, and later to an extent, the car and the culture around the car lay the foundation of many movies. Many movies with the car as a significant part of the story have provided heroes who found freedom rather than duty and hierarchy on the open road. More recently, many changes in popular culture have taken place. New television programmes have given new perspectives on life. This change was very significant in Eastern Europe where television had been state-controlled. For political reasons, opportunities to take part in a Western lifestyle were limited. In these countries, democratization, market forces and the opportunity to adapt to a Western-oriented lifestyle with consumption at its heart came largely at the same time. In Scandinavia, television was also to a large extent state-owned but showed a selection of largely harmless television programmes from the United States and Western Europe – 'Dallas' and 'Dynasty', 'Cosby' and 'Seinfeld' were shown. At the end of the 1980s, the state eased control in many countries and gave room to commercial television channels. In the 1990s, most major programmes were available throughout the Western world. A multitude of programmes were now available: MTV made pop music videos available around the clock; sitcoms such as 'Frasier'; talk shows with Johnny Carson, David Letterman and Jay Leno; and programmes that promoted a glamorous lifestyle, such as 'Sex and the City', emerged. The latter particularly appears to have a strong impact on the values of individuals who grew up during the 1990s. In interviews with the Generation Y cohort (those born in the 1980s)

Popular culture often has its roots in metro areas. Increasingly, in portrayals of a glamorous lifestyle there is little evidence of cars. Metro areas are generally portrayed as desirable and glamorous while rural areas are portrayed as undesirable, so the popular culture has made a significant contribution to one of the car industry's challenges: urbanization. In Times Square in New York, there is much less room for cars now than there used to be: more space is given over to pedestrians, socializing and electronic signs, all being significant aspects of metro living.
(Anders Parment, 4 March 2009, Times Square, New York)

there are many references to 'Sex and the City', 'Beverly Hills' and later 'Gossip Girl' and 'The Hills', to name a few. (See Parment, 2011a, for a further investigation of the influence of popular culture.)

What do these influences, which together are strong in terms of how individuals' values are shaped, have in common? They portray a glamorous lifestyle to teenagers and young adults across the Western world, and now also to other parts of the world. In the lifestyle portrayed there is little evidence of cars, something that reflects a gradual reduction in focus on cars in movies, sales promotions, celebrity exposition, television programmes, etc. In addition, metro areas are portrayed as desirable and glamorous while rural areas are portrayed as generally undesirable, so popular culture has made a significant contribution to one of the car industry's challenges: urbanization. The message to young individuals is clear: if you live in a rural area, you should move to a bigger place with more opportunities, glamour, tolerance and choices. Hence, popular culture has largely contributed not

Metro areas provide an array of opportunities, and living without a car is not only an option – it may make life easier due to the high costs and inconveniences car ownership and use entail in metro areas. For young individuals in particular, the car is less important, both for transport and in terms of image.
(Anders Parment, 29 May 2009, Comedy Theatre, St Petersburg, Russia)

only to urbanization, but also to aestheticization, and a stronger emphasis on brands – individuals who grow up in metro areas face substantially more brand messages than those growing up in rural areas. In addition, the role of the car is different in metro areas: it's less important, both for transport and from an image perspective as there are other arenas that compete for attention.

Fewer young people have a driving licence

A young interviewee argued that there is no reason to have a driver's licence any more – 'If you have seen "Sex and the City", you know how young people want to live, and they don't want to drive their own cars, they want to walk or go by cab.' The car, once a rite of passage for US youth, is becoming less relevant to a growing number of young individuals, something that could have broad implications for the car industry – and many other industries with a strong stake in car transport, such as insurance, fuel and out-of-town shopping areas. In 1978, in the United States 50 per cent of 16-year-olds had a driver's licence and 92 per cent of 19-year-olds – now the shares are 31 and 77 per cent, respectively (Neff, 2010). Certainly it's hard to believe for anyone stuck in traffic on the way to O'Hare airport in Chicago, on a bridge or tunnel into Manhattan, or on any freeway in Los Angeles – but the pattern is clear: the average age of drivers is increasing year by year, thus making the ability to drive less of a symbol for young people.

FIGURE 1.1   Percentage of US population aged between 16 and 19 with a driver's licence in 1978 and 2008

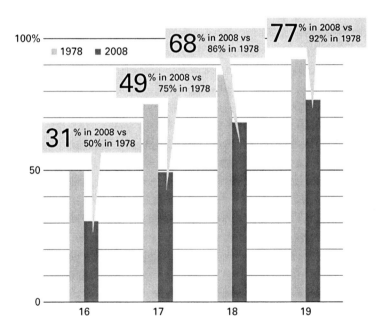

SOURCE: US Department of Transportation

Even though population growth in the United States is, thanks to immigration, among the highest in industrialized countries at 0.9 per cent per year (CIA World Factbook, 2012)[1], the number of miles driven annually on US roads began to decrease in 2004 (Davis *et al*, 2012; Motavalli, 2013). The number of miles driven per person decreased by 6 per cent between 2004 and 2011, primarily down to young people: between 2001 and 2009, the average number of miles per year driven by 16–34-year-olds decreased by 23 per cent – from 10,300 to 7,900 miles per capita. A full driving licence for cars is available by the age of 16 in most US states – 15 or 17 in others and, in North and South Dakota, 14 years and six months!

Similar tendencies have been found in many other countries with the number of citizens with a driver's licence going down and driving rates falling (Sivak and Schoettle, 2011). In addition, the number and percentage of households with a car is decreasing, which may be related to urbanization, an economic downturn, fewer young people having a driving licence or less dependence on the car (Kuhnimhof et al, 2011; Litman, 2012). Regardless of the cause, the fact remains that there is a weaker car dependency among young people.

Several explanations are provided – a 2012 report suggests higher fuel prices, improvements in technology that support alternative transport, and changes in Generation Y's values and preferences (Davis et al, 2012). Solid data prove that while the car has suffered heavily among young people, other modes of transport have gained impact. Bike trips have increased by 24 per cent in the 16–34-year-old cohort referred to above; walking became 16 per cent more frequent and use of public transport 40 per cent more frequent (Davis et al, 2012). This research suggests that the need for transport increased while cars lost impact in relative as well as absolute numbers.

To young people, public transport is more compatible with a lifestyle based on mobility and peer-to-peer connectivity than driving. If the car was once the ultimate symbol of freedom, it is now restricting young people's lifestyles. Bus and train riders can often talk on the phone, text or work safely while riding, while many (state) governments are outlawing using mobile devices while driving – and the tendency is to ban use (which, of course, is a great idea from a safety perspective), something that has a negative connotation from the perspective of the car being a symbol of freedom. In addition, some young people purposely live in ways that reduce their driving as a way to fulfil their personal commitment to a cleaner environment. However, the car is still an important status symbol for young people, as the data from The Car Buyer 2013 Survey presented in Chapter 4 indicate. But the car now competes with a broad range of other products and artefacts and has lost its primacy; it sits alongside many other symbols of progress, success and prosperity.

Global shifts in consumption cultures and economic power

Current global developments appear to move industrial and economic power from the United States and Europe to China and the Middle East. Many

US and European companies how been acquired by owners from Russia, the Middle East and China. With the Asian and Middle East economies getting stronger while the United States and several European countries are having severe financial problems, at least with regard to state budgets, trade (im)balances and budget deficits, the direction for the future seems to be clear.

However, with regard to consumption, the Western world still has a very strong impact. When asked to name leading Chinese companies, like the generations before them, many Western individuals have very little knowledge. An increasing number of products bought in the West are developed and manufactured in these emerging countries (which is now the wrong terms for countries like China and India – they are dominating economies, not emerging ones). Despite this, what happens in the Western world is better known and recognized. This particularly holds for popular culture, with a flow of TV programmes from the Western world to emerging countries, but hardly any flowing back. The same holds for fashion clothing and other lifestyle products. It has been proven that many Asian consumers admire premium products from Europe in particular (Batra *et al*, 2000; Park *et al*, 2008; Zhou and Hui, 2003) but this may change so car makers and dealers have to be attentive and open-minded in their marketing intelligence efforts.

The emergence of branded society

Auto brands have constituted an important part of the branded society as long as cars have existed – the car industry was one of the first to use branding on a broad basis, something that underlines its strong position in 20th century societal history. Annual product upgrades were introduced in the 1930s but more pronounced in the 1950s and gave car buyers incentives to change cars frequently (see, for example, Scherer, 1996). This, supported by strong state support for improving infrastructure and other measures, gave the car industry a strong role in the emerging consumption-oriented society. The car, just like fashion clothing that gained strong support from the emerging youth culture and popular music, took the lead in the increased consumption that was facilitated by strong economic growth. Later, the car lost its unique position in conferring status on its owner, a development paralleled by the emergence and growth of the branded society. Now, the car is one among a number of products that are subject to extensive branding.

Before the 1970s and 1980s, many environments that individuals came into contact with on a daily basis were free from commercial messages: they were non-commercial zones. Gradually, these environments disappeared and were replaced by an ideology that gained solid ground during the 1980s. In the 1980s, the decade of Reaganomics and Thatcherism, centre stage was taken by the 'small state', free markets (Bienkowski *et al*, 2006; Jenkins, 2006; Niskanen, 1988; Pratten, 1987; Skidelsky, 1988; Vinen, 2009; Wood, 1991), privatization (Ferlie *et al*, 1996; Hood, 1995) and individualism (Freeman and Bordia, 2001; Triandis, 1993, see also Schimmack *et al*, 2005). The interest in brands took off: not only were commercial businesses running brand management programmes but also NGOs, cities, employers and societal institutions, which discovered the benefits of profiling the brand in an increasingly competitive environment and in a crowded communication landscape. As a consequence, consumer companies such as car makers and car dealers had to compete with a broader range of actors that worked with their brands. Generation Y grew up in the emerging branded society and see branding efforts of municipalities, public transport services, churches and, a more recent trend, individuals (often referred to as 'personal branding', see for example, Goldsmith *et al*, 2009; Purkiss and Royston-Lee, 2009; Spillane, 2000; Vickers *et al*, 2008; Wilson and Blumenthal, 2008) as something natural, a development that parallels the increased focus on individualism at the cost of collectivistic values (Parment, 2011a).

Canadian author and sociologist Naomi Klein presented many thoughts on our branded society in her influential book, *No Logo: Taking aim at the brand bullies*, published in 2000. Klein describes the negative effects of brand-oriented activities and the methods individuals and movements have used to fight back against companies that use their brand power unfairly. Klein argues that there has been a shift in the usage of branding, from putting a recognizable face on factory-produced products (when multinational corporations had limited market power) to the idea of selling lifestyles and, since the 1980s, there has been a new era with brand names and logos appearing everywhere. Klein describes how brands like Nike and Pepsi attempt to have their names associated with everything from movie stars and athletes to grassroots social movements. The brand name gradually becomes more important than the actual product, according to Klein. Klein also discusses the structural change from local manufacturing to production in low-cost countries where few or no labour laws exist. Klein does not mention the car industry at all, maybe because it luckily did not apply the innovative marketing approaches of Nike and Pepsi at the time, possibly because of a lack of interest in cars.

Aestheticization

The car's role in society and how it has evolved over time is related to aesthetic issues and the interplay between the car and the space in which it appears. The entire range of opinions about the car – from being a gorgeous lifestyle item and a natural and integrated part of a happy life to being something that is consistently stuck in traffic jams, creates enormous amounts of emissions, causes death and destroys cities both from a practical and an aesthetic point of view – have strong connections to aesthetic aspects of society.

An increasing number of human activities are undergoing aestheticization (Löfgren and Willim, 2005), ie the growing significance of aesthetic perception in processes of consumption. More aspects of everyday activity are subject to the principles of aesthetics (the appreciation of beauty and art) and even the most mundane forms of consumption can be expressive and playful. The emerging digital economies of the 21st century have exacerbated this shift, supporting Mike Featherstone's claim that the 'aestheticization of everyday life' has arrived (cited in Flew, 2002). The resulting consumption is part of an emerging experience economy (Rifkin, 2000) where entertainment, information and communication technologies, and lifestyle products and services, combine to shape our identities in ways not seen in the modernist era (Southerton, 2012).

The car industry has to deal with this development. In one sense the car industry has been truly proactive. The design of cars has long caught the attention of those interested in aesthetics and cars are being displayed in many aesthetic contexts: house, clothing and travel advertising and magazines; conceptualizations of efficient and environmentally friendly societies; popular music; movies, television programmes and other popular cultural contexts. Aesthetics is intertwined with social processes such as fashion, identity and identity construction (Dobers and Strannegård, 2005). When these and other societal phenomena change, the general understanding of the car and its role in society is likely to change accordingly.

The emergence and growth of aestheticization as a decisive factor in creating competitiveness

Ever since corporate identity was introduced and developed in the beginning of the 20th century it has been a key factor in developing competitiveness.

An early contribution to this field was the work of the German architect Peter Behrens, who in 1908 created a consistent design for the AEG company. The work applied to products and catalogues but also details such as the design of fonts, cards and the annual report. At the time, one person could create the entire design process, and Behrens is known as a key person in developing a consistent graphical profile: a corporate identity (Kadatz, 1977).

The need for emphasizing the corporate identity has been the focus of many companies in the 1980s and 1990s. BMW was one of the first auto brands to develop a strong corporate identity, a process that included showrooms, workshop fronts, and other visual expressions of the BMW brand worldwide. This added to the consistent product design that has characterized BMW over the years. There have been some significant exceptions that may have irritated customers in the short run but certainly contribute to the brand heritage in the long run, for example the Bangle design era, starting with the controversial 6 Series in 2002.

Another key concept in the context of aestheticization is industrial design. The concept 'industrial designer' was first used in the United States in the 1920s (Ahlklo, 2004). Trained decorators, set designers, graphic designers and advertising professionals started to promote the necessity of styling products to make them more attractive, desirable and modern (Dobers and Strannegård, 2005). This contributed greatly to making consumer appeal part of corporate decisions in designing new products. One example is General Motor's decision to change car specifications every year – model remakes became necessary to stay competitive. In 1928, Ford introduced the A-Ford that replaced the T-Ford, and from then on, industrial design became an important competitive factor in the car industry. After World War I it became increasingly important to make the corporate brand more distinct, visible and distinguishable (Dobers and Strannegård, 2005). Complete corporate style programmes for products, logotypes, advertising and packaging were implemented and became increasingly important (Dobers and Strannegård, 2005; Kadatz, 1977). Much later, during the 1980s, companies began marketing their products through lifestyle, attitude and passion (Adams, 2004). Accordingly, products were bought for reasons of delivering lifestyle and self-realization, and brands, representing aesthetic dimensions, were judged by buyers for their capacities as lifestyle carriers.

One significant example is the Mercedes-Benz advertising in the 1980s: you are what you drive. Controversial at the time in some countries –

a Mercedes-Benz driver would even have been seen as arrogant by his (less likely her at the time) very existence – the message 'you are what you drive' is too vague and boring today to create any significant reactions at all. Importantly, there were few premium brands in the 1980s and Mercedes-Benz was one of the most significant – today the Mercedes-Benz brand creates more mixed associations, partly because of the multitude of premium brands that now exist, partly since Mercedes-Benz went mass market to an extent and now competes in many markets with a limited price premium in the compact and mid-size segments ie A, B and C class cars. In the 1990s, marketing and consumption became increasingly immaterial and customers' experiences became key to promoting the aestheticized environment in which purchase and consumption took place (see for example Salzer-Mörling and Strannegård, 2004).

Aesthetic consumption

With the abundance of product offers in the Western world, companies increasingly engage in efforts to differentiate their product offers from an aesthetic point of view. Aesthetic offerings – products and brands – are now the key to competitive advantage and commercial success, so companies have to infuse meaning into their products and transform commodities such as cars into concepts and lifestyles. Mike Featherstone has argued that Western societies are becoming increasingly aestheticized: companies' marketing efforts have led consumers to constantly search for new fashions, new styles, new sensations and new experiences (Featherstone, 1991). This is a key explanation as to why consumption has become more fragmented, differentiated and trend conscious. Products and services accordingly signal a particular lifestyle, and style has become a project, where consumers' individuality, or ambitions in that respect, is displayed in an assembly of artefacts, practices, experiences and appearances. Some commentators argue that we live in a global image economy (Mau, 2000; Schroeder, 2002):

> Life doesn't simply happen to us, we produce it. That's what style is.
> It's producing life. Rather than accepting that life is something that we passively receive, accept and endure, I believe that life is something we generate. We use our capacities. And that all boils down to style...
> fundamentally style is a decision about how we will live. Style is not superficial. It is a philosophical project of the deepest order.
>
> (Mau, 2000: 27)

Bourdieu's classic concept of cultural capital (Bourdieu, 1977a, 1977b) may thus be reinterpreted: Holt argues that cultural capital is no longer associated with goods consumed, but that the accumulation and proliferation of cultural capital is becoming a matter of practice, ie eating at particular restaurants, staying at particular hotels or choosing particular means of transport. Cultural capital is thus a matter of practice, consumption and choice (Holt, 1997).

Consumer spheres such as the home, the body and the soul are now subject to individual design and have lifestyle implications. The number of magazines on gardening, lifestyle and interior design has exploded (Parment, 2011a) and university programmes on design have grown rapidly. Research and surveys on what constitutes attractiveness emphasize design and other aesthetic factors as important factors (Ahlklo, 2004). Aesthetic performances have long-lasting effects – think of the Sydney Opera House.

Aesthetics, design and taste cannot be treated as something superficial: they are drivers of consumption and, increasingly, people are taking them into consideration when buying. Although there is a strong tendency among older consumers to argue that they are rational rather than emotional in making purchase decisions, emotional factors increasingly have an impact (Parment, 2011a; 2013). Corporate aestheticization is a concept that signifies the systematic conception and deployment of aesthetically rich systems of signification in the pursuit of corporate advantage. Such systems can take an array of forms, from the design of organizational buildings such as corporate HQs to the ways in which individual employees are expected to look, dress, walk and sound (Söderlund *et al*, 2010).

For car companies – regardless of whether they are car makers, NSCs or dealers – aestheticization is an important part of understanding buyers and it is an important input into how to develop business models, branding programmes, employee training programmes and customer approaches for the future. Aesthetics is an integral part of our everyday lives and it is experienced in the high street, the supermarket, in the workplace and at home. This is nothing new but increasingly important for car companies as competition is getting tougher.

Schmitt and Simonson (1997) argue that companies such as Cathay Pacific, IBM and Starbucks have all improved their market positions in part through a strong emphasis on design, stylization and other aesthetically-oriented approaches. More recently it has been argued that employees are cultivated as aesthetically significant carriers of a corporate ethos (Parment and Söderlund, 2010). Organizational branding and dress are part of this development and something that really took off in the 1990s. It has become common to expect staff to reproduce the characteristics of the brand through physical self-presentation, potentially reducing them to the status of embodied corporate artefacts, and through the attitudes they hold and express (cf cultural control). One example is Land Rover: employees in the United States were expected to wear clothes associated with a particularly English type of rural life, an activity that became spontaneous as the employees came to identify with and internalize the mythological brand identity (Harquail, 2006). Dress codes can be understood to convey important symbolic and aesthetic messages such as the white clothing of health service workers, deemed to be indicative of cleanliness and purity, or the dark blue uniforms of police and other security organizations that project a sense of power and tradition (Rafaeli and Pratt, 1993).

Numerous car makers and their NSCs have attempted to force dealer employees to wear a certain clothing style. Rural dealers in particular complain about the car maker's strategy to implement high standards of facilities along with demands on dress codes and salesperson education (in a few

In sparsely populated rural areas, retailing faces challenges such as finding a critical mass of clients and competent staff, and fulfilling manufacturer requirements on facilities. However, dependence on the car is high and solid in rural areas, and there is less criticism of the car per se from politicians, media and other stakeholders. (Anders Parment, 27 June 2013, Aldeburgh, UK)

instances, salespeople must have a business degree). Dealers don't like this approach; as one rural dealer with great success in terms of market share and profitability, but limited understanding of manufacturer strategies put it: 'The experience centres which they want dealers in the countryside to build, with marble floors and guys in black suits and red ties, a yokel from a rural town won't go in there, he won't, he's smart enough to understand that he has to pay.' Again, the tension between car makers, their NSCs and dealers – those operating in rural areas in particular – makes it difficult to implement a coherent strategy across all dealer sites.

Car design, marketing and the use and ownership of a car have long had aesthetic implications, but marketing channels did not really latch on to the aesthetic aspects until the 1990s, when car makers began demanding their dealers invest heavily in showroom design. Research into marketing channels, an area that emerged in the 1950s and 1960s, had a very mechanistic and static view of their role in creating demand (see for example Alderson, 1957; Bowersox et al, 1961; Bucklin, 1966, 1967). At that time, economic optimization was seen as the overarching goal of marketing channels. With the benefit of hindsight, these theories appear to be framed on the assumption that markets are characterized by a shortage of goods rather than overcapacity, and so marketing and branding were not seen as necessary functions. For instance, Bucklin identifies the following marketing channel functions:

- transit of goods;
- inventory;
- search: activities required to communicate offers to buy, sell and transfer title;
- persuasion: activities to influence buyers and sellers; and
- production.

The very meaning of 'persuasion' alludes more to a chatty salesperson than to well thought-out marketing and branding strategies. The role of the marketing channel was to bring the product to the customer in the most efficient manner with no or little consideration given to emotional, branding and aesthetic aspects. Surprising? Yes, considering the focus on aesthetics in other aspects of the car industry; but no, considering the nature of dealerships – at the time largely local, entrepreneur-driven businesses, sometimes selling tractors, garden products and light trucks as well as cars, or the supply-demand conditions at hand: most Western economies experienced two decades (the 1950s and 1960s) of very significant economic growth, and supply did not really catch up with rising purchasing power. If today's society is characterized by a multitude of aesthetically-oriented consumption areas that reflect high living standards (despite economic downturns in some countries) and fragmented consumer interests, buying and owning a car was a primary goal of many families at the time. Fewer people were living in city areas, public transport was not very well developed and the car's role as a symbol of freedom and status was very strong. Postcards at the time often portrayed cars in a variety of environments: parking spots, happy families stopping somewhere along the road to have a picnic, or they were of motels or even traffic intersections and roundabouts – nobody would come up with the idea of selling postcards of intersections and traffic jams today.

Consumption now is more fashion sensitive, dependent on aesthetics and well-designed products, services and offers. Proactive car makers attempt to have a strong presence in popular culture to understand what is happening and evolve with their customers. Mercedes-Benz fashion week, which is run twice a year in several capitals, is an example of this. When BMW introduced the i3, metropolitan cities were likewise chosen – New York, London and Beijing – and Hollywood stars Sienna Miller and James Franco were there to make sure the new car got an adequate association with success, glamour, young people and the popular culture.

Aestheticization of marketing channels: an extension of car makers' corporate identity programmes

After a long period of scant attention being paid to car showrooms, most car makers introduced extensive corporate identity programmes in the 1990s to improve the customer experience. BMW was one of the first companies to start doing this in the late 1980s[2] and the goal was clear: to implement an aesthetically appealing environment where customers could enjoy the BMW experience in line with how the car maker wanted the brand to be communicated. At the time, the move was clever and contributed to making the products more attractive, but it took several years until the strategy was fully implemented worldwide.

Around the turn of the millennium most car makers had succeeded in implementing extensive corporate identity programmes at the retail level. Many dealers complained and the car maker strategies sometimes forced dealers to close down their operations. Investing in profiled showrooms, with a lot of space to display the entire model range, was more than weak dealers could manage.

How important is the showroom and how much could it cost?

A number of trends raise questions about how much effort should be put into costly showrooms. On the one hand, aesthetically appealing showrooms in line with the corporate identity are crucial in providing a consistent brand experience. On the other hand, fewer showroom visits are made during the purchase process, now that buyers use other means to get information, eg the internet, which implies profitability challenges. In addition, expanding model ranges may make the costs overwhelming while not resulting in higher sales. The direct effect of stagnating demand and increasing model diversification is, to a rural dealer in particular, more complexity, higher costs and market share being at best maintained rather than grown. If the market is saturated, great showrooms may have an impact on individual brands' market share but are not likely to affect overall demand. If the industry has profitability problems because of overwhelming investments, it's not good for car makers, for retailers or customers.

There is little doubt that car makers and dealers that address two inherent problems in contemporary marketing channels will gain an advantage over competitors: showroom design and (lack of) showroom activity. Why car makers and dealers? Dealers are running the retail business and appoint their employees. They are responsible for activities where car makers place fewer restrictions, but in terms of showroom design, dealers operate under heavy car maker restrictions – and some brands run their own dealerships so they are both makers and dealers.

Showroom design

A general impression of car showrooms that people in the industry would not agree on, but many people outside the industry would, is that they are boring. Nicely designed but not very lively. As a car dealer consultant put it:

> A car showroom is like a mausoleum; extremely quiet and reclusive.
> I use it as an example of a dying industry. Sales people are sitting in tanks
> like aquarium fish – where can I try the sound system, different suspensions,
> experience engines or get an idea about options that would appeal to me?'

Is it the case that the intense focus on customer satisfaction makes car makers and dealers reluctant to come up with innovative design and experience elements in the showrooms? There should be greater investigation into how other industries are making customer-facing areas lively and appealing. Some have succeeded. Fiat's showroom on Marylebone Road in central London has a unique design and has sofas designed in line with the car design – in addition, the personnel are very attentive. Visbil on the Gotland island outside Sweden is constructed in transparent plastic that makes it possible to vary the colour of the dealership facility with the season or particular events: red and green when it's Christmas time, yellow and blue like the Swedish flag when that's appropriate and appealing (Sweden may win football or hockey competitions), or sparkling on New Year's Eve. And it wasn't expensive to build.

Making high demands for showroom design is a problem in rural areas particularly. And there are customers who complain, not only about the male-oriented facilities with very little activity, but also because they suspect they have to pay for it. If that's the case, the same would apply to grocery stores, travel agencies and fuel stations providing great shop interiors to stay competitive.

Showroom activities

An underexplored opportunity is using the car showroom for activities that don't necessarily have to be immediately driving sales. By increasing the level of activity, a number of good effects would arise:

- The threshold for visiting the dealership would become lower.
- More people in the showroom – directly through the events and indirectly through the increased activity level that results (people coming for planning events, increased showroom traffic because of lower threshold, etc) – reduces the stress caused by investing enormous amounts of money in something that generates very little footfall.
- Through co-branding, events with other companies could be created, allowing the car dealer to make use of the partner's client list and vice versa.
- Events organized for target audiences that are reluctant to come and see a car dealer are likely to be an effective way of reaching profitable and underexplored segments.

- Creative approaches – art exhibitions, secondary school class visits, night events with a fashion clothing company, a food retailer profiled on ecological products etc, may result in free attention from bloggers, journalists etc – at least until they become common practice.

It will require an increase in administration and marketing to raise the number of activities, and it will certainly increase cleaning costs and result in more wear and tear. The latter should not be much of a problem as, since car makers started engaging heavily in the design of dealerships, retail facilities have rarely been renovated due to being run down but because car makers have decided that it's time to improve the style and update the corporate identity. On the other hand, dealers spend a lot of money on advertising (often partly paid by the NSC) and other marketing activities, so the option of working with other companies to create events is worth considering.

The software is more important than the hardware – but more difficult to control

Typically, car makers and their NSCs run extensive programmes to implement and control showroom design, but comparatively little effort is spent on making sure the attitudes in dealing with buyers keep up with the showroom standards. In customer surveys, the 'software' – attitudes, customer treatment, salesperson's knowledge, etc – is normally seen as more important than the hardware. Figures 1.2 and 1.3 show data on how young car buyers, born in the 1980s, value different dimensions of car purchase – and attitudes are more important than facilities and showrooms. This does not, of course, mean that the latter are unimportant, but there is undoubtedly an imbalance in car manufacturers' control of marketing channels: much effort is spent on making sure showrooms are in line with corporate identity – normally an enormous investment for dealers – while only a few measures are taken to control attitudes. Mystery shopping is typically applied twice a year in an average-sized dealership to control whether customers are addressed and treated properly.

Dealers have a strong incentive to treat customers well, and there is no reason to believe a proactive dealer wouldn't strive to do that. The problem with car maker attitude control is that dealers and car makers may have different ideas and goals when it comes to how to treat customers. While dealers,

FIGURE 1.2 Factors considered very important for young car buyers in choosing car brand

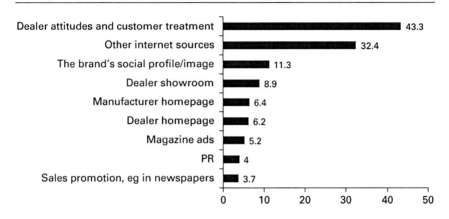

FIGURE 1.3 Factors considered very important by young car buyers in choosing car dealer

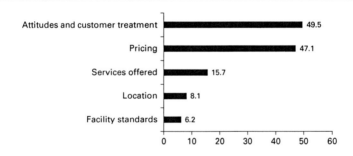

and small ones in particular, apply a local approach, car makers go for a standardized approach – no surprise given the different roles of dealers and car makers.

Generational differences and the paradox of car image

A clear pattern in today's markets is the strong discrepancy between the intended profile of car buyers and reality. Car makers benefit when the car is seen as a very emotional item and bought using emotional criteria. Many cars are designed for young couples with good incomes but bought by buyers aged between 55 and 70. This is obviously a paradox but there are explanations. First, consumers in general want to be about 10 years younger than they are (Evans *et al*, 2009). The car is a great product for this purpose since it could be used to strengthen an individual's social position by projecting an image of being young. Second, older consumers care more about cars than younger consumers, so while older people spend a large part of their disposable income on this 'symbol of freedom', younger consumers emphasize the car's role as primarily a means of transport by spending money on other areas. Third, older buyers to a large extent trust the dealership in choosing the right car, while younger individuals first make the choice of the product they want, then look for an appropriate channel where it can be bought (Parment, 2013a).

Notes

1   The UN suggests 0.96 and the World Bank (2009) 0.86 per cent.
2   The BMW Corporate Identity Programme and its implementation are excellently described in Birkigt *et al* (1992).

Competition, market structure and global challenges

02

This chapter focuses on competition and market structure conditions and how global challenges have actualized a number of crucial strategic issues of concern to car companies. New fuel technologies, changes in car taxation policies, the effects of state subsidies for different industry sectors, and the increased cost of land, making retailing in bigger cities expensive, are examples of challenges that must be dealt with through applying proactive strategies, forward-looking marketing intelligence systems and thought-through incentive systems to control behaviour in different types of markets.

The market and industry structure of the car business is undergoing considerable change. The number of car makers – 40 in 1970 and 24 in 1980 – has continued decreasing over time in the aftermath of consolidation and there are now only 10 major manufacturers left. Former competitors are now in the same company group. As in many industries, mergers and extensive cooperation at the manufacturer level, even among direct competitors (cf BMW and Mercedes-Benz's cooperation on hybrid technology), will continue and grow in importance. The same holds for the retail level: small operations will close down while big, international retail groups will grow. Economies of scale are extensive not only for car makers but also for insurance, finance, retailing, repairs and other areas.

The changes have far-reaching implications for competitive forces in the car industry. Successful companies understand what is going on and find new ways to compete and cooperate, and new patterns of competition emerge. The large manufacturing overcapacity – estimated to be between 50 and

60 per cent – puts strong pressure on marketing channels to sell cars, and it raises many concerns about profitability, market share and the choice of direct car maker-owned channels or indirect channels. Overcapacity creates a huge opportunity for companies that find new ways to create offers that make use of flexibility in the market, eg car fleet companies, insurance companies or even banks that supply mobility items. A smart approach can generate high margins by offering customers a deal on a car that has been acquired on attractive terms from a car makers' overstocked supply.

Herd behaviour: car makers apply similar strategies

Like many other sectors, there is an element of herd behaviour in the car industry, so there is a risk that many companies will try similar solutions to challenges that emerge. If the strategies – a new LED design, free roadside assistance, the design of dealer showrooms, warranties, etc – don't work, discounts are the solution to slack sales.

Although there may be a number of reasons for car makers to use strategies different from those of competitors, they tend to apply similar distribution strategies, which strongly indicates herd behaviour: if one car maker applies a specific strategy or activity, competitors will soon follow to avoid being competitively disadvantaged. Overcapacity appears to be a main explanation for herd behaviour. In this regard, two interesting findings appear. First, dealer networks may appear to be similar but behind the scenes there are substantial differences in terms of car maker-dealer relations, customer satisfaction, customer treatment, culture and profitability. To really make use of the advantages inherent in implementing a consistent brand image, car makers must secure differentiation in both the visible and the invisible. While it is relatively easy to copy and implement consistent showroom design, it is difficult to implement consistency in attitudes and customer treatment across the dealer network. A customer who visits a number of dealerships of a particular brand in different areas will see striking similarities in terms of what is visible and similar, but is likely to face striking dissimilarities in terms of what is invisible.

Car makers' tendency to copy each other's concepts indicates that there is an industry logic that defines a standard of retailing. As one industry expert put it: 'They're all going to do the same thing, because that's all that there is to do. There are obvious things and they have to do them.' Car makers in general have put a lot of effort and money into brand management and corporate identity programmes in order to communicate differentiation and uniqueness. To an extent, car makers adjust the concept to their own brand, but those with little market power will find it difficult to recruit dealers willing to invest in a brand-specific, differentiated distribution setting. More powerful brands are likely to differentiate through the marketing channel.

Customers are getting used to high standards of facilities and services. When a car maker implements a new service throughout its dealer network, others soon follow. This herd behaviour may be explained by the competition which makes car makers nervous about losing relative power. Basic customer requirements increase as car makers do very similar things, such as CSI programmes and measurement, showroom design, and standardizing customer treatment processes.

Being proactive – a sign of competitive and sustainable strategies

There are two principal ways of relating to new developments, regardless of industry and one's position in it: by being proactive or reactive. Throughout this book, numerous examples of successful strategies and implementation are given, with a look at how companies in other industries may have something to teach the car sector.

Once upon a time – and in many instances not a very long time ago – it was argued that one should support local suppliers by buying groceries, fuel, clothing, cars, etc from them. Very few buyers do so now – another effect of urbanization and a weaker rural economy. Value for money seems to be the overriding criterion in making purchase decisions. Car makers attempt to control dealers by applying thought-through margin systems. While sales volume or numbers used to be the main basis of margins, kick-backs and other incentives, since around the turn of the millennium margin systems now give incentives for providing an appropriate product mix, great product display, keeping a sufficient number of demonstration cars with appropriate specs (the higher the spec, the more likely buyers will opt for factory options), how customers are addressed (through 'mystery shoppers'), customer satisfaction, etc. Such systems reflect changes in the business environment and customer demands: intensified competition and increased demands on quality, not only in products but also in the customer process and the services provided by a business. Hence, the change in margin structures was a late but necessary adaptation to changes in the business environment.

The car industry's dealer side, which is characterized by intensive intra-brand competition, reacted differently according to their attitude to change. Reactive dealers responded by complaining about not knowing the size of the final margin: 'We are only guaranteed 10 per cent, so we can't give more than 5 per cent.' Proactive dealers argued differently: 'We do everything the factory wants us to do. It will certainly cost more money, but we'll also get more satisfied customers and higher standards in terms of facilities and processes. We can give away 8 or even 10 per cent, since we know we'll get the highest margin offered, 18 per cent, or close to.'

The reactive dealer sees the change as a threat to the viability of the dealership and can't see any good reason to implement it, indicating a lack of understanding of what is happening in the business environment. Viability is lost and many customers go elsewhere. Young and up-to-date customers in particular see the reactive dealer as very old-fashioned while the proactive dealer applies a fresh and innovative approach. Changes are seen as opportunities to make the business model more viable while increasing customer orientation. The proactive dealer enjoys at least two other benefits: it is more in tune not only with the world around it but also with the car maker in terms of strategies and priorities, and it has more market and negotiation power to exert if, for some reason, the relationship with the car maker runs into trouble.

One may ask whether car makers would not end up applying a similar attitude as the reactive dealer. It's hard to imagine. Car makers by nature apply a more general approach with more market intelligence and situations that require an orientation to the world around them. Car makers might be slightly reactive to changes, as we've seen in instances such as Opel/Vauxhall, Saab, Cadillac and Fiat. Dealers might be very reactive as their market, their local customers, may have critical views about central politics, headquarters, metropolitan areas, etc – the context that car makers normally operate in (see Parment, 2009, on the mental distance between manufacturers and rural dealers). This also explains the difficulties car makers have with rural dealers: their attitude may be part of a more general attitude in the rural area towards bigger cities, head offices and other elements running the country.

When BMW's factory showroom, BMW Welt, opened in Munich in 2007, the architect said: 'The building does not have the boredom of a hall; it is not only a temple, but also a market place and a communication centre and meeting place for knowledge transfer.' Car maker-driven investments in facilities along with control and margin systems that address a broad range of product display and customer process issues together constitute a clear top-down control of the dealer network. One of the rationales for a car maker investing in top-notch showrooms is to provide an example for dealers to follow. Reactive dealers don't like that, and their reactive attitudes apply to more or less everything, including their views on politics, societal change, etc; hence the attitudes of these dealers are embedded in a complex web of reactiveness that is very difficult to change. Car makers should consider getting rid of reactive dealers: even if they represent significant sales in the short run, they are likely to leave a bad impression of the car makers' brand and hinder change in the long run.

Marketing intelligence and driving markets

It may seem an easy thing to gather, albeit somewhat difficult to implement: marketing intelligence. We all know that it's crucial for any viable and successful business to understand what is going on around it and to understand which macro environmental forces provide challenges and opportunities. However, there are many reasons to question the approach that has traditionally been used for marketing intelligence purposes; the problems that marketing intelligence inherits have to be considered.

First, an industry is not an easily defined entity. Theodor Levitt presented in a very influential *Journal of Marketing* article more than 50 years ago the 'marketing myopia' insight: companies tend to define the industry in which they operate too narrowly (Levitt, 1960). Hence, train transport companies might believe they are in the train transport industry while they actually are in the moving people and goods industry. Film producers in Hollywood are not in the movie industry, but in the entertainment industry. These insights are still highly relevant. The car is to an extent, of course, in the transport industry, but it is also a product bought for reasons of showing off, a hobby, a way of belonging, self-realization, etc. Industry definitions are closely linked to purchase criteria – and purchasing power. Understanding to what extent different motives drive a car purchase may be crucial in knowing how to deal with environmental and competitive forces, falling demand, competitors' moves, etc. Assuming a high percentage of Audi drivers buy the car for functional reasons – high quality, reliable four-wheel drive system, great rust protection, high scores in safety rankings, etc – may be dangerous for the Audi brand. Representatives who neglect the functional side and only talk about design, road performance, engine sound and the feeling of having 'made it' are also a problem. This reasoning also applies the other way round: Skoda Yeti owners may have bought the car for its design and emotional appeal – while the Skoda advertising emphasizes reason and not emotions. It may even portray emotional car buyers as out of touch and vain.

But how can we know? At the end of the day, a car purchase is a complex decision and represents a lengthy decision process. The car has a multitude of characteristics and appeals, and the use of the car includes – even for one user – a multitude of applications that may be very different in attitude and underlying rationale. The same woman may use her Holden Commodore to get to work; to transport a sofa from IKEA; to help uncle Matthew visit the doctor; to go to a meeting with old student buddies and show how success- ful one has been (the car is slightly more expensive and extrovert than the buddies' cars); to go to church with her husband and kids on Sunday morn- ing; or to take the kids to school. Customer surveys do not give the full picture of purchase rationales – this also holds true for academics attempt- ing to understand the motives behind car purchases (Evans *et al*, 2009). Surveys may, as we will see, hinder the development of customer-oriented solutions and attitudes.

Second, classic marketing intelligence is based on a reactive approach since the focus is on needs that have already been defined – the approach is market-driven (listen to what your customers say and do what they want). A typical sequence in marketing intelligence may follow this pattern:

> Turning data into information → Turning information into knowledge
> → Turning knowledge into actionable plans.
>
> (Loshin, 2003)

It's about systematically analysing information, qualifying it and adapting it to the organization's needs. But it hardly helps companies that really want to think in new ways. Many companies in the car industry are desperate to reach high customer satisfaction scores, since they think that will create loyalty and profitability. But in the real world, too heavy a focus on cus- tomer satisfaction through measuring what customers say may result in the opposite. Customers get irritated when they have to fill in surveys, and it's shown in studies that the very fact that they are filling in a survey makes them discover more flaws than before (Christensen and Bower, 1996).

Car buyers express very negative attitudes towards extensive use of surveys: a premium car buyer received six surveys in the first year of owning a

€55,000 premium car. One survey dealt with image analysis, one with the purchase process, two with the delivery and the salesperson's performance, one with the first service department visit, and one with the car's characteristics. After six surveys, the car buyer gently asked: 'Is something wrong with the car? I told you five times that I was happy with it but now I don't know.' Typical buyers don't understand what lies behind the surveys being sent to them. The car maker wants information about the image of the car and the delivery. The dealer wants information about the workshop visit and on how the customer is going to answer the survey sent by the NSC (which is normally factory-owned) to map customer happiness with the dealer – so the dealer sends a similar survey to the client to get to know what he or she will say in the forthcoming survey. This explains the two surveys on the very same matter indicated above. The system is not coordinated to minimize customer irritation and time consumption. The fact is that filling in surveys activates the customer's critical faculties. Just think about going to the Alps, to New York, Hong Kong, London or Paris over the weekend – a great experience until the detailed survey from the travel agency or hotel arrives, asking you about everything from the supply of TV channels to the ease of finding a parking spot and the breakfast hours. The more companies ask their clients, the more critical clients will get.

Third, truly successful firms are often driving markets rather than market-driven. The difference between the approaches is crucial. Amazon, Body Shop, Dell, FedEx, Ikea, Swatch and Virgin are examples of companies that have shown a driving markets approach to customer needs. It's about creating customers rather than satisfying them (Berthon *et al*, 1999). To succeed in driving markets, companies may even have to make sure there is a certain distance from customer opinions (Kumar *et al*, 2000; Schindehutte *et al*, 2008). Marketing research, including surveys, can still be used to give clues about how a driving markets approach may be created, provided the research is based on an open, curious and explorative attitude, but it can't be the primary channel of input for developing new products and offers.

Real innovations are difficult for customers to describe since they don't know what their needs look like (Baker and Sinkula, 2007; Bennett and Cooper, 1981; Leonard and Rayport, 1997; Tauber, 1974). Not many clients would have exactly described a need for an iPad. Moreover, at the stage a product is developed, it's difficult to know how it will be used. Who thought about iPads being a mobile baby minder? The same for SMS, originally developed for the military – how the product would be used wasn't known until customers started using it.

There are several examples of marketing research suggesting that a planned product wouldn't make sense to customers – but was nonetheless brought to the market and became very successful (Lynn *et al*, 1996). This underlines the importance of applying a driving markets approach. One significant example is Swatch watches, introduced in 1983 and now sold in hundreds of Swatch stores around the world. Originally seen as standard plastic watches, they were soon perceived by the market as trendy – supported by celebrities and frequently featured in popular culture, etc. Hence, Swatch developed an attractive brand identity. The unique design constituted a substantial competitive advantage since it could not be matched either by Swiss or Japanese competitors.

Swatch was originally intended to recapture entry-level market share lost by Swiss watchmakers to Japanese companies such as Seiko and Citizen and to repopularize analogue watches at a time when digital watches had achieved wide popularity. This combination of marketing and manufacturing expertise largely contributed to helping Switzerland maintain its position as a major player in the world wristwatch market. Synthetic materials were used for the watchcases as well as new ultrasonic welding processes and assembly technology. Despite the success, Swatch watches didn't gain acceptance in marketing research. Watches with the most radical design received the lowest purchase intention scores in the exploratory phase, but nonetheless these were the most successful when brought to market (Kumar *et al*, 2000).

Companies that drive markets have a tendency to be cool and therefore give customers and other stakeholders an impression of confidence. When did you get a survey from Apple, Four Season or Lufthansa? They know they provide great offers and, given the fact that only some 5 to 15 per cent of people answer surveys, the idea of asking every customer for an opinion seems to have lost some of its relevance.

Being market-driven or driving markets is, at the end of the day, not an either/or choice; it is possible to combine the two approaches. Striking a balance between being market-driven and driving markets may be the most successful market approach (cf Baker and Sinkula, 2007; Jaworski *et al*, 2000).

Transparency

A key characteristic of today's markets in which car buyers make their decisions is high transparency – a multi-faceted phenomenon with a range of effects on markets, buyer behaviour and car companies.

Transparency protects buyers and may improve industry reputation

Over time, transparency has increased and it has become more difficult to sell a car with a poor reputation: information about inspections, mileage, repairs, owners, etc is available to buyers through services such as CarFax. Workshops compile information about warranty repairs, trouble shooting and upgrades. Dynamic databases calculate combinations of registration date, factory options, car history, colour and model to add precision to car valuations. For buyers this development means the risk of getting a 'lemon'[1] is lower than ever before – and from an overall market perspective, price-setting gets easier.

In addition to the fact that car salespeople have a poor reputation, something confirmed in several studies, it appears to be acceptable to say just about anything about car dealerships and salespeople – the same holds for insurance brokers and estate agents. 'How to avoid car dealer tricks', 'Car salesman: still sexist, still stupid' and, 'Why do most car salesmen have a reputation for being total dirt bags?' are a few of many examples of articles found on the web in 2012 and 2013 (see Quick, 2012). In a 2012 US survey, car salesmen along with members of congress and lobbyists received the worst results in terms of reputation, even worse than for telemarketers. Only 8 per cent in the survey study had a high or very high belief in the honesty/ethics of car salespeople – and no improvements have been achieved over time. In 1977, the first year the survey was run, it was also 8 per cent and never more than 9 per cent in the 28 surveys carried out since 1977.

Why do car salespeople have such a poor reputation? It has been suggested that the sales techniques used are impersonal and that products – even those that buyers do not want or need – are being forced on them, but at the same time we know that many potential buyers visiting a dealer are ignored. Salespeople may be overselling and customers in general don't like that – the same applies to other professions at the bottom end: stockbrokers, advertising practitioners and, to an extent, members of congress; see Figure 2.1. The car is a complex product, and expensive to own and run – maybe that could explain why customers get frustrated when seeing a car salesperson.

Is there a way out of the consistently poor reputation that car salespeople have? Considering recent developments in terms of dealer quality and training, in combination with increased market transparency, there are strong reasons to have high hopes for the near future. The quality of car retailing

FIGURE 2.1   The honesty and ethical standards of different professions – US 2012 Gallup survey

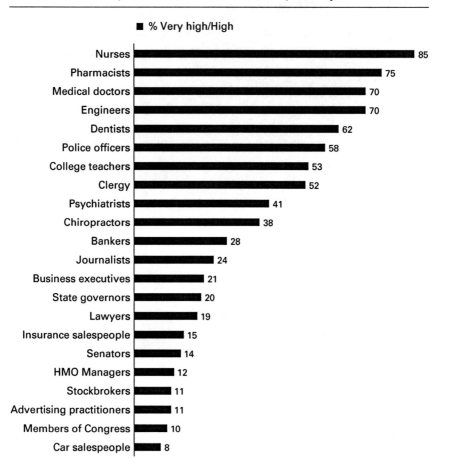

■ % Very high/High

Profession	%
Nurses	85
Pharmacists	75
Medical doctors	70
Engineers	70
Dentists	62
Police officers	58
College teachers	53
Clergy	52
Psychiatrists	41
Chiropractors	38
Bankers	28
Journalists	24
Business executives	21
State governors	20
Lawyers	19
Insurance salespeople	15
Senators	14
HMO Managers	12
Stockbrokers	11
Advertising practitioners	11
Members of Congress	10
Car salespeople	8

has improved significantly in recent years. While customers were once left to their own devices when in dispute with a dealership on service quality, delivery time or product issues, they now benefit not only from stronger legal protection but also from dealership attempts to create, implement and gain customer relationship advantages by establishing 'customer promises' and such like. And customers do benefit from increased transparency – if they are unhappy they can discuss and get feedback on their experiences from other customers on web forums, etc.

Dealerships in general now have great product displays, clean toilets, and a lot of customer care processes in place to make sure nobody falls out – of course it may happen, but less often than before. The 'software', however, does not always live up to the standards: 'I dealt with the husband on engine size, factory options and then I turned to the wife and asked what colour they'd want. You only make that mistake once' an experienced car salesman stated.

'Software' more important than hardware

Car buyers value attitudes and how salespeople address them higher than facilities and showroom standards – see Figure 2.2, which represents car buyers born in the 1980s, something that might explain the strong influence of the social image of the brand. Hence, car companies should give dealership salespeople training the same priority as the hardware. The reason it doesn't happen is simple – it's easy to standardize and measure the physical appearance of an auto brand, but more difficult, complex and expensive to measure the attitudes that dealers convey. In addition, attitudinal preferences may differ across geographical locations and customer segments, and the likelihood of a person failing to deliver appropriate service is higher than the risk that the facilities won't work.

FIGURE 2.2 The 'software' is more important than the hardware

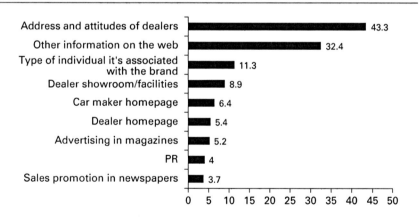

Even though it is difficult and complex to follow up and measure the software, proactive car companies should consider increasing the emphasis on the software in measuring dealer performance.

Transparency makes it increasingly difficult to maintain high margins

One of the major challenges of our times is the transparency that now characterizes almost any business and the environment it operates in. This high degree of transparency has a multitude of roots and effects, for example:

- User-provided information (eg websites that provide hotel reviews, client-based ranking of banks or car workshops and student-based university rankings) gradually gains power and contributes to making buyers question company-generated information unless it's fair and relevant.

- Companies that want a dialogue with their customers and other stakeholders to get invaluable feedback on their operations have to apply openness and transparency in their marketing operations. Communication should be transparent and fair and companies should accept constructive criticism from customers and other stakeholders.

- Companies have to explain significant product or service risks, component substitutions or other foreseeable eventualities that could affect customers or their perception of the purchase decision – if not, the company will lose customers, reputation and, if not immediately then later, profitability.

- Active web forums and similar ensure that prices are fully disclosed and, increasingly, financing terms, price deals and discounts. There are websites specializing in discount codes and sites that run price comparisons – at the end of the day, transparency will promote further transparency and companies that attempt to hide their prices, terms and conditions will lose buyers, attractiveness and profitability.

- An increased transparency about what people are doing (social media makes a contribution here!) and the willingness of young people in particular to make requests at short notice and not being afraid of making demands of companies, salespeople, bankers, employers, etc has created a new situation for selling and employing (see for example Parment, 2011a; 2013b).

- Openness, transparency and trust are necessary foundations of a communications strategy when buyers use new and fast communication tools, can easily find information elsewhere and expect full and honest information to be provided by companies.

- A more open attitude, particularly among young individuals, and better tools to share information, mean that few young people hesitate to share information about discounts on a new car or on a mortgage with other people – making it a lot easier to compare offers.

- Under-performing staff will face a tough time: customers are increasingly evaluating the personnel they meet, hence providing the company with direct market feedback. This happens both through existing systems and with new techniques. When there was less openness 'voting with my feet' was the likely consequence of customer dissatisfaction.

- The new transparency reflects the transition from companies being in power to consumers (and employees) increasingly having the upper hand in negotiations and purchasing (employment) decisions.

For many decades, transparency has to an extent characterized new car sales as well as the market for used cars. Some complications exist because of variations in the quality of used cars, but apart from that both the new car and used car markets have provided great opportunities for buyers to compare prices.

At the turn of the millennium – slightly later in some markets – it was still possible to charge high prices for services bought in connection with a car purchase, eg inspections, repairs, insurance and finance. For many years, a couple of car makers earned more than 50 per cent of their profits from finance (Parment, 2009). Through internet penetration and a number of other developments, market transparency increased rapidly and it became difficult to overcharge consumers for any type of services as a direct consequence of changes in consumer attitudes and the ease of running price comparisons.

Business overlap – competition gets tougher

The increasing overlap of businesses will have important implications for car buyer behaviour and the way the car industry and related businesses respond. Rental car companies are providing cars on a long-term basis, competing with fleet car companies. Finance and insurance are increasingly infringing on each other's territories – and not just in the car industry. Non-franchised repair shops not only offer inspections and repairs but also windscreen repairs, tyre services and roadside assistance, sometimes in packages.

This is obviously a sign that competition has got tougher – when there is less room for profitability and growth, businesses tend to expand into other businesses and industries' territories. And in this case, it makes sense, since the more services are offered by each player, the higher the competition, the better the market coverage, the lower the prices and the easier for the customer: he or she will have the choice of purchasing each service where it's cheapest, or seeing a dealer – or other service provider – to get an overall car ownership package, in which case there is likely to be a price premium.

Transparency, competition and price-setting

Not even the taxi business is free from competition. Political ideology and users' willingness to pay create very different situations in different markets. Some countries, eg Sweden, allow cab companies to charge whatever price they want, which results in businesses that charge 5 to 10 times the normal market price – not good for the reputation of Stockholm when tourists are being hugely, but legally, overcharged. In China, cab fares are fixed and each cab gets an annual subsidy from the state – hence fares are very attractive and tourists are rarely ripped off. Prices vary among cab companies in many countries, but in the United States, for instance, differences are normally small.

The German taxi industry is heavily regulated, so foreigners need not worry about being overcharged. All taxis in Germany are required to have a visible meter and fares are set by local laws within a designated local tariff zone *(Pflichtfahrgebietes)*. Rates vary by city but are never unfair. Although many German cab drivers complain about poor profitability, the rental car company Sixt has founded My Driver, which offers a limousine service that charges cab fares. Since March 2013, My Driver services in four classes – Eco, Business, First and Van – has been available in 11 German cities. How can a limousine service be provided at cab fares? Again, the answer is manufacturing overcapacity in the automobile industry, something that gives Sixt and other rental companies very attractive leasing terms for a variety of new cars. The heavily subsidized cars can be used for the limousine service.

There is little doubt that heavy industry overcapacity has had a major impact on transparency, and an increasing overlap of businesses supported by aware and demanding customers.

Balancing traditional and emerging countries

There are strong reasons for car makers to apply a portfolio perspective that balances traditional and emerging countries. Different brands do well in different markets, for purchasing power, consumption culture and other reasons, and downturns in different markets happen at different times. Governments may impose taxes and increase regulations, which makes selling in that market difficult, and crises that affect particular countries may result in new car sales going down by 40 or 50 per cent at short notice – Spain, Greece and Ireland are relatively recent examples of how a financial crisis hurts car sales.

Relying on one or a few markets for a high percentage of sales is therefore a risk. Even better than diversifying the portfolio within a country or continent – ie across the United States or the EU countries – is to have diversification that considers traditional and emerging markets. The risk of both being hurt simultaneously is more limited than in the case of selling to one country, continent or region only.

Companies that are proactive and establish marketing channels with good market coverage at an early stage in emerging markets have a chance of benefiting from 'first-mover advantage'. When a market grows, the first-mover advantage will be translated into higher brand awareness, larger market share and, in many cases, higher profitability, something that facilitates further expansion. After the *Wiedervereinigung*, when Germany became one country again in 1990, the Volkswagen Group enjoyed the benefits of great market coverage in the former East German states. When Skoda was introduced in Sweden in 1994, it was sold solely by Volkswagen dealers, which made it possible to reach 5 per cent market share within one year of introduction. Considering Skoda's history as a car with poor quality and road performance back in the 1970s, this was impressive – and the main reason, of course, was access to great dealers with great locations and a good reputation.

China's high economic growth (even if it slowed down remarkably in 2013, it still exceeds that of most other countries) and a population of almost 1.4 billion inhabitants make it a crucial market in creating growth for the future. China is also the world's largest motor vehicle producer measured by the number of vehicles produced. Out of the 84.1 million cars and commercial vehicles produced in 2012, 19.3 million were made in China, followed by the United States (10.3), Japan (9.9) Germany (5.6), South Korea (4.6), India (4.1) and Brazil (3.3). Having a presence in China is a great growth opportunity – but also demanding: most car makers put a lot of effort into gaining a strong position in China, competition is tough and buyers at this stage are very keen on buying products with a strong emotional content.

Note

1 In 1970 in a paper in the *Quarterly Journal of Economics*, economist George Akerlof presented an influential paper within the used car market as an example of quality uncertainty. The essence of the paper is that owners or good cars – cherries – will not place their cars in the used car market while cars for sale – lemons – are in less-than-average condition. These insights have been widely criticized but the word 'lemon' for undesirable used cars (wrong model and spec, below-average quality etc) is extensively used.

Marketing channels

03

Marketing channels are crucial to making the offer available to customers. Due to the complexity and size of a car, there is a need for a physical point – for delivering, maintaining, and repairing the car. These services have often been provided by the dealer, and it's likely that automobile dealerships will constitute a major part of the marketing channels in the future too.

Marketing channels fulfil many more functions for car makers and buyers than just giving access to car ownership. Marketing channels make sure car makers provide good market coverage when it comes to after-sales services, get their products adequately exposed, and get access not only to buyers overall but, in the best case, buyers with a profile that fits with the car maker's brand intentions. The more intensive the competition, the more important it is for a company to have great marketing channels.

Dealers will be necessary for the foreseeable future

There is and will be a need for a dealer from a number of perspectives. First of all and maybe most important, the buyer wants a dealer. Even for bicycles and lawnmowers – compared to cars, very cheap products – customers want a place to go for information, support, product demonstration, etc. In many industries, low-cost providers offer relatively complex products – white goods, brown goods, garden tools, etc – at low prices with very limited service. Over time, however, they tend to add personnel and expertise to be able to offer services many buyers want. Their cost advantage may remain, but it's derived from scale advantages in marketing, procurement and administration and, very important, negotiation advantages with manufacturers gained through market power.

In addition, dealers have an absolutely crucial role in pushing cars to buyers through active salespeople and good market coverage. The competitive situation makes it essential to have marketing channels that display products in a consistent and attractive way, have great and relevant market coverage, address customers in a proper and adequate way and treat them well.

From an efficiency point of view, which has been the main argument for eliminating the dealer, it's hard to believe that it would save a lot of costs to sell cars at Carrefour, Hornbach, Tesco, The Home Depot or Amazon, since there are many activities that must be carried out anyway. In addition, a good dealer can put together a great package and give the customer a clear benefit: one point of contact, convenient and competent.

For a dealer to survive, there must be motivation. A senior Volvo representative once asked me: 'Why is there a need for the local dealer to put his name on the sign? He's selling Volvos, that's something to be proud of.' The fact is that brands are not, like some other entities, competing for attention but may rather strengthen each other, ie a strong local Volvo dealer will strengthen the Volvo brand, while the Volvo brand will strengthen the Mr and Mrs Smith dealer brand (Parment, 2008, 2009). It's hard for companies, not only in the car industry, to understand this. Several meetings with senior managers in different industries involved a discussion on this, and it is common that top management lacks an understanding of what really motivates dealers and individuals. If ISS, primarily known for cleaning, facility and catering services, is running the reception for a very attractive company, why would the reception staff, as suggested by ISS, state that they work for ISS, while they in fact spend eight hours a day for the highly ranked company and one day a year with ISS training? Why would a very successful dealer, which has been selling cars for generations, want to represent a car maker that, for unclear reasons, wants to eliminate the dealer's name in every type of marketing communication? This approach has two aspects: arrogance and stupidity. The people buy a Volvo, a Holden or a Toyota from Andersson Bil, Parramatta Motors Company or Hans Klein GmbH, ie from franchised dealers who by contract, commitment and tradition put a lot of effort into selling the car maker's cars in the local market. If the car maker wants to set up its own manufacturer-run retail operations in the area, it can, but it can't then expect commitment from the locals or from the franchised dealers it is undermining.

What about eliminating NSCs? They are neither the final link to the customer nor crucial to the creation of competitive products. They've slimmed down over time. The label sometimes used – 'national sales offices'

– is highly relevant since these actors are dealing with 'push issues', ie making sure dealers take on cars, and that sales numbers are as high as possible, as well as attempting to translate the car maker's overall marketing strategies into domestically relevant communications and campaigns. Again, overcapacity in the industry – and the substantial economies of scale – makes it necessary to have a marketing and sales function per key market area. But it's striking to see how the size of the NSC differs across brands. It's partly explained by the division of work between the factory and the NSC, but also by a management attitude with efficiency implications.

Tensions between car makers, their national sales companies and dealers

All types of organizations that work intensively together, deal with each other or cooperate in any sense, are characterized by tensions and conflicting perspectives. In the car industry, the tension between product development on the one hand and marketing and sales on the other is still there, but not as strong as in some other industries, since there is little interaction between the two sides. There is a clear division of responsibility and products are seldom designed for a specific customer's needs as is the case with medical equipment, manufacturing machinery and IT systems. Special vehicles companies, which may be partly or fully owned by car makers, build ambulances, police cars, funeral vehicles, armoured vehicles, etc so they are not built in the normal factory, which is designed for efficiency and scale advantages.

In addition, downstream channel members may have opinions on products, quality issues, etc but are in general quite happy with what the car maker creates in terms of product design. There are a lot more complaints about pricing, margins, inspection scheduling, marketing campaigns, demands on dealer facilities, etc than about the cars themselves. With premium brands in particular, dealers are often proud of the cars they're selling.

Since the debate about reducing the impact of, or even eliminating the need for dealers in the 1990s, the general quality of dealers has improved a lot. This debate, however, is not the only input to the improvement that has taken place – business in general shows a higher interest in, and buyers increasingly require, fair and clear price-setting, short waiting times, clean repair shops and showrooms, certified quality when buying used products, generous warranties, etc. Such matters apply generally, but the car industry in particular underwent a rapid and strong reorientation from being not very customer-friendly to relatively good standards. Extensive cost calculations presented around the turn of the millennium suggested that the elimination of the dealer would save a lot of money. By realizing pull orders and reducing pushing, about €1,000 a car could be saved (Ciferri, 2002; Parment, 2009). However, this line of reasoning did not take into account the competitive situation and heavy manufacturing over-capacities. It was based on a restricted analysis that looked at push vs pull as if it were a choice between selling pre-produced cars from stock and selling cars made to order.

When the discussions on reducing the reliance on dealers started, not surprisingly dealers complained and said that there was no way it was going to work. This discussion was intensive in the late 1990s and what at first seemed to be a typical reactive attitude turned out to be a good response: 15 years later very few new cars are sold to customers through channels other than a retailer – and the phenomenon of heavily discounted new cars flowing across EU countries has gone on for several decades.

Why was the dealer input not used in this discussion? The problem is that: a) dealers often complain about car makers' ideas – justified or not, and b) car makers, for this reason, rarely listen to their dealers although they sometimes say they do. If we try to understand this tension, we need to appreciate the advantage of car makers – they spend more time on scanning the environment, and managers are normally responsible for a limited part of the business (price-setting manager, product manager for Toyota Avensis, CRM manager, etc) – while managers of small dealerships have a variety of responsibilities. Thanks to the role of the car maker or NSC, managers, far removed from the everyday struggle to maintain margins and develop long-term sustainable and profitable relationships with buyers on the retail side, know more about trends, changes in consumer behaviour, etc at a more general level. They also have the capacity to carry out and collect more systematic market research and analysis. On the other hand, and very im-portant for the way this industry works, car makers and NSCs tend to apply a one-size-fits-all perspective whether it's appropriate or not. There are several reasons for this:

- A general tendency in business is to prioritize standardization over local adaptation.
- People working for car makers and NSCs normally live in or close to a large city and often socialize with others who have typical HQ jobs

– and rarely jobs in retail. They will often have a university degree and see the position they're occupying as part of a larger career plan, as opposed to retailers who often stay in one business for many years, sometimes their entire working life.

- A general lack of understanding of the retail side. There are sometimes a few staff members with retail experience but that's the exception rather than the rule.

- Relationships between HQs and retailers are often very complex – but less so with companies that: a) own all retail operations and/or b) apply a standardized approach, eg McDonalds, Starbucks or H&M. The Spanish fashion clothing retail group Inditex runs around 3,500 retail stores, 2,500 of them Zara stores. Inditex owns all the stores – and the entire supply chain from product design to retailing (except, of course, creating raw material) – something that makes controlling a lot easier. Due to the complexity of the retail business with all the financial, branding, information and social relations between NSCs and manufacturers, from a car manufacturer's perspective it's a lot easier to run a one-sided approach that will focus on implementing its ideas and translating them into appropriate strategies in each country, forcing dealers to implement them, than to apply a bottom-up approach. For all car makers, to varying degrees, the top-down mechanisms are a lot stronger than the bottom-up ones.

There is a variety of positions in this respect. NSC sales managers are more knowledgeable about retailers since they deal with them on a daily basis and they know they're highly reliant on the retail sales force to accomplish sales goals. NSC marketing, CRM or dealer network development managers may overemphasize the manufacturers' perspective in attempts to develop the retail businesses. Car makers and NSCs have by their very nature an advantage in understanding the industry and important trends and tendencies overall. But it's crucial to have the right people in place to secure a good feel for what is happening in the market to hand.

The vice-CEO of a large brewery that was nearly bankrupt in the late 1970s had a strong position in popular culture and implemented a number of challenging innovations that people didn't believe in at the time. The vice-CEO says he is now too old (65) to understand emerging trends in popular culture but he did an excellent job back in the 1970s and 1980s. A red Porsche 911 turns up in the company's car park during the discussion and the vice-CEO says: 'This is the guy I need absolutely the most. He hangs out twice or three times a week in high-profile bars and clubs and he knows everything about emerging trends. He's also an ambassador for our company in social spheres we normally have very limited access to. His input to new products is invaluable.' That type of guy makes more sense for HQ than for a retailer. He may not be the most hard-working person – he obviously spends a lot of time and energy on social activities – but his input could be invaluable.

Marketing vs selling – a tension that prevails in the car industry

Many businesses experience significant tensions between designers and manufacturing, and in consulting, enterprise systems, etc between product development and sales. The most significant conflict in the car industry is that between marketing and sales. There are few complaints about the cars' characteristics per se and the same holds for general marketing, corporate identity programmes, etc. There are complaints on margins, dealer investments, etc, but the strongest tension is that between the sales and marketing functions.

Marketers are under pressure to achieve revenue goals and want the sales people to sell on product characteristics and capitalize on the brand and not sell on price. An excellent idea if it weren't for the fierce competition that forces all car brands to discount and give away factory options, extended warranties, guaranteed resale values, etc for free. Marketers know exactly what to do to maintain a price premium, create demand, avoid discounts that reduce resale values and brand attractiveness, etc – but manufacturing overcapacity and low marginal production costs force car makers to push cars through the marketing channels with incentives to dealers and buyers. A car maker that would relax and wait for supply and demand to get back in balance would lose sales and market share since a pure pull strategy creates fewer sales than a mixture of push and pull (these mechanisms are extensively discussed in Parment, 2009). Unrealistic sales forecasts on top make things even worse.

Although many – professionals and the general public – see marketing and selling as tightly interconnected, they represent fundamentally different roles, which largely mirror the car industry's inherent tension between marketing (creating great products, building strong brands, developing marketing campaigns with a strong appeal among the target audience, etc) and selling (reaching high sales targets which, depending on product attractiveness, the state of the economy, etc may be less or more difficult to accomplish). The terms 'sales manager' and 'marketing manager' may appear similar, and in some sectors (eg the medical industry) there may be positions that are responsible for both sales volume and marketing efforts of a particular product line. But it's difficult to get sales and marketing on the same page. Kotler *et al* (2006) discuss the war between sales and marketing and how they are feuding like Capulets and Montagues: 'Marketers insist that salespeople focus too myopically on individual customers and short-term sales at the expense of longer-term profits.' In the car industry, too, marketing and selling are always in a symbiotic but conflicting relationship. Almost every decision is influenced by, and influences, what marketing and sales people do. In NSCs, the sales manager position is normally a lot tougher – car companies are under pressure since they are not selling as much as they have budgeted, and the factory has ambitious sales goals for the future. Marketing is easier since local adaptation of global strategies, including corporate identity, brand profile and marketing programmes, is limited.

In a grocery store, in a hotel, in a hospital or school, regardless of whether it's private or publicly owned, the marketing function strongly influences the opportunities to sell, but the functions are normally separate and sequential: marketing is more centralized and comes before selling. In a consultancy company, ie a firm of lawyers or auditors, the consultant carries out both marketing and selling but within the (normally not very rigid) overall marketing set-up. Because of the tough situation in the car industry, the tension is a lot greater than in many other sectors.

Marketing as a discipline has its roots in sales, and has gained acceptance and relevance as the need for seeing the bigger picture has grown. Despite this, marketing and sales managers may be very different. Marketers hang out with PR and advertising agencies, and discuss the latest trends in feel-good activities like gala dinners, product introductions and presentations, branding summits, etc while we do the hard work: making sales happen – that's the sales department's argument. Marketers, on the other hand, claim to be oriented to the long-term and strategic while sales people are short-sighted and undermine attempts to create strong brands, a price premium, and building relationships with the desired customer segments. So it's no surprise that tensions exist!

A web of tensions – a marketing and sales perspective on car maker-dealer relationships

The tension between marketing and sales is key to understanding relationships between car makers and their dealers. While car makers have a strong focus on overall marketing, and NSCs have to deal with simultaneous pressure on implementing marketing programmes and attempts to strengthen the auto brand, they are at the same time expected to implement high or unrealistic sales goals. Dealers are by their very nature more focused on sales than on general marketing issues: they can't influence the car design or car maker marketing and branding programmes. They focus on building a strong reputation in their local markets, something that is closely linked to sales efforts.

Hence, while car makers and their NSCs put a lot of effort into standardizing dealer processes, and measure and evaluate how dealers behave, which provides input into car maker processes, dealers are focused on making sales happen. According to a South Australia small multi-franchised dealership:

> Because of this competition, sometimes you need to be a little bit tough with clients; the dealer with perhaps a worse CSI report will be selling more cars because they are asking the stronger questions and perhaps cornering people, and perhaps that's not the sweet way of dealing with people, but in business, people would buy from someone else for $50, you know you have to sometimes get tough with people, in a nice way. It's one thing to have a CSI percentage of 90 per cent, but you have to ask yourself, is it worth what you have to do to get the CSI to 95 per cent, because you'll never have 100 per cent, but the cost of getting these extra 5 per cent, is it worth what it's going to cost for your business overall? I don't believe it is.

From the car maker's perspective, having more data is an advantage – and the disadvantages of asking buyers too often and too much are borne by the entire marketing channel, including customers who do the job of filling in surveys, not by the statisticians and mathematicians employed by car makers or NSCs to take care of and process the data. While dealers interact with their clients largely on an individual basis – a typical salesperson perspective – car maker marketers are heavily geared towards the bigger picture. And they like standardization, which makes follow-up easy. Combined with a fairly negative attitude towards dealers, tensions are strong, in particular between car makers and small, rural dealers. A car maker CEO puts it thus: 'We take the customer relations, that sort of thing, probably much more seriously than a lot of our dealers. Generally, the dealers are very nervous, and they have every reason to be, because most of them haven't changed the way they operate for the last 30 years, and the world has changed.' In addition to the negative attitude towards dealers, the car maker CEO expresses a very strong preference for seeing the dealer's relations with the customer as a standardized process: 'From the customer's point of view, one of the key points in retailing is to always dream of this as a factory, to have standard processes. So when the customer goes to a dealership, any dealership, they get handled properly, every time.'

Relatively few people have been on both sides of the business: the dealer side and the car maker side. An experienced person with decades of experience from each side states that a tendency over time has been for car makers to avoid people staying in the same NSC position for years, since this can result in too strong social ties between the NSC and the franchised dealers. Such a situation would make it more difficult to implement car maker decisions. A similar approach is found in embassies – people employed in a US Embassy are not allowed to stay in a country for more than three years, since that may create too strong connections to that country.

Most car companies have clever ideas about long-term strategies for their brands and product portfolios, but the battle in the marketplace is very tough and there are few signs it will get much better in the foreseeable future. New car makers arise in emerging countries and make cars that, after a couple of years of experience, can compete not only on price but also on other buyer-relevant criteria. Kia and Hyundai, for instance, were selling on price when they expanded heavily in the 1990s but later caught up – the luxury Hyundai Equus is now in general terms comparable with a Mercedes S Class or Lexus LS.

Planning horizon – top-down and bottom-up perspectives

There is an inherent paradox in the planning horizon of car makers, national sales companies and dealers. The first two argue that dealers are short-sighted in their approach. Car makers and NSCs certainly have a better overview and normally staff are more highly qualified, with university degrees and experience working for a couple of companies; dealers' staff tend to have lower formal qualifications and little experience in other companies or industries. The average duration of employment is, however, much shorter at the car maker or NSC level while it is not uncommon for people in dealerships to stay for many decades and there are several instances of the third or even fourth generation running a dealership. From the car maker side, the only known example is Ford Motor Company: Henry Ford I (1906–45) and Henry Ford II (1945–60) ran the company, and the MIT graduate William Clay Ford Jr, the great-grandson of Henry Ford I, acted as CEO (2001–6) and later Chairman (2006–). It's paradoxical to argue that people who are heavily involved in or even running a business for decades are short-sighted. It is, however, true that dealers often don't see the bigger picture and are less aware of changes in the macro environment. Car makers and NSCs, on the other hand, by their very nature, have difficulties understanding local markets.

Dealer control and channel power balance

The power balance in the supply chain is shifting in many industries. In the car industry, the power balance has long been weighted heavily in favour of the car maker. Dealers are dependent upon the car maker for the delivery of competitive products, general marketing, finance, etc. The dealer agreement gives car makers the upper hand: the possession of coercive sources of power – sanctions when the dealer does not achieve sales or corporate identity targets, and ownership of the brand. Car makers' tactics of control are based on five areas: the dealer agreement; training provision; dealer assessment procedures; the communications systems; and the car maker's general support (Rafer, 1997).

Powerful and growing retail groups have the negotiation and market power to counterbalance car makers' control. The ideal situation for a retailer, that can offset the car maker's power advantage over dealers, is to have:

- a proactive attitude, and see changes in the environment such as other dealers going bankrupt as an opportunity and not as a sign of poor industry profitability;
- representation of many brands to achieve diversification;
- the financial capacity to take on unsold cars, buy fleets of used cars and take other opportunities that may emerge, eg buying 200,000 tyres when a tyre retail group goes bankrupt;
- the courage to challenge car makers, apply a portfolio approach and not be too loyal to car makers without being rewarded for that.

For some franchised operators, it's very important to emphasize that the operation is 'proudly' locally owned and operated, as opposed to manufacturer-owned operations. (Anders Parment, 30 November 2010, BP Gas Station, Sydney, Australia)

Manufacturer-owned or franchised dealers?

A crucial question in designing marketing channels is, from the car maker's perspective, whether to sell through its own, direct channels or through indirect channels, ie franchised dealers. Traditional wisdom suggests manufacturers should concentrate on manufacturing and retailers on retailing, and the idea behind outsourcing the sales function to a franchised dealer is that with a strong business, social and cultural ties to the local area, the franchised dealer has a greater chance of selling higher numbers than a manufacturer with limited knowledge about the local market (Helmers, 1974). There are other rationales, too. Manufacturer investment costs are kept at a minimum and, through franchising, fast market penetration can be reached, something that has been emphasized more recently (Winter and Szulanski, 2001). McDonald's and 7-Eleven are well-known examples of this.

Nonetheless, direct channels, ie manufacturer-owned stores, increase in number and importance in many industries. If earlier manufacturers started their own outlets because they couldn't find an entrepreneur willing to invest, many more advantages have been emphasized recently. First, and maybe most important, direct channels give the opportunity to control stores in terms of product display, localization, personnel, etc. A manufacturer-owned store can thus work as a guiding star for other dealers to follow. Moreover, it will drive the manufacturer closer to the market since its own staff are in direct contact with end-users. In all industries with manufacturer overcapacity, manufacturer-owned stores give an additional advantage: they can be used as outlets for overproduction. It makes a huge difference from a car maker's perspective. Rental cars, car pools and other relatively short contracts of 6 to 12 months are great opportunities for moving excess stock. The same holds for manufacturer-owned outlets: instead of fighting with 100 dealers to make them take on 2,000 cars, cars can be distributed to the manufacturer's own outlets without a lot of hassle. Manufacturers in all industries share this experience. Assume Apple, or another computer manufacturer with strong dealer control has 10,000 unsold items from last year's production to get rid of at the same time as it wants the 100 dealers to display its new computer in the showrooms. With its own outlets, it's easy to make a decision on showroom disposition and discounts on old products. With franchised dealers, it may take a lot of time and result in a lot of irritation and complaints.

Car makers have taken standardization of dealer facilities and showrooms very far. Dealers largely look the same regardless of location and surroundings, reflecting the car maker's corporate identity but not necessarily the local architectural heritage.
(Anders Parment, 29 June 2013, Motorhaven Peugeot, Hastings, UK)

Indirect channels that are small-scale independents often suggest that they are forced to be customer-minded and do whatever they can to close a sale; it's also easier for a buyer to complain about products and services provided by a manufacturer. This goes back to the basic reason why car makers went for franchised dealers in the first place: to get rid of problems involved in recruiting and managing people, running a complex set of businesses that may be in conflict with each other (intra-brand competition) etc, in markets that car makers have limited detailed knowledge about. The expectations placed on a manufacturer-run dealer are hence higher.

When dealer groups grow, they may become large multinational enterprises with hundreds of dealerships and billions of dollars in turnover, thus taking on a role that is not very different to that of the car maker. Large enterprises with many organizational layers, specialist functions and large geographical (and mental) distances across units end up being somewhat formal and bureaucratic, running the risk of losing the entrepreneurial spirit that once characterized them.

In some instances, car makers have got tired of the drawbacks of having many dealers selling their products in a specific market area – intra-brand competition drives sales but reduces prices and hurts margins (see Parment,

2008; 2009). In an attempt to improve margins, strengthen the brand and create better relations between dealers and buyers, among dealers, and between dealers and the NSC, car makers and their NSCs have taken a stake in the franchised dealers. By taking control over them, principles for discounting have been established. The evidence is clear: prices have gone up, margins have improved significantly, but sales have slowed down by up to 50 per cent. The first explanation to this is the reduction in intra-brand competition. The second is the loss of incentives that go back to the owner-ship of the dealership. An entrepreneur running his or her own business has stronger incentives to make a sale than a car maker-owned vs NSC-owned dealership run on principles of limited discounting and attendance to cus-tomer care. In recent years, however, car maker-owned outlets have engaged heavily in discounting although the incentive structure remains different. The enormous pressure from car makers to sell more applies to all dealer-ships, regardless of location, competitive situation or ownership.

Solus, dual or multi-franchising?

Manufacturers in general prefer solus franchising since it implies that not only dealers but also other parts of the marketing channel are fully dedicated to the brand. Dealers, on the other hand, derive a lot of benefits from selling more than one brand:

- It's more likely that the dealer will have a car that appeals to a customer who walks into the showroom.

- It may – given that the size and turnover of the dealer are considerable – give a negotiation advantage. According to common belief, loyalty should result in advantages, and it does: commitment advantages arise when a dealer grows and becomes very important for the NSC in realizing sales, growth and branding goals. But in very competitive environments, negotiation power that results from having a portfolio of brands in a multi-franchised dealer may be at least as powerful.

- Risk diversification in a number of dimensions: less dependent upon the pricing and delivery capacity of a particular brand; less dependent upon product attractiveness; exchange rates, taxes, etc may vary as well as country-of-origin effects that arise from political and cultural events in particular markets.

A key dimension in marketing channels design is to address the need to take the invisible or hidden parts of the solus-multi dichotomy into consideration. Although the design and layout of showrooms and other customer-facing areas may convey a clear and brand-specific image, areas not apparent to the customer are likely to influence customer perception too. Separating brands or bringing them together has a strong influence on management attention. Hence, the choice of a solus, dual or multi-franchising channel – to the extent the car maker is in the position to choose – goes far beyond customer-facing areas. The more separated the marketing channels, the more dedicated people at all levels in the channel are likely to be to the brand. This underlines the fact that from a branding point of view, solus franchising is best accomplished in a channel owned and managed by dealers only selling one brand.

From the car maker's point of view, a substantial argument for solus is that multi-franchising steals the dealer's focus of attention. When a dealer starts to take on other brands, all decisions are weighed with regard to what is best for the dealers whereas in a solus setting, the dealer is focused on the one and only brand. Even worse, the NSC's efforts to pull buyers to the dealer showroom may result in the purchase of a competitor's product, something that would not happen in a solus channel.

The difference between solus and dual or multi-franchising is evident throughout the marketing channel. Solus strategies emphasize the brand and the cooperative interplay between channel members committed to the same brand. In contrast, multi-strategies emphasize market forces manifested in channel members striving to find profitable cooperation partners, with little or no hesitation in changing partners if a better opportunity emerges. Solus chains are more stable over time, while multi-channels are continuously changing – although it may be a slow process – in response to new opportunities emerging in the market. Solus chains are manifestations of commitment and a shared goal to strengthen the brand and derive advantages from a consistent brand appearance and experience. Multi-channels are manifestations of channel members' power and search for profitability. These mechanisms appear at all levels in the marketing channel (see Parment, 2008; 2009):

- *At the NSC level*: An NSC that represents more than one brand always has to prioritize between the brands. For instance, if two brands introduce new models at the same time, the importer organization may put more effort into one of the products at the cost of attention paid to the other.

- *At the dealer ownership level*: The owner of a multi-franchised dealership must prioritize between the brands. If a number of brands are sold by the dealer, owners are likely to see the business as a portfolio of franchises, and the attention on each brand is reduced to a part of the business portfolio. Moreover, profits from a successful brand may be invested in another brand, or used to take on an additional brand. This is bad news for the successful brand since it would prefer to have the profits invested in it for securing future success.

- *At the retail level*: In the showroom different brands always compete for attention. Hence, car makers are vulnerable to what is happening with the other brands sold at the dealers, unless excellent and outstanding products are offered – something that is difficult to maintain over time in a very competitive market.

The last problem is even more marked if a small volume brand is exposed in the same showroom as high volume brands. The more separated the brands, the more brand-specific the experience – but the management attention span adds to these mechanisms.

Salespeople's remuneration may be based on gross margins, which gives them incentives to direct the customer's attention to specific brands and models. Salespeople are likely to sell the products that are easiest to sell, or generate the highest salaries, thus an inherent characteristic of a multi-franchising environment is that salespeople could not be expected to be loyal to a particular brand. And remember – if any professional group is controlled by incentives, it's salespeople.

To capture the full advantages of brand separation, a separate solus organization should be put in place, from the car maker via the NSC to the dealers and their internal organizational structures. With a strong focus on solus dealers, car makers could aim at letting proactive dealers grow intra-brand instead of taking on other brands supplied by the car maker. Hence, dealers could grow through extending the market area by merging into or purchasing dealers in adjacent areas. A Volkswagen dealer could thus grow intra-brand through taking over other Volkswagen dealers instead of taking on Audi, Seat, Skoda or Porsche franchises in a nearby area. The benefit of growing intra-brand is not primarily about back-office cost savings – such savings are generally overstated. Advantages are rather based on being skilled in managing a particular brand.

Multi-franchised dealers: conflicts with car makers

Solus vs multi-franchising marketing channels are key to understanding the power balance in the supply chain. Despite the strong connections between large multi-franchised dealers and car makers that may exist, the mechanisms for solving conflicts, potential conflicts or friction are different.

Both the car maker and the dealer may see termination of the relationship as a solution to conflicts and friction. Relationships in a solus channel are to a larger extent based on mutual commitment. The weaker part – often the dealer – may be very vulnerable to the moves of the strongest part – often the car maker. A multi-franchise dealer group may have a power advantage over some car makers, not hesitating to exercise that power if conflicts arise.

Power balance

Car makers supply products that vary in terms of attractiveness, and dealers supply advantages in terms of local market share, market power, knowledge and reputation. By its very nature, the power balance will vary substantially across brands and marketing channels. Viable and growing solus dealers may see more costs than benefits in taking on another brand, hence they enjoy commitment advantages. The dealer may have power through its position as a committed high-volume dealer that represents a significant part of the car maker's sales in a particular market. It could be a metro area Ford or Skoda dealer with a large market share and a range of outlets. As the dealer has a strong position in the market, the car maker is highly dependent on it for sales volume. The dealer's commitment has proved strong over the years and the car maker would lose market shares if the dealer were to start selling another brand. Accordingly, the car maker will not interfere too much with the business arrangement but respect the dealer and make sure that terms are fair.

Car makers want proactive and innovative dealers on the one hand, and committed and loyal dealers on the other. Hence, they prefer dealers' intra-brand growth to inter-brand growth: growth in sales in a multi-franchise environment may mean that dealer profits from one brand are invested in competitors' brands. When inter-brand groups grow, the commitment advantage of solus dealers becomes clearer. Thus, the power shift that the growth of dealer groups entails may make solus dealers stronger as well, as their importance for the car maker becomes more evident.

Market mechanisms force portfolio-based models through

The increasing strength of dealer groups constitutes a significant shift of power in the car industry. Marketing channels used to be characterized by fairly stable relations and cases where car makers threatened dealers with franchise contract termination, or dealers suggested that they would take on further brands unless they get what they want from the car maker or the NCS were relatively few. The combination of stronger dealers, more market forces, and less loyal car makers and dealers – although there are clear exceptions – creates a new situation. The portfolio view is most likely here to stay. Car makers are increasingly willing to explore multi-channels while dealers are increasingly willing to consider multi-franchising.

Dealer groups applying a multi-franchising strategy may acquire power associated with a portfolio view that transforms the thinking about multi-franchising of a small dealer who considers taking on an additional brand to broaden the customer base and spread risks. Hence, there can be substantial market and negotiation power that can offset car makers' influence. From the dealer's point of view, increasing local market power, economies of scale and the spread of risks have been identified as the most important driving factors for multi-franchising (Hoffmeister and Huneberg, 1998). By acquiring significant market and negotiation power, competitive dealers with great locations and a strong brand may have the upper hand in dealing with car makers and customers alike.

With a portfolio approach, all car makers and dealers act in a market for contracts, and the stronger that large, powerful multi-franchised dealer groups get, the more often car maker-dealer relations will swap. Through commitment to the dealers, a car maker may create a hedge against the supply-demand mechanisms that guide the allocation of franchise contracts. To become attractive to dealers, car makers have to offer a strong brand, an attractive product portfolio and good terms.

There are a number of aspects to understanding the portfolio of franchises perspective, which gets stronger over time as market forces get stronger and car makers and dealers have to strengthen their market offers. Car makers have a number of areas to consider in dealing with dealer groups:

- Being dual or multi with attractive brands may generate showroom traffic and make it easier to access target segments. This applies in particular to brands with a low brand awareness and unexplored market potential. If the brand has a high awareness and a considerable market share, competing brands in the showroom would distract customers. German Volkswagen dealers would not benefit from having Ford and Opel cars in the showroom while a brand like Jaguar, Alfa Romeo, Volvo or Porsche may find new customers, who hadn't thought about the brands or didn't know about the surprisingly high availability and practicality of the cars, and the attractive terms offered. When Saabs were still being sold, around the turn of the millennium, a sports car dealer in Bristol was selling Saabs and argued that it would create sales that would not have taken place had the Saabs only been available through solus Saab dealers: 'A lot of people come in to look at a Lotus, and find that it's really impractical, and walk past the Saab convertible, that is cheaper, and they might not have thought about a Saab, we sell a lot of cars that way so it helps Saab, it attracts more people into the showroom, I think it's very good.' The multi-franchise approach forced the dealer to continuously evaluate whether the Saab business made sense: 'Bad management, bad marketing, very poor focus on the marketing, inconsistent marketing, basically just management that stays in the head office and never comes back, they don't really know what is going on in the marketplace. If the Saab business shrunk enough, I would obviously let another brand in, so it depends on the business, I don't want to, but Saab at the moment is going quite badly wrong, so we have to be flexible.'

- Being dual or multi with unattractive brands may have an adverse effect on customer perceptions of the brand, eg Saab sold with Kia in Spain a couple of years ago. In some cases, being dual with less desirable brands may be the only way to sell the product. This may happen if the product is not very attractive or has low brand awareness.

- Being the dealer's core business is a way to secure appropriate management attention over time. If another brand dominates the dealer's business, the dealer may lose sight of the second, 'less important' brand.

- A powerful car maker, with attractive products and resources to invest in the distribution network, will have the choice of using only solus dealers. Dealers applying or approaching a portfolio view may emphasize their own benefits from expanding the base in terms of the number of brands.

- It's always important to remember that while car makers prefer solus dealers, multi-franchising is a way of servicing customers better through offering a broader range of products. It is certainly true that buyers see more knowledgeable salespeople and a more consistent brand experience in a solus environment. However, it's unclear whether the higher level of expertise is really appreciated by buyers. Having the opportunity to compare a broad range of products and brands makes multi-franchising environments buyer-friendly, since it saves time and makes direct product comparisons across brands possible.

- Multi-franchising might strengthen the dealer's brand as the dealer becomes less associated with a particular brand. The dealer may benefit from the looser coupling between car maker and dealer inherent in multi-franchising, since the dealer can drive its own branding forward with fewer restrictions than in a solus chain.

- Multi-franchising is a way to diversify the business in relation to the state of the market: various brands do better in different economic climates. Product attractiveness may vary over time for each brand, as may terms and conditions, allocation policies (car makers may allocate cars to other dealers and/or other countries), exchange rates, supply-demand conditions, etc. The logic of diversifying through multi-franchising is the same as in any business: Volkswagen with Up!, Polo, Golf, Beetle, Touran, Passat, Sharan, CC, Amarak, Touareg, etc is substantially more diversified and less dependent upon the success of one model than for example Smart or Maserati – or Saab and Maybach, two brands that can't be bought anymore. Lack of a diversified product portfolio proves to be very challenging – if two out of three models are doing badly, how can the company survive? And if almost nothing happens in terms of product development for a couple of years, how can dealers stay motivated? Not surprisingly, most car makers are very much into diversification – Jaguar Land Rover and Porsche are instances of former niche car makers that are now offering relatively broad product portfolios. With too little portfolio diversification, as a car maker or as a dealer, one is a lot more vulnerable during periods of recession because of the lack of a hedge against lost sales for a particular brand or product.

Industry structures differ across countries and so do the attitudes towards and incidence of multi-franchising. The United Kingdom and Australia have a high incidence of multi-franchising groups, which suggests a strong retail side. In Australia it's largely a consequence of being a vast country with only 20 million inhabitants – only a few car makers could manage to run a dealer network with sufficient market coverage while keeping it solus throughout. In Germany, there are fewer multi-franchising dealers, which might be explained by a high interest in cars leading to customers valuing specialized solus dealers, high population density and relatively strong loyalty (see Parment, 2009). While buyers in other countries go in for a lot of shopping around, Germans appear to show a greater loyalty.

Many or few dealers – a tricky issue

If dealers are (too) small and weak the car maker will have a great number of small independent dealers. Hence, the car maker and its NSCs will have to deal with a large number of dealers that from a NSC perspective are not very professional and result in high dealer servicing costs. Small dealers may not have the resources required to invest in their businesses, at least not in the areas car makers see as crucial. Car makers can, to a large extent, put pressure on the small, independent dealer which in many cases has no choice but to stay with the car maker. But poor conditions will result in unprofitable and dissatisfied dealers that don't represent the brand in a good way.

Small dealers' ways of thinking may be very different from that of car makers, which implies communication problems and different views on what characterizes a successful dealer strategy (Parment, 2009; Witttreich, 1962). Moreover, small independent dealers are often managed by people who are seen as reluctant to change or to invest. An industry expert with four decades' experience in different roles in the car industry sees this as a crucial point in understanding problems in marketing channels relationships:

> They've got fragile goals, and it's very hard to get down to the real essence in discussions with them; they can be defensive, they don't like people telling them that they are wrong, some are very good and very rich, they have been used to giving orders in their own dealerships, you never hear about criticism.

In the worst case, people working for the NSC are the only ones who question the dealers, who may be 'local heroes' in the geographical and social contexts they operate in.

On the other hand, if dealers are too large, powerful and strong the car maker will have a comparatively small number of dealers to deal with. Dealing with a small number of professional people is beneficial from the car maker's point of view: the parties are more equal in negotiations. However, dealer groups may become too strong in terms of negotiation power and market power. The dealer side is then likely to make a claim for higher margins or any other term that neutralizes the car maker's initial power.

Based on this reasoning, power relations can be described in terms of franchise desirability. The more desirable the franchise, the stronger the car maker will be. Hence, car makers will get the dealers they deserve, and vice versa. Market mechanisms guarantee the survival of good dealers and car makers, and the disappearance of poor ones. Companies' self-interest and search for profits will drive out lacklustre management and weak players from the market, or they will end up in less desirable situations in terms of location, reputation and profitability. These mechanisms work irrespective of whether or not car makers apply controls to direct dealer behaviour. Customers do not accept poor dealers, nor do car makers. And of course, the same holds for car makers and the products they offer.

Entrepreneur-driven and portfolio-based multi-franchising

It's obvious that multi-franchised dealers have a couple of advantages over solus dealers. When the different brands come from the same car maker group, administrative systems and stock-holding of spare parts could be shared across brands, and a competitive advantage based on flexibility and quality could be reached. On the other hand, the high investment necessary to acquire a further franchise may not be repaid by an increase in sales volume. Dealers are fairly reluctant to take on further brands as long as they are small and stay with one or a few brands, but they are willing to take on further brands and dealerships if they have already reached a substantial size.

Multi-franchised dealers range from small-scale, entrepreneur-driven dealerships that see every opportunity to grow as a big decision, to large dealer groups that view the business as a portfolio of brands and dealerships as profit centres. The former are entrepreneur-driven, operating with an instinct to survive, while the latter are based on portfolio considerations and corporate discipline as the controlling philosophy.

To car makers, the latter are far more dangerous. The former may in broad terms contribute to market share and be difficult to replace due to their strong social and market position in the area in which they operate. On the other hand, they also constitute a substantial problem for car makers since they are reluctant to implement car makers' ideas and see the world very differently (Parment, 2009). But they may have few choices other than to stay with the car maker, hence they tend to be loyal. Powerful dealer groups operate based on what makes sense from a profitability and growth point of view, and have few emotional ties to car makers. They may be very tough in negotiations and make use of their negotiation and market power and, in general terms, they can get stronger and become an unstoppable threat to car maker dominance.

Power balance and margins

Margin renegotiation downwards is an extremely sensitive issue. The net margins reflect an actor's power and contribution to the added value of the marketing channel. Gross margins are largely seen as indications of net margins, although experience in different industries suggests that high gross margins in retail may be associated with low net margins. The car industry is a typical 'buyer bargaining industry' so, not surprisingly, auto brands with a strong market position can offer dealers low gross margins and still be considered very attractive, while weak auto brands may offer dealers very high gross margins and still get little or no commitment from dealers: net margins are wafer-thin for weak brands in very competitive segments. A strong market position, based on successful and desirable products and qualified dealers in prime locations, is likely to result in a wheel-of-fortune with a steady flow of buyers walking in to showrooms with buying intentions, limited bargaining, substantial net margins, high dealer and car maker profitability, happy buyers and resources to invest in new products, great showrooms and client relationships.

As mentioned earlier, around the turn of the millennium there were a lot of discussions on the future of marketing channels and whether cars would be sold through supermarkets, international arbitrageurs, internet-based intermediaries, and so on. Car makers – and retailers – that invested heavily in internet sales lost a lot of money and internet sales never took off. Retailing cars is a complex business with the physical distribution of cars, trade-ins, test drives, warranty repairs, etc so the buyer wants to see a qualified dealer. Also it's a lot easier to sell additional products and services in a car dealership than in a supermarket or on the web: leather upholstery, panorama roofs, hi-fi systems and large alloy wheels are often bought after the buyer has seen the options on a demonstration car. The same holds for additional services: after discussions with salespeople, many buyers recognize they want additional insurance, winter tyre storage facilities, extended warranties or prepaid service schedules included in the finance or leasing package of the car.

Car leasing and subscription

Increased difficulties in making young buyers interested in buying a car along with the lack of attractiveness of existing finance and leasing approaches have forced car makers and dealers to develop new ways of making cars available for the younger audience. Key in these approaches is removing risks to the buyer and offering flat monthly rates – it may be called leasing, subscription or full service finance. To reduce car buyers' or users' fear of having to pay for defects, eg scratches or dents, when the car is handed back at the end of the period, criteria for judging the value of the car may be offered. This is also linked to court cases which stipulate that car dealers are not allowed to charge clients for 'normal use'.[1] It is unlikely that politicians will reduce consumer rights in the future, so it can be assumed that consumers will enjoy protection when they hand in the car they've been using for a couple of years.

Mercedes-Benz in Germany has provided a great solution to fears buyers have over possible disagreements they will have with the dealer when they hand the car back. Criteria for what will be accepted in terms of car condition are published when the contract is signed; they are even published on Mercedes-Benz' homepage (see Figure 3.1). For instance, stone chips of 3 mm and up to six dents (maximum of two per door/bumper, etc) no larger than 2 cm will be accepted – a generous policy since a car with six dents and a couple of stone chips would normally have a lower trade-in value. It's important to note that Mercedes-Benz owns around 40 dealers across Germany so it keeps more control of concepts offered at the dealerships than any other brand with a substantial market share in Germany.

A crucial question from the customer's perspective is whether residual values will be guaranteed – if not, the customer bears a substantial risk (less so for a Toyota Yaris or Volkswagen Polo – cars that have high and stable residual values in all markets where they are on sale), and the attractiveness of the leasing/subscription concept will be undermined. In some

FIGURE 3.1 Mercedes-Benz, Germany, provides criteria for what will be accepted in terms of car condition when a leased car is handed back

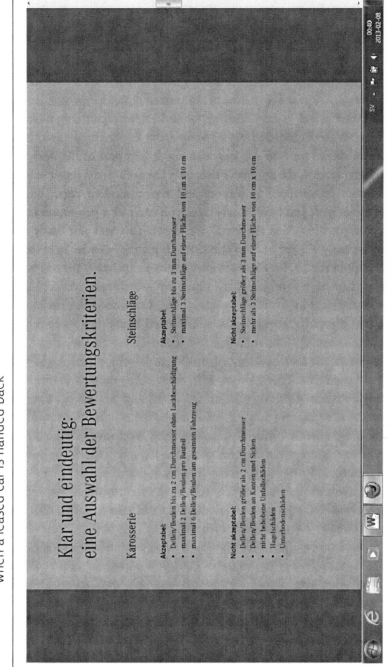

Klar und eindeutig:
eine Auswahl der Bewertungskriterien.

Karosserie

Akzeptabel:
- Dellen/Beulen bis zu 2 cm Durchmesser ohne Lackbeschädigung
- maximal 2 Dellen/Beulen pro Bauteil
- maximal 6 Dellen/Beulen am gesamten Fahrzeug

Nicht akzeptabel:
- Dellen/Beulen größer als 2 cm Durchmesser
- Dellen/Beulen an Kanten und Sicken
- nicht behobene Unfallschäden
- Hagelschäden
- Unterbodenschäden

Steinschläge

Akzeptabel:
- Steinschläge bis zu 3 mm Durchmesser
- maximal 3 Steinschläge auf einer Fläche von 10 cm x 10 cm

Nicht akzeptabel:
- Steinschläge größer als 3 mm Durchmesser
- mehr als 3 Steinschläge auf einer Fläche von 10 cm x 10 cm

markets, interest is deductible from the value, which gives financial leasing a disadvantage.

Competition from unauthorized actors

Car inspections and repairs is a huge market that used to be characterized by low quality and high prices in authorized repair shops, and less cheating and lower prices in free-standing, unauthorized repair shops. Two factors protected the authorized repair shop from competition: first, it was the natural choice for new car buyers, since it was part of the dealer's service package; second, the argument that only the authorized repair shop had the necessary competence to inspect and repair modern cars. 'With all the electronic stuff you have in cars now, you can't let a guy around the corner inspect your car' was the usual argument. This was not really true until very recently – a car built in the 1990s is normally easier to inspect than a car built in the 1970s: there are fewer parts to exchange (eg contact breaker points had been eliminated), oil filters are more easily accessible, there are no mechanical adjustments to make, etc. Later, software updates became part of a regular inspection and advanced computers were required for trouble shooting. Free-standing, unauthorized repair shops can buy these computers but they are very expensive and – along with higher demands on environmental compliance, HR policies, cleanliness in the workshop etc – contributed to neutralizing the initial cost advantage. These factors, along with a general tendency in businesses for a higher threshold volume to make a business viable, contributed to small workshops closing down while larger ones grew, merged or became part of a chain that engaged heavily in marketing. For both these reasons – car buyers see the dealer's workshop as a default choice and buyers think it has a competence advantage – unauthorized workshops, often parts of a chain, have to spend a lot of money on marketing to convince car owners.

In addition, while the unauthorized workshops must be profitable to stay in business, a dealer can run the workshop at a loss and see it as a part of the overall offer. Since the dealer's businesses are related, a lot of benefits may be derived. When car owners visit the dealer to bring their car in for inspection, a certain percentage of them will take a look in the car showroom and talk to the salespeople – it normally costs several hundred dollars in advertising to make a potential buyer visit the dealership. And the authorized dealership may offer a car as a test drive or a promotion to market a new model while the owner's car is in for service. It normally means that the customer will get a newer and nicer car, too, instead of the free-standing workshop's used little run-about.

Small, unauthorized repair shops may not have the competence and skills required to do repairs and many of them are likely to close down. Or if they are large, multi-brand operations with high marketing and training costs they will be vulnerable to changes in the environment. Car buyers looking on the internet for the lowest price may find better prices elsewhere. The government may introduce measures that make life difficult for small, free-standing workshops, as was the case in Germany in 2009 with the scrappage premium of €2,500. And a profitable auto brand may relatively easily drive non-profitable workshop chains out of business by reducing its prices.

Model range expansion and complexity

A strong trend in recent decades has been car makers' attempts to maintain and increase market share by expanding model ranges, something that has contributed to high complexity in marketing channels. A typical example of this is Mercedes' small family car – an entirely new segment for the brand when the first A Class was introduced in 1997 (W168). The second generation, introduced in 2004 (W169), was launched as two models using the same platform: the A Class and the B Class. The third generation (W176) introduced in 2012 added a stylish CLA to the A and B Class, with a small SUV (GLC) and a CLA Shooting Brake expected to be launched. For car dealers, range expansion such as this means a significantly increased complexity that requires smart logistics to deal with more spare parts, more demonstrators, larger showrooms and higher operating costs, resulting in higher threshold volumes required to represent and sell a particular auto brand.

The car of the future comes in many different shapes. We've seen an enormous expansion in model ranges over the years, not only in automobiles but also in other industries, eg white goods, fashion clothing, consumer electronics and airline travel. An increased diversification of offers signifies high competition. Car makers have at least three reasons to broaden their model ranges:

1 As buyer preferences become more diversified, creating new products is a way to meet those wants and needs. Unless this happens, the car maker is likely to be competitively disadvantaged.

2   As other car makers are expanding their model ranges, not offering cars in new segments is likely to result in lower sales and market share.

3   Offering a portfolio of models means a significant risk diversification, which has many facets: a) different models do well in different economic climates, b) as the product is moving along the product lifecycle, it normally becomes less competitive, meaning it's an advantage to have products at different stages in the lifecycle, c) if a new product is not very successful, it's a tragedy for a company with one, two or three models, while car makers with 10 to 20 models are more likely to survive competition. If a new Volkswagen Polo or Mercedes C Class were not very successful, these car makers have around 20 other models so they are likely to survive.

In 2008, Audi introduced its first SUV, the large Q7, followed by the smaller Q5 and Q3. In 2015, the plan is to offer a Q1, Q2, Q3, Q4, Q5, Q6 and Q7. BMW will soon provide an X1, X2, X3, X4, X5 and X6. Mercedes will have the MLC, ML, GL, G, GLK and GLA Class. An interesting development, and car makers are even competing with themselves. In addition to all the SUVs, BMW offers, in about the same size as the X1 and X3, the 3-series saloon, the 3-series touring, the 4-series coupé, and the 3-series GT, which is larger than the touring but not an SUV. Mercedes provides the CLA and C Class, both competing with BMW 3 series and the Audi A4. Or is the CLA competing with the A3 saloon? Staying out of this game of expansion might cost market share!

The implications of this are challenging. Dealer operating costs will increase while all the available car models should be available for customer inspection and test drives, and the dealer structure becomes urbanized – it is difficult to run a rural dealership for a brand with 20 models. The effects of the latter will result in an ever stronger metro-rural divide. If rural dealers only offer the lower-range models – very few car makers would be happy with that, and they're currently applying measures and incentives to make sure it will not happen – the brand will be perceived differently in rural areas. Another option is to reduce or even eliminate dealerships in rural areas and rural hubs with a market of fewer than, say, 100,000 inhabitants. In 2002, Audi implemented a plan to improve dealer quality and adjust the business models to new realities in some countries. In Sweden, for instance, the number of dealers was reduced from about 150 to 50 in a few years. The effect was higher dealer quality and an urbanization of the buyer profile:

market shares were largely kept but increased in metro areas while fewer sales were made in rural areas.

Broadening model ranges obviously increases costs in an industry that is not known for its high margins. Car makers compete on volume and market share, for both long-term market position and reasons of prestige, so staying out of this game and focusing on a few models appears very risky.

Push and pull: a key indicator of industry health?

A key factor in understanding the car industry is push and pull. As there are several reasons to move towards a pull system, while the evidence in recent years speaks for an increased application of push, one may ask why the theoretically superior pull strategy is not used to a greater extent.

Push and pull rationales

In striving for reduced distribution costs, stock-holding of cars at different stages in the marketing channel has been questioned as it is assumed to entail significantly higher costs. A complete conversion of automobile production from a push to a pull system has been estimated to yield savings of up to 20 per cent in the cost of providing cars to the market (Ciferri, 2002; Dettmer, 1998). Car makers say that they are trying to move towards a leaner distribution system in order to complete the transformation that started with lean production. However, the transition to a lean distribution system has proven to be very difficult. Logistically it's doable, but the enormous industry over-capacity in combination with intensive competition makes it hard to realize. In addition, the complexity inherent in supply and marketing channels with an NSC implies coordination and cooperation among an extensive network of dealers, authorized repairers, parts distributors and the logistics companies responsible for delivering vehicles. Organizing the system involves both optimizing the sub-processes and coordinating flows of information and physical goods in a complex web of relationships. It would have been doable if competition were limited, but as long as factories keep producing and supply far exceeds demand, it is difficult.

A research report from 2001 suggests systems are put in place to support an efficient and transparent vehicle supply:

Most car makers have developed an online link between dealers and the national sales companies (and with the factory), which makes the ordering process much more efficient and reliable, along with better transparency. Leaner and more frequent ordering implies a lower intermediating role of national sales companies... where production can be more fine-tuned with market demand as perceived by dealer operators. To this respect many activities of national sales companies are being automated, outsourced or centralized, hence their role is gradually evolving, with more and more focus on value added activities such as marketing and network relations.

(Buzzavo and Volpato, 2001: 11–12)

Hence, theoretically, pull is superior and definitely doable, but implementation is difficult. In addition, competition and oversupply have made the role of the national sales company more complex and resource-hungry, contrary to the expectations of more qualified order-to-delivery systems.

Difficulties in implementing order-to-delivery

Numerous attempts to implement customer-pull systems have been initiated in recent years – no surprise, since the arguments for doing so are strong and multifaceted. Calculations suggest that building to order could save substantial amounts.[2] The buyer gets exactly the desired car spec, and the car is newly built with the latest hardware and software adjustments as opposed to a car that has been kept in stock for a couple of months or longer. With the right spec, both seller and buyer make better deals since there will be no discussion on the extent to which the buyer should pay for an unwanted sunroof or Bose hi-fi system – or even worse, getting the new car in an unsuitable colour combination.

Order-to-delivery eliminates costly stock-holding – in addition to the cost of stock there are substantial costs involved in the space used for storing cars. Selling costs are also likely to be higher since the customer process will be less lean and customer-focused: the salesperson keeps the overstocked cars in mind in discussions with the buyer. An Audi dealer had a new A8 in stock for 13 months and finally found a customer – but the car didn't have a sunroof. The buyer wanted a sunroof and ordered a new car. The dealer grew irritated as the car in stock grew older and older – and the customer process was infected by this attitude. The – according to the buyer – wrongly specced A8 stays in the showroom as a reminder of a demanding customer who couldn't live with an A8 without a sunroof – but why should he? The car cost more than $100,000!

One of the most serious problems with keeping cars in stock goes beyond the higher costs per car involved in order-to-delivery: depreciation. When there is a strong push as in the car industry, there is downward pressure on the value of cars in stock. The more cars in stock, the higher the accumulation of depreciation will be. The more the NSC is under pressure from the car maker to push produced, stocked and unsold cars to dealers, the larger the problem. A dealer may optimally have 20 to 30 new cars in stock, but strong incentives from the NSC to take on more cars have increased the stock to 60. What happens then? It's likely that other dealers selling the brand are likewise overstocked, and have to give large discounts to get rid of the cars. Attentive buyers will start bargaining over prices and, in a situation similar to a reverse auction, dealer net margins will get wafer-thin or even negative since cars may be sold at a loss. By tradition, the practice of discounting is seen as an indispensable part of some industries but is very rare in others; in the car industry it has a long history. Needless to say, residual values get lower as a consequence of heavy discounting, something that hurts the brand.

Intense competition makes lower prices a common tactic to maintain market share. In 2013, face-lifted Opel Insignia, BMW 5 Series and Mercedes E Class models were introduced with lower prices in many markets. Hence, pre-facelift cars that had been in stock for a while lost value. NSCs then had to pay part of the depreciation to save dealers from financial problems.

The only way out of this negative spiral is to attempt to restore the balance between supply and demand. The defensive strategy would be to scale down production – something that will result in fewer cars sold as the brand in question will have less push than competitors. The aggressive approach would be to introduce new, attractive models and expand the model range – as competitors do so to maintain their market share, not doing it would result in fewer opportunities to find customers in the increasingly fragmented car market.

A great advantage to cars in stock is that the dealer will have cars ready for immediate delivery. Buyers these days don't want to wait, and if the spec is close to optimal, many prefer a car that they can see and touch before delivery to an unseen car that will be delivered 10 weeks after the purchase decision. But it comes at a cost: order-to-delivery is a lean approach; keeping cars in stock is not.

In sum, there are some significant and inherent problems involved in an order-to-delivery approach which, given the current market circumstances, makes it difficult to put into effect. A great deal of research has questioned the predominant push approach without taking these factors into account, arriving at the conclusion that a transition to a pull system would entail substantial cost savings that can be passed on to the customer (see Parment, 2008; 2009):

- Immediate delivery drives volume. First, having products in stock means immediate delivery – an advantage for the customer; second, the push pressure forces dealers to sell cars already on the forecourt.

- Intensive competition, particularly for volume products. Buyers who are not very loyal are not willing to make sacrifices to get a particular brand, eg wait a few months for a car. For premium and luxury cars, buyers are more likely to be prepared to wait to get what they want. A Jaguar F-Type buyer is unlikely to buy a Mercedes SL purely because of the shorter delivery time.

- Intra-brand competition drives competition and volume. Dealers are forced to develop intra-brand competitive advantages to sustain competition.

- Marginal costs for building a car are low while costs for development and factory facilities are high; thus car makers have incentives to boost volume, as long as they don't have any serious ambitions to go upmarket.

- The marketing channel overall is focused on volume, from the car maker CEO to the dealership salespeople. Unless there are profitability problems, senior car managers talk more about sales volume and product strategies than they do about profits. Overcapacity has strengthened the position of volume and sales figures in the last decade. A serious transition to pull thinking would mean a radical cultural change with a lot of management effort to get to a situation of balance between supply and demand.

- There are strong reasons to emphasize sales volume. All channel members are likely to benefit from higher volumes since more cars means more profitable after-sales services, including more spare parts. An increase in volume is also likely to increase future sales. In this respect the actors' interests may differ. Even a zero-margin sales transaction may be profitable for the dealer since it entails an increase in the demand for after-sales services. However, selling too many cars with high discounts reduces margins and may reduce residual values.

Ideal push share

The higher the share of pull, the more likely there will be a mismatch between cars in stock and buyer preferences. This particularly holds for upmarket cars, where the car spec is more important to buyers than for low-end vehicles such as the Peugeot 208, Vauxhall Astra, Volkswagen Polo, Chevrolet/Holden Cruze, etc.[3] This may result in a very slow turnover of cars with unusual specifications, and the customer's desired vehicle specifications cannot be met very well. A range of unwelcome consequences are the likely result of too high push share:

- Buyers don't get the car specs they want. Heavy promotion may result in real pull with buyers asking for high-margin factory options such as a powerful engine, sunroof, sound system or LED headlights. When they visit the showroom, however, the dealer attempts to force cars with the wrong spec onto the buyer, since that's what's in stock.

- Factory efforts to sell overproduction to the dealer get increasingly difficult, since the stock tends to expand and push creates a downward pressure on its value.

- Every push effort will irritate dealers since they are an indication of oversupply and problems for the dealer getting rid of existing stock.

- Car makers, NSCs or dealers will never face the real market demand, since push prevails over pull. Hence, there is a risk that products are always sold for a price less than real market price.

With a strong push, the buyer has the upper hand; with strong pull, the seller has the upper hand. This is very obvious in car retailing. An extreme example of real pull is in the UK in the first few years of the first generation BMW X5. Waiting time for a new car was around a year. When buyers asked for a valuation of their trade-in car, the dealer said: 'Let's do that when you get the new car. If you're not happy with what we offer, we won't punish you, we just pass on the new car to somebody on our waiting list and you are welcome to order a new car and wait another year to get it.' It's still the case that when new, very desirable models are introduced, for a while there will be more demand than supply – it's a very uncommon, and very desirable, situation for a dealer.

The ideal push share largely depends on a number of factors:

- The state of the economy in general and of the car industry in particular: a higher push share is reasonable in a recession, and the distribution system, ie dealers and NSCs, could thus balance the lack of market demand by keeping the factory running.

- The distance from the factory to the buyer. Selling Asian cars in Europe means a considerably lengthier delivery time, hence most Asian cars are sold from stock in Europe while Germans buying Germany-built cars could expect delivery in a couple of weeks at best.

- The brand profile and the product portfolio. For lower-end cars such as a Skoda Fabia, Toyota Yaris or Ford Fiesta, push is the rule and few customers would complain if their car has been kept in stock for a couple of months. In fact, they enjoy fast delivery and often don't even think about the opportunity to customize the new car – even a colour other than the preferred one may not be a problem.

Regarding the latter point, even lower-end premium cars, eg BMW 1-series, Audi A1 and A3, Mercedes Class A and B, and to an extent BMW 316d, Audi A4 1.8 TFSI, Mercedes C 200 CDI etc, may well be sold from stock. Although factory people working for premium brands often state that 'premium brand is an attitude, not a car size', these particular premium cars are direct competitors of slightly cheaper, more well-equipped and still competitive volume brands such as Ford, Toyota, Volkswagen, Hyundai and Peugeot. Working for a premium manufacturer and stating that a 316d, A4 1.8 TFSI or C 200 CDI in no way competes with a Peugeot 508, Volkswagen Passat or Volvo V60 proves the person has a poor understanding of competitive mechanisms.

There are by its very nature some inherent advantages in a pure pull system, where no cars are built until they are sold. For the factory it means risk reduction: planned production volumes are supported by orders, which minimizes manufacturing costs. All output is financially secure for the car maker since the cars are paid for by the dealers on delivery. The desire of dealers to minimize stock is believed to lead them to maximize sales at the cost of retained margins. It may well be argued that buyer needs are not the critical element in a push system (Whiteman *et al*, 2000).

In principle there are many advantages in a pull system compared to a push system but it might be hard to put in place a pull strategy as long as overcapacity is substantial. For a car maker, overcapacity is a key reason to run its own outlets, which work as a safety-valve and take care of over-production in a smoother way than franchised dealers.

Push drives sales volume

Official car sales statistics lay the foundation of market share, one of the key signs of success in the car industry. Car makers, importers and dealers are constantly tracking not only their own but also competitors' market share and they follow competitor moves closely. The downstream pressure on sales volume is enormous – particularly for markets that constitute a significant share of the car maker's total sales volume – and, which is one of the strange characteristics of the car industry, in many cases appear to be more important in the short run than profitability, product quality and happy buyers (of course, a car maker or NSC would never confess something like that!)

There is little doubt that push drives volume for two reasons. First, some customers want fast delivery. It is argued that this is the spirit of the time: if the car can be delivered within 24 hours, the customer wants it now. Waiting times have gone down and there are web shops in almost every industry that compete on fast delivery: order before noon or 2 pm, and you'll get delivery the next day. Particularly in the case of budget and volume cars, for which there are a lot of close substitutes, they are easier to sell if there are cars in stock for fast delivery. As a rural dealer argued: 'Opel Astra, you must have cars in stock, the customer is shopping around during the weekend, if you have the red car in the showroom ready for delivery, they will buy it; if it's an Opel or Peugeot or Renault or whatever, I think most people won't care.' Second, overstocked marketing channels, ie many cars kept in dealers' and national sales companies' stock, force all actors involved to close a deal and sell, with the drawbacks it entails in terms of low margins, residual values going down, etc.

Car makers push sales

It's quite understandable that car makers use the push button to boost sales. There are numerous strong advantages to selling many cars:

- The costs of developing new cars are enormous, but the marginal cost of producing more units is relatively low. Over time, marginal costs have gone down in general terms, since parts have become cheaper and manufacturing is increasingly carried out by machines.

- New cars provide a basis for selling finance, insurance, inspections, repairs, etc, which generate profits for car makers and dealers alike.

- Cars sold means that, assuming buyers like the products, the brand gets ambassadors who may be walking-talking advertisements – more efficient and, in a strict sense, cheaper than other types of marketing communications.

- High sales figures add prestige, give motivation to salespeople and purchase-decision confirmation to buyers.

There are basically three types of new car buyers: companies and other legal entities, consumers and car dealers. Under a pure pull regime, the first two represent the absolute majority of sales. Under a push regime, car dealers represent a significant part of sales: they take on cars and keep them in stock, either because they got a good deal or they want to have cars ready for delivery when buyers show up.

Push is a very effective way of boosting short-term market share. Car makers do force their dealers to take on cars by requiring them to place orders for the upcoming year in advance. Until the 1980s, Mercedes had a 5 to 6 per cent market share in Sweden. Quality and rust problems, and competitors that offered cars that were comparable in terms of comfort and safety and ran aggressive marketing campaigns made Mercedes appear not to deliver value for money. The importer was integrated into the Danish organization, something that emphasized the lower priority Mercedes gave to the Swedish market. Market share eroded and for many years Mercedes had 2.5 to 3.5 per cent of the market. Recently, the potential of the Swedish market with 250,000–300,000 cars sold per year – one tenth of the German home market but still important – forced Mercedes to use the push button: in 2012, 67 per cent of sales (7,930 out of 11,774 cars) were sold to Mercedes dealers for pre-registration, demo cars, etc. In this way, a 4.2 per cent market share was reached. This practice is normally not used by premium car makers (Parment, 2008), since it undermines the genuine demand that attractive products are expected to generate, but it's a very effective way to boost short-term sales. And if there is a high global sales target, communicated to everybody and tracked narrowly by competitors and journalists, the car maker is likely to do what it can to reach it.

What happens, though, when cars are pushed onto importers in the first place (by car makers) or onto dealers (by importers)? Natural or automatic demand is undermined since cars are not sold based on pull, but on push in combination with oversupply. A number of disadvantages with a strong push may be identified:

- Residual values go down. In the first place, a new car buyer thinks he or she has got a great deal because of the high discount provided; however, the discount is a sign of lack of demand at the suggested price, something that is going to generate further discounts and a reduction in residual values along with lower desirability of the brand.

- New, nearly new and to an extent older used cars in the dealer's stock lose value when discounts on new cars increase. The dealer may thus lose money when margins and discount levels rise, since they are lowering the market price of the new cars.

- If a car maker starts overstocking the marketing channels with new cars, there is a significant risk the problem is never eliminated and natural marketing forces will never come into effect.

The market is very transparent, so increased dealer margins are likely to have an effect on discounts given. Many car buyers – consumers as well as business buyers – do extensive price comparisons and dealers, regardless of the state of the economy, want to sell cars. Hence, they tend to give away increased margins to buyers.

In sum, balancing pull and push strategies is a tricky question that can be managed if the brand and the products are attractive. Without an inherent underlying attraction neither pull nor push will work.

Pushing premium brands – a questionable practice

Although push in general terms makes more sense for the lower end of the market, there are some premium dealers who argue that keeping an assortment of cars in stock is advantageous, since it drives volume:

> We buy cars and place them on the yard before we try to sell them. It may be cheaper to order the car directly from the factory and wait six or two weeks, but I think we would lose a lot of sales. Here, you get immediate delivery. When you buy a television set, for instance, you don't like to wait two weeks, you want it now.

If there is stable demand, a system to coordinate a balance between push and pull is likely to work. The mix may be different for different brands depending on model range, exclusivity, customer profile, etc. In broad terms, a push strategy suits volume brands whereas a pull strategy suits premium brands. For upmarket models and premium brands in particular, the disadvantages of customers getting the wrong car spec are important: buyers are paying for options they don't want and not getting options they do. Hence, on a larger scale, push contributes to reducing customer satisfaction and profit margins; but in a market with heavy competition, manufacturers may have no choice if they aim to maintain and increase sales volumes.

Increased push means a larger percentage of new cars come with a 'business package', 'premium package' and similar from the factory, so buyers are less likely to order a car with an individual spec. Car makers' practice of loading rental cars with many factory options contributes to the commoditization of factory options.

Commoditization of factory options

When car leasing, subscription and fleet cars are a large part of sales, there is a risk that the very lucrative factory options become subject to commoditization. Rental cars used to be very poorly equipped – a Sixt Audi 80 rental car in the early 1990s typically was equipped with a radio. That was it, not even a compact cassette player. In the BMW 5 series e39 generation, German rental cars had a few factory options: automatic air con, sunroof and metallic paint; the 523i also got leather seats. Five years later, in 2004, the e60 5 series generation 525i rental car was equipped with these options, *plus* xenon headlights, parking sensors, and a GPS. Another five years later, a French Peugeot 407 rental car had all the available factory options (GPS with voice control, adjustable leather seats, adaptive xenon headlights, telephone, hi-fi system, etc). The marginal costs for the car maker of adding these features are typically lower than the nominal plus in residual values. So in the short term, it's profitable for car makers to load fleet cars with many factory options, even if the fleet customer doesn't pay a higher cost to get them.

NSCs typically get a list price from the factory, based on which the retail prices for factory options are set. Cost calculations make it clear that even by using the NSC list prices, which are substantially higher than the factory costs, fleet car depreciation in nominal value (ie not the percentage) is considerably lower for cars equipped with business and sports packages, xenon headlights, metallic paint, larger wheels, etc. The reason is clear: it is very difficult to sell a one-year old 'basic' car without the factory options most buyers see as mandatory. That is a clever strategy. But what about overloading fleet cars with factory options – the most expensive GPS, adaptive chassis, leather upholstery, LED headlights, hi-fi system, sunroof, etc – that are very expensive in the retail price list? Fleet cars (over)loaded with factory options are highly depreciating cars that soon reach the used car market, and buyers are unlikely to be willing to pay for more than a few of the options. The problem is similar to that of pre-produced cars that are pushed to buyers: the buyer can't change the spec and is unwilling to pay for unwanted options, so dealers have to offer them for free or at a large discount to get the sale.

Another problem in some markets is when the opposite happens – all but a few cars delivered in a market area have the same spec. Sweden has long had a limit on the taxation of official cars with a price of up to about SEK 360,000 (€42,000), adjusted for inflation each year – above that level a luxury tax is added. Intense competition and a strong desire among all brands to be part of the official cars market, even at the cost of heavy discounting, results in an undesirable situation, for premium brands particularly: 85 to 90 per cent of the cars delivered in a broad model range (Audi A6, BMW 5 Series, Mercedes E Class, BMW X3, Volvo XC60) are standard spec cars with a 'business package' – sold at heavy discount to get below the tax price limit. After three years, the typical duration of a leasing contract, dealer showrooms are full of standard spec cars with the weakest engines. This harms the premium brand experience.

These examples underline an inherent problem in car maker strategies: if a very high percentage of new cars delivered are standard spec cars, there will be too little variety in the used car market, something that reduces the (premium) brand experience. If cars are overloaded with options buyers don't want to pay for, the residual value of the factory options goes down. Intense competition and industry overcapacity give car makers strong short-term incentives to give away factory options – but in the long run, it may hurt the brand experience, reduce the price premium and constitute a danger to the brand.

Overcapacity makes car makers inconsistent

All in all, car makers are not entirely consistent in their approaches. On the one hand they implement programmes to strengthen the brand and create a demand for the product in order to get rid of pushing and discounting; on the other, car makers force pre-produced vehicles through the marketing channels.

The pressure created by industry overcapacity induces car makers to maintain sales, partly through product strategies, ie broadening the model range, and partly through intensive marketing. Car makers implement measures to secure commitment, primarily through creating solus chains dedicated to the brand, both in terms of management attention and brand-specific investment. Car makers also explore different ways of selling their cars, eg to leasing and rental companies, to push the cars to the market. This multi-channels approach may undermine attempts to create a dealer network dedicated to the brand. In addition, overcapacity undermines the preconditions for order-to-delivery – as long as the marketing channel is overstocked with pre-produced cars, it is very difficult to maintain pull strategies with cars ordered to delivery. Even worse, overcapacity impacts badly on residual values.

In sum, many car makers can be inconsistent in their marketing channel approaches under the pressure of industry overcapacity. They tell dealers not to sell cars from stock but rather to order a vehicle that is specified in accordance with the buyer's preferences, based on the argument that a customized vehicle makes the customer more satisfied, which reduces the need for high discounts. With an order-to-delivery approach, the dealer does not have to carry stock, which saves money. However, car makers offer incentives to persuade dealers to take on more cars than there is a need for. This inconsistency irritates dealers and harms residuals: it is difficult to deal with a situation of products not being desirable at the retail price. Dealers under pressure create a situation similar to an auction with buyers receiving bids from dealers looking to reduce stock.

Push and pull cultures

There is a substantial difference between countries when it comes to push and pull cultures. While US customers have been used to buying cars from stock, Germans in particular but also many other European customers have been used to having the opportunity to get the car to the spec they want. With the introduction of the BMW X5 in the United States in 1999, order-to-delivery was introduced on a broader basis, made possible by the fact that the first X5 was produced in Greer, South Carolina.

The distance from production point to the dealer is a key factor in push and pull considerations. The longer the distance, the more difficult it is with pull systems since it will take a long time to get the car delivered. Hence, with few exceptions, Asian-built cars get delivered in Europe with just a few specs available. Typically, options such as an automatic gearbox come with sunroof and/or satellite navigation. Another key factor is the price and luxury level of the car: buyers of cheaper cars are less likely to want to customize the specification of their cars: this option is primarily appreciated by premium car buyers.

Balancing supply and demand

It could well be argued that car makers should scale back production to get a reasonable balance between demand and supply. In an industry with no overcapacity problems and demand stronger than supply, such an approach would work. In the car industry, however, push increases sales since over-stocked importers and dealers have strong incentives to get rid of their stocks, even at low margins. Moreover, cars in stock are ready for delivery, which provides an advantage for some buyers over order-to-delivery – and the percentage of buyers wanting immediate delivery appears to increase over time due to a lower interest in cars and increased push pressure from the channels.

To sum up, a healthy push may be necessary to avoid overproducing competitors that are desperate to get a sale from increasing their market share (at the cost of brand strength and margins). If it's based on a truly attractive product offer, a great brand, competent channel management and hence happy dealers and buyers, the mainly pull-based strategy is likely to be successful.

Notes

1 This has been discussed in Germany and the tendency in contracts is to stipulate that normal use is included in the leasing rate – if not, customers are afraid they may have to pay a large sum when they hand the car back, something that would undermine the attractiveness of the leasing concept.

2 Calculations (which may be out of date), eg Ciferri (2002) and EMCC (2004), are for cost savings of €900 a car.

3 In this respect there is a significant difference between countries, see KREF.

04 Car buyer behaviour

With few exceptions, companies that have been successful in recent years have founded their ideas and strategies on an understanding of how buyers think and behave. This chapter discusses the car buying process based on recent research and puts the process into a broader framework where car makers and their dealers can relate the insights to their own business models and strengths, thus identifying potential improvements in their dealings with customers.

Customers may not know why they like, prefer and buy a particular auto brand or product, so understanding consumer motivation and how that translates into profitable marketing, product packaging and sales strategies is crucial for proactive car companies. The dangers of not understanding consumer motivation are many – often resulting in poor profitability and dissatisfied buyers.

Buyers being less loyal – driving forces and effects

There is little doubt that over time, buyers in general have become less loyal. This tendency is strong in all industries and car buyers are now applying a different attitude in all types of purchase situations.

The fall in loyalty has its roots in the strong consumption culture with all the choices and opportunities that it offers. A few decades ago there were far fewer choices in life overall and consumers couldn't choose telephone suppliers, customized educational programmes, car models or holidays to the same extent as today. The internet didn't exist, and price comparisons were difficult. Calling 10 car dealers would take a lot of time which, in combination with a dominant local mind-set, led to a preference for local suppliers.

An important driving force in the transition from loyalty to exercising choice is the globalization of tastes and preferences, with strong influences from popular culture and consumption cultures. In the 1980s, lifestyle consumption became influential and brands could reach iconic status, meaning consuming the brand contributed to the consumer's self-expression and personal identity. For a while, it meant that a brand could build and maintain loyalty and put the seller in a great position. Brands that created a meaningful story and represented a cultural contradiction, a mismatch between prevailing ideology and emergent undercurrents in society, could reach iconic status (Holt, 2004), in contrast to the prevailing focus on product functionality. Few auto brands took up this opportunity and this contributed to cars in general losing their strong influence on, and place in, popular culture.

The combination of a number of societal changes led to a move away from functional, modernistic approaches to a new era of lifestyle and attitude, a fragmentation in consumer preferences and an emerging focus on individuals' self-realization. The multitude of 'reality' television programmes – 'American Idol', 'Britain's Got Talent', 'Big Brother', 'The Apprentice', 'Project Runaway' etc – aired all over the world and sent a message to young watchers: you can be what you want, just take the chances you are given! Television and other channels featured people who succeeded, with beautifully designed apartments, glamorous clothing, etc (Parment, 2011a). How does a car maker or dealer relate to this development? To what extent is the car industry prepared to be an attractive place to work for young individuals? These questions largely remain unanswered.

For a car dealer approaching buyers without thinking about changes in the environment, it may be difficult to understand why customers, and the young ones in particular, are different from before. If earlier – at the time the Baby Boomers came of age – the influences on young people's thoughts about consumption, car ownership and use, education, career, etc were restricted to the family, friends and to some extent the few mass communication channels that existed; influences now come from many sources: a multitude of television programmes and websites, celebrities, social networks, mass media, etc. The sources of influence have become more global. Car companies have to re-evaluate their strategies to understand what is happening and it's more important than ever to know one's customers – the existing ones as well as the ones to be approached.

The shifting power balance between companies and buyers

A key explanation to changes in the marketing environment and its impact on buyer behaviour is the shifting power balance between companies and buyers. Hence, it has become increasingly important to understand consumers and how they will behave. Regardless of age, consumers now have more power than ever in relation to companies. Most companies now offer customer call centres, customer care programmes, generous return policies, extended warranties and other services, created and run either to gain a competitive advantage, thus driving operating costs and customer expectations, or to avoid being competitively disadvantaged. We see this in most industries. A few decades ago, universities seldom undertook marketing activities beyond publishing catalogues with information on courses and programmes. This practice reflected the power balance at the time: there was a scarcity of university courses and admission was difficult. Individuals were happy to be admitted and universities were seen as authorities. Today, everybody offering services is under constant customer surveillance – whether it is a doctor, a car mechanic or a school teacher.

It is not uncommon for companies to be even more generous than they claim to be. Sometimes it takes extreme forms. The hotel chain Radisson offers a 100 per cent guest satisfaction programme. Some supermarkets, well aware of how expensive it is to recruit new customers, honour all competitors' discount coupons. Car companies have to decide whether this development should influence car retailing or not – buyers will take these experiences into account when choosing a car brand and dealer.

Car managers and salespeople who do understand customers, buying behaviour and the buying process derive strong benefits, while those who don't understand customers, how they think, what motivates them, where they live, what music and clothes they like and so on lose competitive power. As customer orientation is getting stronger in many sectors, salespeople who stick with what worked in the past and don't develop can't compete with the new breed of customers – and their existing customer base is likely to erode.

Car buyer preferences

This section introduces the results from the Car Buyer 2013 Survey related to key aspects that have been introduced in this book. Two types of important knowledge for decision making in the car industry can be derived – knowledge about what car buyers evaluate when buying a new car, and generational differences in this respect.

New car purchase – buyer criteria

In the first part, criteria that consumers express when buying a new car are discussed, starting with a generational cohorts perspective. It is important to note that as older people are likely to have more experience when it comes to car purchase, their preferences are more likely to be persistent over time. The 20–23-year-olds are still in the formative phase and may change their opinions substantially.

The question raised was: if you were to go to a car dealer to buy a new car, how important would the following be? The answers are shown in Figure 4.1.

FIGURE 4.1 The dealer is close to where I live. Importance when seeing a car dealer to buy a new car based on age categories.

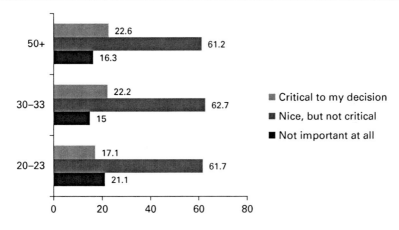

SOURCE: The Car Buyer 2013 Survey

While store location in general is seen as very important, with significant advantages for companies that go for key locations, reflected in substantial variations in rent across locations, it appears to be less so when buying a car. As with other durables, the purchase process is relatively lengthy and based on research, hence the location is not as crucial as for fast-moving consumer goods, which are sold quickly and at low cost. Something that really matters, though, is location convenience: by establishing a car dealership in a cluster

– often called Ciudad Automóvil, Automobilstadt, car plaza, etc – or at least easily accessible by car buyers, the threshold for seeing the dealer is lower.

FIGURE 4.2 Wide assortment of ancillary services (car servicing, tyre storage, etc). Importance when seeing a car dealer to buy a new car based on age categories.

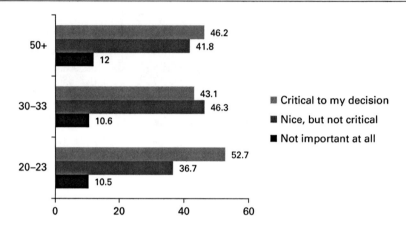

SOURCE: The Car Buyer 2013 Survey

The basic idea of a car dealership, especially among young car buyers, is that it provides a wide range of services. As almost every other car buyer, and even more among the young ones, sees it as crucial, car dealers should make sure they offer or at least can organize just about any service related to car ownership (see Figure 4.2). That will make the dealership stronger and more financially sustainable when cost-efficient solutions that offer a limited range of services at low prices emerge.

A strong argument for offering new cars in key city locations (a practice that has been more common in recent years, long after car dealerships left city centres), is that it will be easier for younger buyers in particular to access them (see Figure 4.3). Young people, often new graduates, with good jobs and living in downtown locations, may be difficult to reach without a city showroom with some dealership services – you need a car to buy a car. Maybe surprisingly, but consistent with the findings in the first question on dealer location, young car buyers are not any more positive than older ones when it comes to dealer accessibility. A reasonable strategy for a proactive dealership could be to offer accessible, but not city centre-located dealerships and then run marketing campaigns on city locations and in cooperation with companies in other industries, eg hotels, fashion clothing, furniture, music and entertainment.

FIGURE 4.3   The dealer is easily accessible without a car. Importance when seeing a car dealer to buy a new car based on age categories.

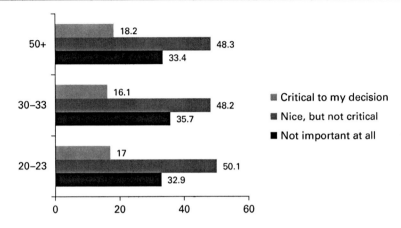

SOURCE: The Car Buyer 2013 Survey

FIGURE 4.4   Attractive showroom. Importance when seeing a car dealer to buy a new car based on age categories.

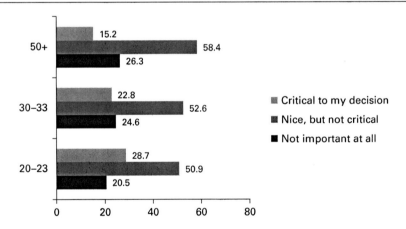

SOURCE: The Car Buyer 2013 Survey

Consistent with the increased aesthetic orientation in the society that young individuals – born in the 1980s and 1990s – grew up in, the attractiveness of the showroom is more important for young buyers (see Figure 4.4). But even more important, and also consistent with clear patterns in dealers' experiences, is that the software appears to be significantly more important

FIGURE 4.5   Buying experience. Importance when seeing a car dealer to buy a new car based on age categories.

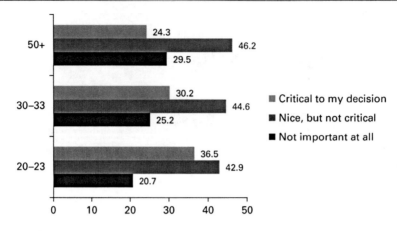

SOURCE: The Car Buyer 2013 Survey

FIGURE 4.6   The lowest possible price. Importance when seeing a car dealer to buy a new car based on age categories.

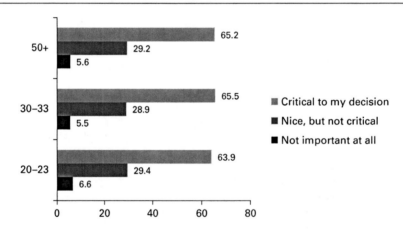

SOURCE: The Car Buyer 2013 Survey

than the hardware; that is, the buying experience (Figure 4.5) is significantly more important to young individuals. The same holds for the dealer's attitude and customer treatment (see Figure 4.7): when potential buyers meet the dealer all generational cohorts find these critical but even more so with young individuals, who are used to good customer treatment, extensive service and many choices (Parment, 2011a; Schewe *et al*, 2013).

FIGURE 4.7 A professional attitude and customer treatment. Importance when seeing a car dealer to buy a new car based on age categories.

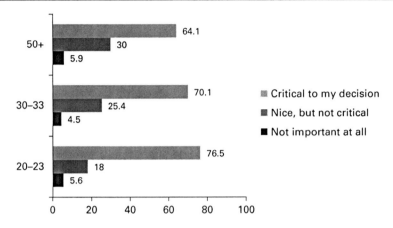

SOURCE: The Car Buyer 2013 Survey

A low price is critical for about 65 per cent of buyers and not important at all for slightly more than 5 per cent – here, no differences related to age and cohort exist (see Figure 4.6). In dealing with the tension between saving costs on the one hand and differentiating the offer and delivering superior, brand-tailored services on the other, it seems that young people expect more from the latter while the desire to make a good deal does not change with the new generation of car buyers.

FIGURE 4.8 Open nights and weekends. Importance when seeing a car dealer to buy a new car based on age categories.

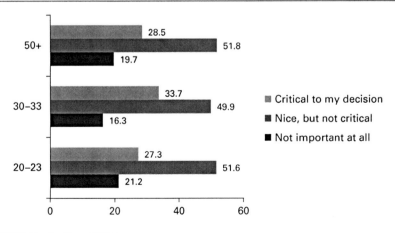

SOURCE: The Car Buyer 2013 Survey

Another aspect of dealership availability is the opening hours (see Figure 4.8). A strong tendency over time in the service sector has been to provide longer opening hours – supermarkets, workshops, dentists, hairdressers, pharmacies and shopping malls all have extended their opening hours (although some countries place restrictions on opening hours). Spanish departmental store chain El Corte Inglés used to be open until 10 pm (in some cases slightly later) but closed on Sundays; it now provides open stores every day for customers looking for the latest fashion and accessories, perfumery, cosmetics, watches, groceries, sports, home electronics, books, toys, souvenirs – or a travel agency, an insurance office or an optician.

The implication for car dealers appears to be clear: longer opening hours! But it's not as valued by car buyers as one might think, and the cost of running an automobile dealership late at night is very high. An opportunity would certainly be to have the showroom and the pick-up from the workshop open late at night – and let other parts of the dealership stay closed. But if the point of seeing a car dealer when other opportunities to buy, maintain and repair a car emerge is superiority in terms of service range and

Long opening hours and an appealing architecture inside shopping malls raise general expectations of the shopping experience – car dealers are forced to follow suit to stay competitive not only in relation to other car companies but also other industries that compete for attention and buyer purchasing power.
(Anders Parment, 29 March 2013, Westfield Shopping Centre, London)

quality, it is doubtful whether the strategy to offer just a limited amount of services is useful. The paint shop and the body shop could certainly be closed at 9.30 pm – but if the customer wants use the dealer's car wash, buy additional insurance, test drive a new model that has been heavily advertised, or talk to a sales person – closing down key activities may save costs but result in missed opportunities. In addition, large facilities with no customers don't give a great shopping experience to most shoppers: a dealership with personnel, activities and customers frequently showing up is livelier and hence more attractive to customers, staff and others – here's the place where things happen! Needless to say, this is easier if the location is good.

FIGURE 4.9   Good website. Importance when seeing a car dealer to buy a new car based on age categories.

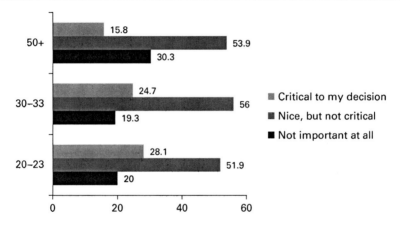

SOURCE: The Car Buyer 2013 Survey

Not surprisingly, a good website is more critical to younger car buyers (see Figure 4.9). Every dealer must have a website, and providing a decent website is not very expensive, but the question is whether a website could constitute a competitive advantage. To a car maker it could; to a dealer it's more doubtful since the dealer is normally accessible through offline means, and customers as well as dealers want the face-to-face contact. Although online booking of inspection slots has been available since the 1990s, very few car owners use it. Strictly speaking, booking through the web saves money for the dealer, but if the maintenance of customer relationships is included in the calculation, talking to clients instead of having web-based communication could be very useful. It is, however, difficult to argue for investing heavily in the website: a website can't be great unless it represents a great organization. And if the organization is great, the website should automatically reflect this greatness.

FIGURE 4.10   Easy to contact through other channels than by phone (eg e-mail, social media). Importance when seeing a car dealer to buy a new car based on age categories.

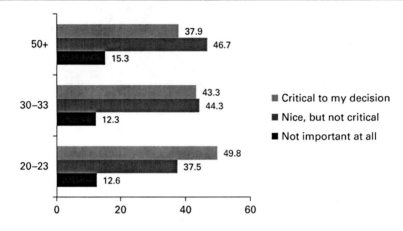

SOURCE: The Car Buyer 2013 Survey

Ease of contact is a key criterion. The opportunity to contact the dealer is appreciated and this certainly holds for young car buyers (see Figure 4.10). Dealing with e-mails, Facebook groups, Instagram, web forums, etc is a difficult venture. First, a car company must know 'the language', the codes of conduct and the culture. It may be a shock to people not used to this type of communication to look at feedback, which is often direct and rough. Hence, a car company, like any other company, can't be too defensive or too offensive in dealing with people in social media. Second, the way of communicating in social media may not be the best channel for offers and discussions with clients on run-down trade-in cars, repairs after an accident, an invoice for a costly 100,000 mile/160,000 km inspection for a car owner who can barely afford it, or whether it's time to change winter tyres or use the old tyres another season. These are sensitive issues that are costly for the car owner and may involve decisions with an impact on safety and resale value. Third, the way the car company appears in this type of channel must be consistent with the overall strategy, and with other communication efforts.

While car companies are forced to communicate through many channels, because of pressure from the competition, high sales targets and buyer expectations, dealers may decide to have a presence in social media channels but don't work with them intensively. Whether that's a clever or (too) defensive strategy depends on the situation at hand, but one thing is sure: companies that deal with emerging channels because they are under pressure to do so, but lack the necessary motivation and knowledge, may not only be unsuccessful but also appear in a way that has a negative impact on the brand.

FIGURE 4.11 Assume you need a new car. How would you prefer to own and buy it?

SOURCE: The Car Buyer 2013 Survey

Numerous car manufacturers, eg BMW at the introduction of the i3 electric car, have announced they will start selling cars on the web. But car buyers don't want to buy cars on the web and this preference is even stronger among young car buyers (see Figure 4.11). Although the typical car dealer location in industrial areas or along ring roads may not be ideal for reaching young buyers, they are very comfortable with this dominant design. The very weak preference for internet sales was also clear in an earlier study in 2009 (Parment, 2011b) and while many car companies have invested enormous amounts of money over the years in internet sales, with few exceptions it has been with very weak results. In metro areas, it's a good idea to run a showroom in a central location as a complement to a larger dealership (see the section on metro, city and rural areas, below).

FIGURE 4.12   I would prefer a seller that is...

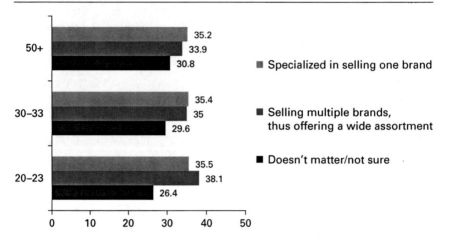

SOURCE: The Car Buyer 2013 Survey

Solus vs multi-franchising is a key issue in designing marketing channels and, obviously, car makers in general prefer the former while strong dealers often prefer the latter. Car buyers in general don't have strong preferences in this respect (see Figure 4.12).

FIGURE 4.13   I would prefer to...

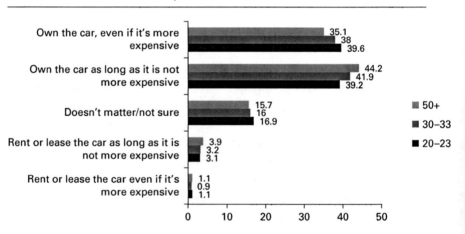

SOURCE: The Car Buyer 2013 Survey

The point displayed in Figure 4.13 is a key issue in marketing cars, now and in the future. General belief suggests that consumers prefer flexibility and not owning products, to the inflexibility that inevitably comes with owning a durable. Why own a motor boat, a summer house, a trailer or an apartment on the French Riviera when you can rent one for a week and don't have to take responsibility for maintenance, insurance, finance, etc? The car does not, it seems, fit with this general belief. Regardless of age, respondents show a strong preference for owning the car. While more than 40 per cent prefer to own the car, if it's not more expensive than renting it, only 3 to 4 per cent prefer renting to owning.

The results on this question suggest that the car has a very strong position as a personal item and also, to a large extent, as a status symbol. Why else would the percentage of respondents willing to pay more to own the car than to rent it be almost 40 per cent while only 1 per cent prefers to rent the car if the cost is higher – in other industries the latter appears to be a popular choice.

FIGURE 4.14   How important do you think the car is as a status symbol in society?

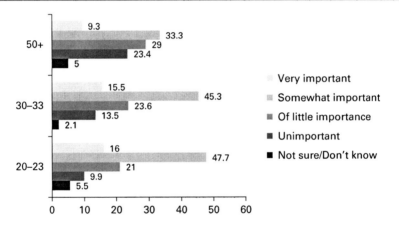

SOURCE: The Car Buyer 2013 Survey

The survey suggests the car to be a more important status symbol to young people than to older people – the younger individuals are, the stronger the role of the car as a status symbol (see Figure 4.14). One thing that is very important here is to consider the wide range of status symbols available to individuals born in the 1980s and 1990s (see Parment, 2011a). Combined with a high level of status orientation and striving for self-realization in life, this makes the car an important status symbol but one that is in competition with many other such symbols. It's important to note that the question might be interpreted by the respondents as the car being too much of a status symbol – more than it deserves.

FIGURE 4.15   How important do you think the car will be as a status symbol in society in the future?

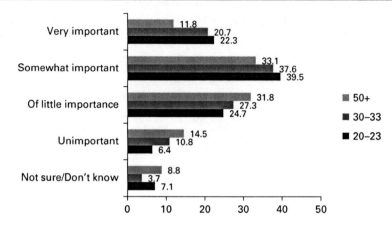

SOURCE: The Car Buyer 2013 Survey

As with their view on the car's role as status symbol today, older respondents have less confidence in the car's role as status symbol in the future. However, all generational cohorts share the belief in the car being a strong status symbol in the future; see Figure 4.15.

FIGURE 4.16   How important do you think the car will be as a means of transport in the future?

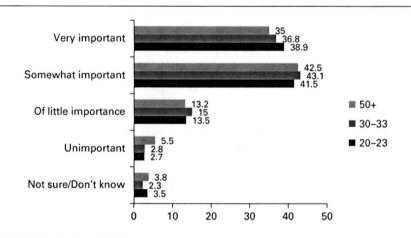

SOURCE: The Car Buyer 2013 Survey

There is a relatively strong belief in the car's role as an important means of transport in the future across the generational cohorts (see Figure 4.16). This is good news for car companies and a strong argument against proponents of a society with less emphasis on the car as a means of transport.

FIGURE 4.17   How important do you think electric cars will be as a means of transport in the future?

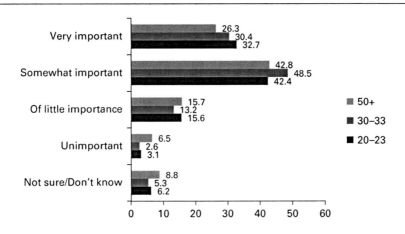

SOURCE: The Car Buyer 2013 Survey

When it comes to electric cars, young individuals show a stronger belief in their future emergence and market penetration although the differences across cohorts are not very strong (see Figure 4.17).

Metro, city and rural areas

Building on earlier research in a variety of industries, and defining characteristics of metro, city and rural areas, this part of the survey explores differences between metropolitan areas (800,000+ inhabitants), city areas (80,000–800,000 inhabitants) and rural areas (fewer than 80,000 inhabitants).

In the economic geography literature, the spatial organization of economic activity and the urban system to which it gives rise are analysed. A general distinction is made between rural and urban areas. Within a particular area, clusters of centres exist with distances between them short enough for consumers to consider several alternative choices for shopping. Such centres perform local functions for the population, but also specialize in the performance of high-class functions for the group, eg a car sales centre (Berry *et al*, 1988; MacDougall and Campell, 1995). Although there is a behavioural dimension to the definition of market areas too, the number of residents is important and highly correlated with many dimensions of economic activity, something that defines an agglomeration of citizens, workplaces, tourism, etc. An example of criteria in defining the prosperity – and hence, purchasing power and consumer attitudes – in different types of market are land use, demography, income and wealth, employment and economic activity, housing, and form of government (MacDougall and Campell, 1995). For instance, a market area with high unemployment rates, high levels of recorded crime and a large number of citizens moving away in recent years (it's difficult not to think of Detroit) may be a very different market area with a similar number of citizens but high entrepreneurial activity, population and financial growth and being an attractive place for a variety of stakeholders including families, companies and tourists. Nonetheless, there are general patterns across market areas that are useful in understanding buyer behaviour, designing marketing channels and marketing activities.

FIGURE 4.18   Assume you need a new car. How would you prefer to own and buy it?

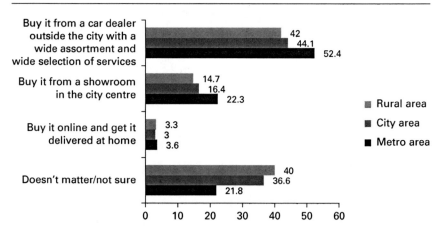

SOURCE: The Car Buyer 2013 Survey

Metro area respondents have a much clearer idea about where they want to purchase the car in the future (see Figure 4.18) – no surprise when considering that 'city centre' and 'outside the city' might be very distinct in a metro area while hardly distinguishable in another area. Online purchase is only preferred by about 3 per cent, regardless of market area.

FIGURE 4.19   I would prefer a seller that is...

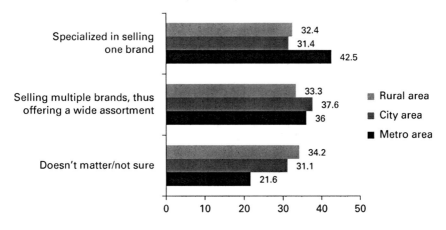

SOURCE: The Car Buyer 2013 Survey

The preference for solus franchising is stronger among metro area respondents, something that fits well with car makers' and NSC's strategies to emphasize solus franchising in metro areas (see Figure 4.19).

FIGURE 4.20   I would prefer to...

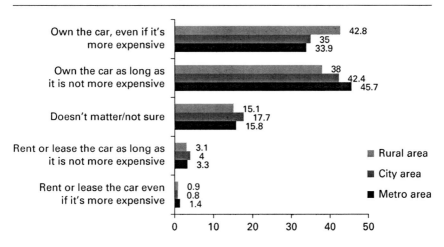

SOURCE: The Car Buyer 2013 Survey

The preference when it comes to owning the car on the one hand, or renting or leasing it on the other, does not show any significant differences across market areas (see Figure 4.20).

FIGURE 4.21   How important do you think the car is as a status symbol in society?

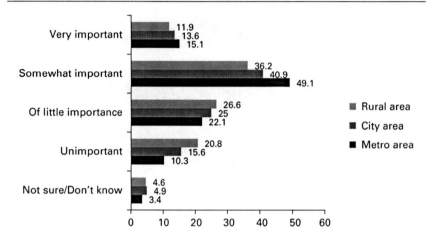

SOURCE: The Car Buyer 2013 Survey

In accordance with common belief, metro areas have a stronger preference for status symbols, affluent living and emotional criteria in buying (Parment, 2011a); see Figure 4.21.

FIGURE 4.22   How important do you think the car will be as a status symbol in society in the future?

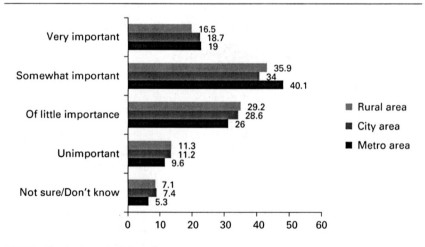

SOURCE: The Car Buyer 2013 Survey

FIGURE 4.23 How important do you think the car will be as a means of transport in the future?

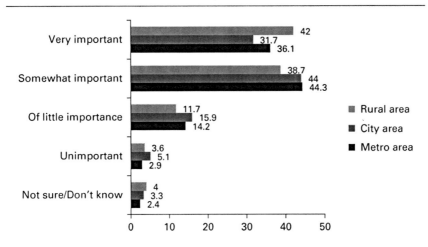

SOURCE: The Car Buyer 2013 Survey

No significant differences were found in the survey study on the role of the car as a status symbol or means of transport in the future; see Figures 4.22 and 4.23.

FIGURE 4.24 How important do you think electric cars will be as a means of transport in the future?

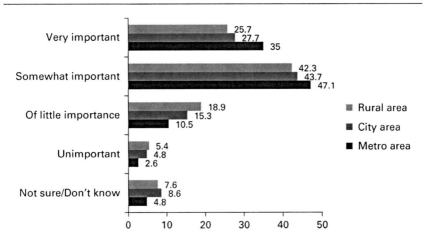

SOURCE: The Car Buyer 2013 Survey

Electric cars are in general more convenient in metro areas where the driving distances are shorter and the availability of charge stations higher (see Figure 4.24). Interestingly, most decisions that would facilitate market penetration of electric cars are made in metro areas: not only are political institutions located there, but also power companies' head offices, trend-setters with high purchasing power, media and lobbyists. There may therefore be a risk that decision makers overstate the potential of electric cars in the future.

FIGURE 4.25   Assume you own a car. How would you prefer to buy services related to car ownership, eg insurance, tyres, inspections, repairs and financing?

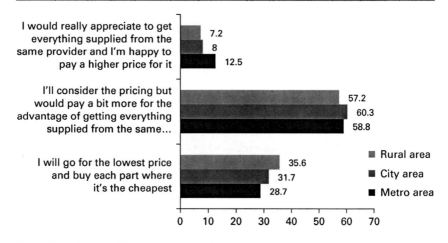

SOURCE: The Car Buyer 2013 Survey

The answers in Figure 4.25 are happy news for proactive car dealers working hard to offer everything related to car ownership and driving: 64.4 per cent in rural areas, 68.3 per cent in city areas and 71.3 per cent in metro areas are willing to enjoy the advantages of one-stop shopping and pay a slightly – or significantly – higher price for getting all services provided in one place. The more services a car dealer offers, the easier it is to build relations and offer additional services, show new products such as new car models, offer test drives and work with marketing efficiently. This will reduce the reliance upon expensive marketing and advertising.

Selling cars in rural areas

Retailing in rural areas has gone down, which can easily be explained by the general economic trend for larger units and increasing threshold costs to keep a business viable. For cars the development is even worse: the complexity in running a dealership remains high; authorities put demands upon dealers to provide adequate information about the business and comply with environmental rules; and they have to live up to customers' expectations (customers are used to high quality service from other industries). Dealer facilities should be large enough to give room to expanding model ranges.

The level of economic activity in rural areas varies by country and region. In general terms, activity has gone down and costs have gone up. In addition, in many cases the once strong consumer preference in rural areas of supporting local business has lost its hold.

A number of conditions make it increasingly difficult to manage an automotive dealership in a rural area. Buyers may not buy from a local dealer unless it provides substantial advantages at a similar or slightly higher price. Demands from car makers on product display, which should reflect the car maker's corporate identity and profile and at the same time cover the model range offered, are a challenge. In addition, having more car models and ranges increases complexity not only in car demonstration and sales (organizing a test drive of a model not kept as a demonstrator is a key challenge), but also in after-sales: higher costs for training car mechanics, more complex handling of spare parts, etc. This is to an extent neutralized by the increased use of common platforms that cover many car models and ranges.

It's common among people working for car makers and NSCs to have a largely negative opinion of rural dealers. A retired former marketing manager, now working as a researcher and industry expert at a university, agrees on the negative attitude but says it's easy to understand given the circumstances that used to exist in rural dealerships. The industry expert, with almost five decades of experience in different parts of the industry, explains what happened when he started working for a large dealership:

> Car makers don't understand people. They understand manufacturing processes, they say 'we have been successful; therefore we're going to translate that to retail people'. You have to be in it to understand it. For eight years, I drove around and contacted dealers. Then I went to the head office for seven years, and I thought I knew what dealers thought and what really happened. But I didn't know until I became the sales manager in this big dealership. What I saw on the inside, I didn't think it was that bad, I didn't understand the sales people; unless people have been on both sides, they're never going to understand... One of my best sales people, I couldn't understand how he could sell anything, he could hardly write his name, his paperwork was terrible, but he sold cars, because he worked with human relationships. How could I explain that to someone in the factory?

Being anchored in the local community is a key advantage for a local business – knowing people, discussions that are going on, issues in the local area, etc may add some flavour to the processes and services provided by a dealership and may give a substantial competitive advantage that is difficult to copy. In a large city like Washington, Madrid, Frankfurt or Moscow, these advantages are limited, but in rural areas, dealers with strong local ties can derive substantial competitive advantages over metro dealers.

In addition, rural dealers often have more opportunities to run a trade-in section at a profit. Used cars are often in a better condition, as car owners in rural areas tend to be more careful with their cars. There is little doubt that the wear and tear of city driving is higher than highway and rural driving, too. Repairs and preparation of cares for sales are cheaper because of lower rents and salaries. It may also be easier to deal with older used cars than in metro areas where the threshold for profitable used cars is higher due to greater costs for premises, preparation, etc. Also, prices may be higher due to cars being in better condition and some local buyers preferring to buy from a local provider, so a higher margin can be achieved.

Country differences

Here, differences between the four countries researched in the survey study (the United States, China, Sweden and Germany) are introduced and discussed.

FIGURE 4.26   Assume you need a new car. How would you prefer to own and buy it?

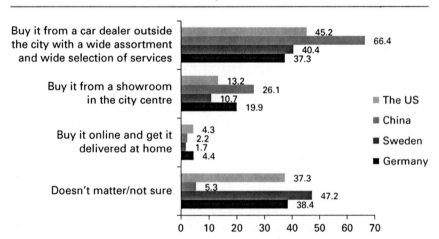

SOURCE: The Car Buyer 2013 Survey

Respondents from all countries in the survey agree upon the low desirability of buying the car online (see Figure 4.26). Chinese respondents have much stronger preferences on how they prefer to buy a car – but the preference for full-service car dealers outside city centres over showrooms or dealers with restricted services in city centres is significant in all countries.

FIGURE 4.27   I would prefer a seller that is...

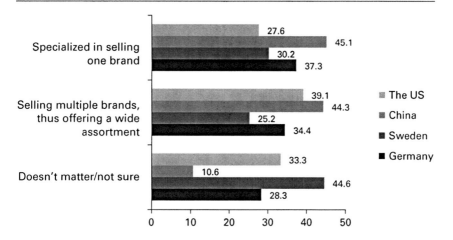

SOURCE: The Car Buyer 2013 Survey

Figure 4.27 shows that car buyer preferences on type of dealership differ substantially across countries. Respondents in the United States have a relatively strong preference for multi-franchising – car makers selling through their own outlets are prohibited in almost every state by laws requiring that new cars be sold only by franchised dealers.[1] This provides an interesting contrast to Germany, where manufacturer-owned dealerships are more common than in most other markets. For instance, Mercedes-Benz has a very strong manufacturer presence in the marketing channels while the factory owns 34 market area dealers *(Niederlassungen)* with representation in 144 locations, distributing cars to franchised dealers. Hence, all franchised dealers have a Mercedes-Benz market-area dealer as a contact point and franchised dealers can't get the status as market-area dealers.[2] BMW has manufacturer-owned dealerships in 20 major cities[3] but also sells through many strong franchised dealers that may have a stronger market position in some market areas.

Overall, buyer preferences on solus or multi-franchising are unclear, something that gives support to possible success for different strategies applied by different dealers. In a well-functioning market, different strategies may be successful and contribute to increasing buyer choice and competition.

FIGURE 4.28   I would prefer to...

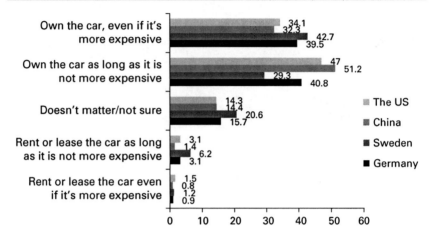

SOURCE: The Car Buyer 2013 Survey

Although Sweden shows a stronger preference for renting or leasing cars than the other countries, it doesn't change the overall strong preference for owning one's own car (see Figure 4.28).

FIGURE 4.29   How important do you think the car is as a status symbol in society?

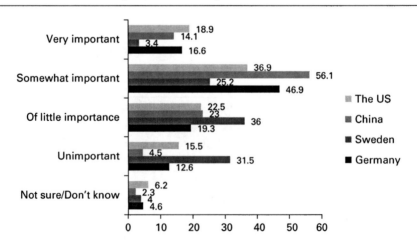

SOURCE: The Car Buyer 2013 Survey

Sweden stands out on the question of status symbols in seeing cars as not being very important in this respect while the opposite holds true for China (see Figure 4.29). German and US respondents see the car as an important status symbol.

FIGURE 4.30   How important do you think the car will be as a status symbol in society in the future?

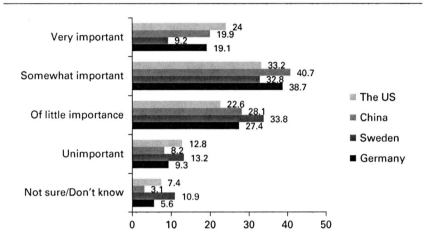

SOURCE: The Car Buyer 2013 Survey

Compared to the former question, across-country differences are less significant when respondents are asked to forecast the role of the car as a status symbol in the future (see Figure 4.30). US, Chinese and German respondents expect the car to become less of a status symbol.

The United States stands out on the question in Figure 4.31 by – surprisingly – expecting the car to be less important as a means of transport in the future. This may reflect a strong debate in the United States that questions the heavy reliance upon cars for society to function properly, and a reorientation of emphasis on modes of transport among young people. A 2012 report proves that among individuals aged 16 to 34, bike trips have increased by 24 per cent; walking by 16 per cent and use of public transport by 40 per cent – at the same time car mileage has decreased by 23 per cent (Davis *et al*, 2012).

The belief in electric cars as a key means of transport in the future – which is relatively high in all countries – is significantly stronger in China (see Figure 4.32). There is extensive debate on electric cars, high political awareness and interest, and a multitude of electric cars manufactured and

FIGURE 4.31 How important do you think the car will be as a means of transport in the future?

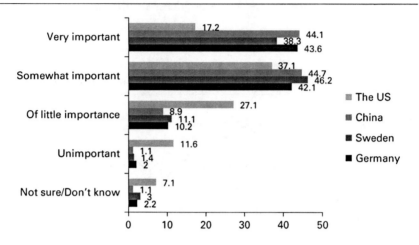

SOURCE: The Car Buyer 2013 Survey

FIGURE 4.32 How important do you think electric cars will be as a means of transport in the future?

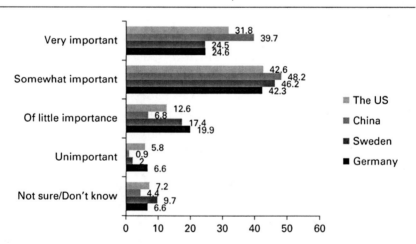

SOURCE: The Car Buyer 2013 Survey

on sale – and a growing awareness of the problems of a high dependency on oil, pollution, etc. The electric car is here to stay – as one among many solutions to the problems that the car creates – and proactivity in contributing to the implementation of new fuel technologies is important for consumers as well as politicians, car companies and other stakeholders.

Notes

1 This rule has been extensively discussed and questioned, for example by Bodisch (2009) who argues that direct channels would result in higher customer satisfaction through better production-matching to consumer preferences to meet buyers' desire for customized cars. In addition, according to Bodisch, distribution costs and costly stock-keeping would be reduced.

2 See www.mbvd.de, retrieved August 2013; Parment, 2009.

3 Bmw-niederlassungen.de, retrieved August 2013.

05 Car cultures

For the consumer, the car is associated with emotional and status values (Merritt, 1998; Sandqvist, 1997), which makes the car a significant expression of culture and lifestyle. To understand the emotional and cultural component of car buyers' purchase considerations, it's important to understand car cultures.

Car cultures are strongly influenced by the overall culture in different countries and regions, which largely may be derived from how people live and the attitudes they express. Although there are still substantial differences within each country, without any doubt one country stands out: the United States. This chapter will deal with a selection of regions and countries, with a strong emphasis on the United States in dealing with the emergence and growth of car cultures.

The car as a cultural expression – a global phenomenon

A key characteristic of the car is its strong representation of different cultural phenomena. Along the road from being a symbol of distinction, typical of the bourgeoisie and the aristocracy, and some professions such as lawyers and doctors, to being a functional item and a work tool, many car cultural events and aspects have taken place. This chapter does not try to cover every aspect of car cultures in different countries and continents, but will give some insights into how car cultures have emerged and changed over time.

As with any cultural expression, it's tightly linked to the societal development of the world around it. Hence, at the societal level, the car has strong cultural expressions and meanings that do differ across countries and consumer groups, although there are also some general patterns. This chapter takes a closer look at automobile culture, its history and recent and ongoing developments.

According to the sociologist Martin Heidegger, machinery 'unfolds a specific character of domination... a specific kind of discipline and a unique kind of consciousness of conquest' over human beings (Zimmerman, 1990). During the emergence and growth of car cultures, particularly in the 1930s to 1960s, modernistic society is manifested very clearly in the system of production, consumption, circulation, location and sociality engendered by the car.

The car has also contributed to globalization through flows not only of cars but also parts, financial transactions, knowledge and expertise, and management principles. Consider the extensive exchange of management, ideas and product development knowledge within a manufacturer group. Shortly after Daimler and Chrysler merged in 1998, the corporation founded a new subsidiary company, DaimlerChrysler Aviation, and ordered an Airbus A319 with 50 business class seats to ferry managers between Stuttgart and the conglomerate's second headquarters in Detroit.[1] As expensive as it may sound to provide flights every weekday between Stuttgart and Detroit, it shows the global character of the car industry.

One billion cars – will there be even more in the future?

The desire to own automobiles had been recognized in the 1920s but was put on hold during the depressed 1930s. During World War II, production of the automobile for the civilian market was halted and tight restrictions were placed on vehicle use. The transition during the 20th century of the car from being an expensive luxury for the rich into the mass market transport vehicle it became in most developed countries reached its height in the 1950s and 1960s. We are now witnessing a similar pattern in many developing countries, but under a different set of restrictions and challenges due to the lack of confidence in the car as the key solution to transport problems. Even though many developing countries may only have witnessed limited problems related to car use, the awareness of such problems globally is high.

There are currently over 1 billion cars worldwide,[2] a figure reached in 2010 and expected to rise further in the future. Growth will primarily take place in countries with a short mass market history, eg China, India and South America. In many Western economies, the number of cars is expected to decrease. In France, for instance, a research report suggests that when today's young French adults are in their 60s, the likelihood that they will own cars is about half the rate of those who are now in their 60s. In 1983,

35 per cent of 18–19-year-old French individuals held a driver's licence, but in 2010 only 19 per cent did. Of all age segments, only retirees are driving more now than earlier generations. Young French people – like young people everywhere – want a car but it must compete with many other potential purchases like travel, fashion clothing or buying one's own home. Car sharing, which has taken off in France, does not only reduce costs but also reduces the problem of finding a parking spot in metro areas.[3]

History of car culture

A key explanation of the growth of car culture is the increasing need for transport; another is the car's profile as a luxury product in the first decades of the 20th century. The transport revolution, started by railways, largely paralleled industrialization in many countries, and entailed a fundamental shift in the need for transport for work, goods transport and distribution, and later social interaction and movement. Industrialization created a massive increase in the need for transport, and transport was linked to movement that further increased the need for transport.

Until the emergence of cars, workers lived close to the factory where they were employed or travelled by shared transport, sometimes provided by the factory. At the time, the service sector of the economy was a lot smaller – nowadays many service workers are highly dependent on the car to get to work, and increasingly so as a greater proportion of service businesses, driven by strong competition, have long opening hours which makes public transport a difficult option.

Through the often explosive development of cars and roads in the 1950s and 1960s, it became more convenient to live in suburbs (Jackson, 1985). Interestingly, the cleverly named Chevrolet Suburban, the car produced under the same name for the longest period in the car industry, followed this development since its introduction in 1934, with a twelfth generation introduced in 2014. Needless to say, the enormous size and relatively high fuel consumption of the Suburban doesn't make it a great city centre car – but a great car for suburban use!

The end result of the emergence and development of the car and supporting infrastructure, including roads, motels, fuel stations, etc is clearly visible: increased distances between home and work brought about by industrialization and urban sprawl have led to traffic congestion and high costs of living in geographical areas that are seen as functionally and emotionally desirable, with short distances to attractive jobs.

Notably, governments in the early stages saw investment in roads as a progressive way of investing for the future, particularly during economic recessions, since it created jobs and economic activity. Such approaches are based on Keynesian political ideologies. In Europe, extensive freeway programmes were initiated by governments in the 1950s and 1960s to create economic activity and jobs and make the car available to the masses. Similar arguments are now being used – and questioned – as many countries invest heavily in fast trains.

The car and other means of transport

Although the car until a few decades ago increased access, particularly to remote places, and reduced travel times, we now see a development in the other direction. Travel times have increased in large cities, particularly in Latin America, as a result of traffic agglomerations, and public transport has become more efficient, particularly long distance trains that often compete with cars and domestic flights. Flight times have largely remained the same since the late 1960s when modern aircraft such as the Boeing 737 and 747 were introduced with cruising speeds of around 900 km/h – attempts to reduce the cost and impact of air travel, eg green landings, and increased agglomerations around major airport hubs may even have contributed to slight increases in aircraft travel times. Long distance trains typically had a top speed of 130 to 160 km/h in the 1960s, 200 km/h in a few instances, but now most developed countries offer trains travelling 200 to 350 km/h – it's difficult for cars to compete on travel times and in many cases also for air travel, given the high convenience of train travel. Madrid–Barcelona (slightly more than 600 kms) takes 2 hours 38 min by train. Spanish fast trains, like the Japanese Shinkansen trains, travel up to 320 km/h. Paris to Lyon – almost 500 km – takes 2 hours 10 min by TGV train and Paris to Marseilles – 800 km – 3 hours 20 min by train. It may be a faster option than a domestic flight if a traveller wants to travel between city centre locations.

The tendency is clear: car companies have to take changes in the larger environment into account. Flights get slightly more comfortable over time thanks to reduced noise levels, while travel times remain largely constant. Aircraft product development certainly takes passenger comfort and convenience into account but safety and fuel consumption considerations are more pressing. It may be argued that a new Boeing 737 or 747 is very different from the same models built four decades ago – both were introduced in the late 1960s and are still on sale in updated versions based on the same body – but passenger space is constant and the main focus is on making air travel more sustainable.

High jet fuel prices, congested airports and highways, and increasing airport security all contribute to making high-speed trains an attractive option. A study conducted by the International Union of Railways indicated that high-speed trains produced five times less CO_2 than automobiles and jet aircraft.

Although a significant number of people across the world have a genuine interest in trains and aircraft, that can't compete with the solid car cultures in most countries. While train and air travel are collective modes of transport, with no personal ownership of the vehicle, the car may be chosen, customized and personalized in a way that gives room for strong individual and cultural expressions. In addition, the development of the automobile has contributed to changes in shopping patterns, social interactions, and urban and landscape planning, something that underlines the dynamic nature of the car as opposed to trains and aircraft that normally travel through hubs and on fixed (and occasionally delayed) time slots.

More recently, particularly in the last decade, there has been less room for driving and parking cars in city centres. Typical political interventions are:

- Introducing/increasing car tolls.
- Driving into city centres not allowed on certain days – or at all.
- Making double-lane roads single-lane roads to give room for bicycles, trees, flowers and pedestrians.
- Introducing one-way streets, something that could actually improve traffic flow but also make room for pedestrians and green areas.
- Limiting parking space and/or making it very expensive. In many countries and states, the city controls parking fees along roads and city administrations may even run their own parking garages.
- Not allowing cars with high emissions to drive in city centres – Germany has implemented Green Zones in all major cities, and Denmark has Low Emission Zones for heavy traffic. The idea is to reduce traffic and pollution by offering better terms for cars (and trucks) with lower emissions.

A good example of the above measures is Times Square in Manhattan, New York. Urban planners have succeeded in reducing car traffic to give room for activities that are natural in a big city. Times Square is New York's very hub of tourism, cultural activities and marketing communications – few places in the world show a higher density of signs. But it has in recent years been subject to traffic restrictions, a measure most other cities would have implemented much earlier. Step by step, space for traffic has been reduced and space for pedestrians, cafés and social activities increased. The effect is clear: it is less convenient to go by car and more convenient to walk, and Times Square's role as a place of social get-togethers has become (even) stronger: politicians and urban planners – and many citizens these days – in general prefer social activities and shopping in city centres to high traffic flow.

City branding scholars and marketers emphasize the strong preference in attractive cities to give room for shopping, restaurants, cultural activities and recreation environments and other expressions of modern lifestyle, something that gives the city a safe, social and vibrant character – with higher safety and less emissions (at least in the city centre) compared to a city that gives priority to traffic flows (see for example Govers and Go, 2009; Greenberg, 2000; Moilanen and Rainisto, 2009; Morgan *et al*, 2002; Rainisto, 2009). The effect of these changes and measures is clear: there is and will be even less room for car cultures in bigger cities, a development largely paralleled by less interest in general among car drivers in driving around just for fun, a common practice in the past.

Differences across countries

Driving culture says a lot about a country. Without doubt, car drivers in Southern Europe are a lot more careful than they used to be, but their reputation lives on: traffic is lively and cars have an endless number of scratches and dents. Parking bays are smaller and roads narrower – and obviously it is more difficult to keep a car in great condition when the car culture is focused on the car as a functional and social item. People care less about the car, that's at least how an American, a Scandinavian or a German would put it, and when that's part of the culture around the car, it requires more attention and causes more frustration and effort to keep the car in a great condition. It's difficult to find solid international data on the extent to which people take care of their cars. Two studies from 2010 and 2013 suggest that 58 per cent of German car owners state that they wash the car once a month or more often.[4]

Safety has improved across European countries with the most significant improvements in Southern Europe where extensive investment in infrastructure has been made in the last few decades. Information, safer roads, better train-ing, and the economic downturn in Spain, Portugal, France and Italy in recent years, contribute to making less traffic: when people have little money they drive less and go slower for fear of getting a ticket and to reduce their fuel consumption. There is normally less stress and fewer overcrowded streets when there is a downturn in the economy.

By 2025, India's middle class is expected to approach 600 million people – about 40 per cent of the population. This is a major change for India which, in 1985, saw 90 per cent of its population living on less than a dollar a day. When the middle class grows the demand for affordable automobiles takes off. At the same time, mass motorization could result in increased pollution and heavy traffic congestion – heavier, maybe, than in any other country given the enormous population density in India.

In Cuba, about 60,000 pre-1960 US cars cruise the streets of Havana. The often rusty – but obviously long-lasting and robust – cars are symbols of pre-revolutionary US influence and half a century of embargoes.

The United States

Treating the vast United States as one country is difficult but in terms of car culture, the tendency to think big is pronounced not only in rural and city areas but also in metro areas. Until the last Ford Crown Victorias were delivered in 2011, it was by far the most common cab in metro areas since the Chevrolet Caprice was discontinued in 1996 – the Caprice largely replaced the Checker that was built until 1982. The Crown Victoria is, like the Caprice and the Checker, a full size sedan that always comes with a 4.6 litre V8 engine. As opposed to many other cars with six to nine gears, the Crown Victoria always came with a four-speed automatic gearbox. Fuel consumption averages 10 to 12 mpg in Manhattan traffic. Nonetheless, the car has been very popular thanks to its high reliability and great passenger comfort. It's no surprise that the thirsty but spacious and reliable Crown Victoria has been extensively used as a police car in its more power-ful and dynamic Police Interceptor guise, with greater engine power and special shock absorbers. But what place does the huge and fuel-inefficient Crown Victoria have in downtown Manhattan cab traffic? It says something about the United States and its car culture. Going by cab is not very expen-sive in the United States either – substantially cheaper than in Europe, even with US tipping taken into consideration: in no other country would cab companies get away with the predefined 20, 25 or 30 per cent tip buttons that Manhattan cabs typically provide.

The thirsty but spacious and reliable Ford Crown Victoria, delivered until early 2012, was the dominant cab in the United States. but is gradually being replaced by more fuel-efficient vehicles. (Anders Parment, 24 April 2011, 7th Avenue/47th Street, New York)

Recently hybrid cars such as the Ford Escape, Nissan Maxima and Toyota Prius have begun to replace the Crown Victoria, but it is interesting that they didn't do so earlier, given that fuel consumption is better by more than 50 per cent – and even more with the not very spacious but very fuel-efficient Prius. Cab drivers get a tear in their eye when asked about the Crown Victoria – many of them wish it could have been built forever. In 2011, New York Mayor Michael Bloomberg announced that Nissan had won the Taxi of Tomorrow competition, meaning it will replace the city's 13,000 yellow cabs, phased in over five years from 2013. The NV200 is likely to be complemented with a fully electric version later.

US car culture reached its peak in the 1950s, and this has had an enduring influence on US culture overall.[5] The 1950s began with 25 million registered cars, many of them produced before World War II (during the war, no cars were produced between 1942 and the end of the war (Snyder, 2011)) and one decade later, in 1960, 74.4 million cars were registered. This early car penetration explains why the annual car growth rate per 1,000 people has been only 1.6 per cent in the United States between 1960 and 2002 while it has been around or above 5 per cent in Europe, South America and Asia. Only three countries came close to the United States' 411 cars per 1,000 inhabitants in 1960: Canada (292), Australia (266) and New Zealand (271) (Dargay *et al*, 2007). The United States became the world's largest car manufacturer and in the late 1950s, one in six working Americans were employed either directly or indirectly in the car industry.

It's important to note that the strong US car culture is not consistent across this huge country. While Michigan is characterized by a phenomenal auto-related heritage and events, California is certainly very car-intensive but early on started the transition into alternative fuels and was the first US state to implement tough emissions laws in the mid-1970s. The car industry was crucial to the development of Michigan. The innovation and growth of this industry, its good times and bad, have had profound effects on it as the epicentre of the US car industry.

There is little doubt that Michigan and Detroit have experienced a significant decline over time. In 1960, Detroit was the richest per capita city in the United States.[6] Now it has filed for bankruptcy, the largest US city to do so. Sixty per cent of Detroit's children are living in poverty; 50 per cent of the population has been reported to be functionally illiterate; 33 per cent of Detroit's 140 square miles is vacant or derelict; 18 per cent of the population is unemployed (Mathews, 2013). Michigan lost 48 per cent of all its manufacturing jobs between 2000 and 2010.[7]

When the NAFTA (North American Free Trade Agreement) was first signed in 1994, it was argued that jobs would be created in the United States, for example by Nobel Prize winning economist Paul Krugman. Reality turned out to be different, though. Research reports contend NAFTA cost the US millions of manufacturing jobs (Scott, 2011) or, according to another estimation, at least 680,000 US net jobs have been lost or displaced because of the NAFTA agreement. At the same time, the United States has created 1.5 to 1.75 million jobs in the service sector, but a significant proportion of high-skill, high-paying manufacturing and industrial jobs have been lost to Mexico and other global trade partners; the exact number is difficult to assess since estimates differ.

People born in the 1960s have very different experiences of US car culture. If they grew up in Michigan, Detroit's muscle car era was around them – if they grew up in California, they experienced strong emissions restrictions and other state interventions. Los Angeles was founded by the Spanish on the site of a Native American village in 1781, but it wasn't until after the first film studio was established in 1911 that Los Angeles really took off. Soon, a lot of movies were being produced in there. As the box office boomed in the 1920s and 1930s, so did the population. The Hollywood sign, erected in 1923, was built as an advertisement for one of many real-estate developments that began to crop up. The opening of the Arroyo Seco Parkway in 1940, linking downtown Los Angeles with the California network of freeways created a new era for the city. From that time on, car culture flourished in Los Angeles, and auto-friendly infrastructure was encouraged. The growth of the freeways led to the development of Los Angeles' suburban sprawl, turning it into a city without a single geographical focus, making the city very spread-out and car-dependent.

By the end of the 1950s, one-third of Americans lived in the suburbs. All but one of the 12 largest US cities recorded a declining population during the 1950s. The only exception was Los Angeles, with its priority given to cars. (Los Angeles is still known as a city difficult to manage without a car – extensive road work in the summer of 2011 made people more worried about how to survive than in any other US city.) Los Angeles soon became a centre for car culture. The car made the growth of suburbs possible, and the suburbs made the car necessary. As middle-class and more affluent people moved from city centres to the suburbs, city centres lost business, viability, tax revenues, inhabitants and attractiveness.

The heavy reliance on the car as a means of transport created entirely new categories of businesses and services that allowed car drivers to enjoy their products and services without having to leave their cars, eg shopping malls, driver-through or drive-in restaurants and theatres (cinemas). In the United States, zoning laws, which are still in place, required that new businesses provided a certain amount of parking based on the size and type of facility. The effect of this was to create a massive amount of free parking spaces. In addition, companies such as GM, Firestone Tire, Standard Oil of California, Phillips Petroleum and Mack Trucks purchased a number of streetcars and electric trains in the 1930s and 1940s and closed them down as part of a deliberate strategy to increase dependency on cars. Even more innovative was Richard Hollingshead's fly-in theatre. Hollingshead was a young sales manager at his dad's Whiz Auto Products, who had a hankering to invent something that combined his two interests: cars and movies. An interesting innovation was the combination drive-in and fly-in theatre (Cohen, 1994; Friedberg, 2002). On 3 June 1948, Edward Brown Junior opened the first theatre for cars and small planes at Asbury Park, New Jersey, with capacity for 500 cars and 25 airplanes. An airfield was placed next to the drive-in and planes would taxi to the last row of the theatre. When the movies were over, planes were towed back to the airfield. The strong focus on activities built around the car along with the car's natural role as the primary mode of transport help explain the strong role of cars in modern US history.

Many suburbs and shopping malls abandoned sidewalks altogether, making pedestrian access inconvenient and dangerous. Even though pedestrian protection has improved significantly in recent years, walking is still dangerous and something that urban planners have to consider; the result is often a clear separation of cars and pedestrians or, more often in the United States, the removal of pedestrian zones overall. Upon a request to walk to the Golf Restaurant, approximately six to seven minutes' walk from the main hotel at Prince Hotel, Maui, Hawaii, hotel staff referred to the regular golf bus tours and emphasized the danger of walking to the restaurant. Infrastructure obviously has the effect of encouraging people to drive or go by shuttle bus, even for short trips that might have been walkable.

For many decades, infrastructure for the car has been superior in the United States in terms of road quality and density as well as the services provided along the road. The interstate system authorized by the Federal Aid Highway Act of 1956 has made a significant contribution to growth in the United States (Weingroff, 2000). Investment in infrastructure coincided with a rapid growth of availability of affordable cars. In the decade following World Word II, many babies were born and many families got the chance to buy their own single-family home with their own backyard. The Servicemen's Readjustment Act of 1944, often referred to as the GI Bill, provided a range of benefits for returning World War II veterans including low-cost mortgages, low-interest loans for business start-ups, cash payments for tuition and living expenses to attend college or high school, and one year of unemployment compensation. It was available to every veteran who had been on active duty during the war years for at least 90 days. When the programme ended in 1956, 2.2 million veterans had used the education benefits to attend colleges, and an additional 6.6 million for training programmes (Altschuler and Blumin, 2009; Bound and Turner, 2002; Ortiz, 2013). Car buyers became increasingly aware of the fact that the car they drove indicated their social standing and level of affluence. It became a statement of their personality and an extension of their self.

The effect of all this was that Americans spent more time in their cars and began seeing them as an extension of their personal identity, hence making cars a key part of US culture. New designs and innovations appealed to a generational cohort tuned into fashion and glamour.[8]

US buyers prefer large cars

Lack of space is something that characterizes every metro area and Manhattan is no exception. But cars aren't small in the United States: that's obvious to every Manhattan visitor. With the exception of European premium cars – in addition to the numerous Mercedes S Class, BMW 7 series and Audi A8 there are some C Class, 3 series and A4, and you may even see a Mini Cooper – smaller cars are uncommon. As mentioned earlier, the full-sized Ford Crown Victoria is still the most common taxi – at 5.5 metres it's sized between the long version of the Mercedes S Class and a Maybach. In fact, a Rolls Royce Silver Spirit is shorter. The Crown Victoria is a perfect example of a classic US car. It has a very simple set-up: a large engine, a robust but not very sophisticated four-speed automatic gearbox, an enormous trunk, a spacious passenger area, very soft suspension and no unnecessary gadgets. The dashboard looks like a cheap European non-premium car from the 1990s in terms of finish and style – the Crown Victoria did not even have a rev counter until the last years of production. US speed limits are comparatively low and rigorously enforced – it's difficult to find an American who has ever driven faster than 85 or 90 mph – but nonetheless, US car buyers want powerful engines. In fact, the weakest engine in the Mercedes E Class is the E300 (272 bhp) – in Europe it's E200 CDI (136 bhp), in the Volvo S80 the 3.2 (241 bhp) – in Europe it's the D2/1.6d (115 bhp) and so on. A young American with a business degree who has studied in Austria says: 'The bigger the better, the ultimate success is a large car' – no sign of the European 'rather premium than large' attitude.

Another young American states that 'we need to deal with growing income and wealth differences first, then we'll consider the climate and ecological issues'. This attitude is worrying given the fact that wealth has a tendency to accumulate over time and few countries have succeeded in reducing vast differences between rich and poor in modern history.

There are signs of change, though. Cars' fuel economy is improving – in fact, during the 1980s the United States' Big Three car makers were very successful in reducing fuel consumption in all types of car models. The downsizing that started in the 1970s in the aftermath of the oil crisis gained momentum once more in the 1980 and has now started again. And it shouldn't be forgotten that a US state – California – was the first, in 1975, to insist on cars being fitted with catalytic converters to reduce emissions. In addition, cars run on ethanol were already being sold and used in California in the 1990s.

Australia

Australia is a vast country with enormous distances between population centres, which creates a number of challenges when it comes to owning, driving and servicing cars. Dealerships are located in the larger cities – Sydney, Melbourne, Brisbane, Adelaide and Perth – and rural hubs, eg Tamworth, and are most likely to be multi-franchised. Sydney's factory-owned BMW site proudly presents itself as 'the largest premium car dealership in the southern hemisphere' – which is true, but not as impressive as it may sound considering the lack of competition in that area.

Australia is one of the wealthiest countries in the world, with the fifth highest per capita income. Tourism and exchange students contribute to a strong economy – but Australia is also likely to have among the world's highest costs per capita for dealing with natural disasters. For many years the rural economy has been suffering and it's a struggle for auto brands to provide a proper network of service stations across the country. The metro-rural divide is very strong and this huge country with only 22.5 million inhabitants is very sparsely populated outside the coastal cities.

Australia is far away from Europe but doesn't lack European influences. In many respects it shows strong similarities to the United Kingdom, not surprising given the shared history of the UK and Australia, and shares many British institutions such as upper and lower houses in the Parliament. However, in terms of car culture Australia is more similar to the United States. The culture overall has a bit of Europe, the United Kingdom particularly, a bit of mainland United States and a bit of Hawaii, and while it is not particularly friendly towards immigration, it's a hub for tourism and guest students, the latter being the country's greatest income source.

Australia is largely a car-friendly country but with significant car tolls and taxes for luxury cars. Hence, a German premium car gives more prestige than in many other countries. While a BMW 320d or an Audi A4 is certainly premium, but not considered very exclusive in Germany, the United Kingdom, Sweden or Austria, it is an expensive car in Australia. So, as in Thailand, Norway and numerous other countries with luxury car taxes, expensive cars are considered more exclusive.

Although the economy is good and car sales have constantly grown, with about 1.15 million cars per year,[9] the car industry has lost societal influence. In 2013, Ford decided to close down its two factories in Broadmeadow and

Geelong (Melbourne) by 2016 due to high manufacturing costs. Mitsubishi ceased Australian manufacturing in Adelaide in 2008.

Germany

Germany is perceived as being one of the leading car-producing nations of the world, second only to the United States. There is hardly any other country where the car and the automobile industry dominate the culture as much as in Germany. The German car market is characterized by fierce competition and the existence of numerous leading car producers.

Germany is known for high precision, great engineering and high quality products – Miele white goods, Siemens turbines and Porsche cars are just a few examples. Although it's doubtful whether Germany produces higher-quality cars than other countries – there have been many quality issues with Opel cars in the 1990s, Mercedes-Benz corrosion problems and Audi and Volkswagen gearboxes to name a few. But they are well-engineered and some of the quality problems are due to high levels of innovation – new features are more likely to cause problems than tried and tested solutions. German companies are good at bringing things together, and with high functionality they are often attractively designed. Most designers of German cars are non-Germans so the label often used to define Seat – Spanish design, German engineering – applies to many other products, within and outside the car industry. Barcelona is a centre for car design and has a strong influence on the design of many industrial products.

German car owners like station wagons/estate cars and are known for keeping their vehicles in good condition. Inspections are more likely to be carried out before the stipulated service schedule than after. Winter tyres are mandatory and Germans put them on in accordance with the recommendation: plus 8° Celsius, often earlier than car owners in countries north of Germany where it's colder. (There is more about Germany's role in car cultures in the next chapter on auto brands.)

Sweden/Scandinavia

Like in Germany, the station wagon's share of the market is high. Cars were until recently specced according to logic and need: cruise control, xenon headlights, parking sensors and Bluetooth for hands-free phones. In recent years, however, emotional extravagances such as sports packages, have become more popular. Winter tyres are mandatory and more than half the winter tyres have spikes.

While Norway, Denmark and Finland have very high taxes on luxury cars, Sweden offers among the lowest prices for new cars in Europe. Despite its size (9 million inhabitants) it has been subject to a lot of price competition. A three-year warranty against damage is normally included in the new car price, a competitive weapon introduced by Volvo in 1975. To survive cold winters and extensive use of road salt, seat heating, upgraded rust protection and heating system, etc were offered to car buyers. A key explanation to the comparatively low new car prices is that the official car tax threshold is around €37,000, above which the user must pay luxury taxes, which would make it impossible to get a full-size premium car at normal European prices. However, Audi, BMW and Mercedes offer full-sized station wagons below the threshold (c. 20 per cent below mainland Europe prices) – a consequence of intensive efforts to reach their global sales targets, and Volvo and some others also want to be in the game. This is the reason why Swedish sales reps drive an Audi A6, Mercedes E Class or Volvo XC70.

Canada

The car industry in Canada consists primarily of foreign car makers running assembly plants, dominated by the US Big Three and Japanese car makers Toyota and Honda. At one time Canada was the world's second largest car producer but by 2012 it was 11th, with approximately 2.1 million cars produced.

Canada has a strong car culture that in many respects mirrors that of the United States. Many Canadian cities are very spread out and, as in the United States, many roads lack pavements. Also like the United States, getting a driver's licence is relatively easy and cheap; in most states 17 years is the lowest accepted solo driving age. Taxes on cars and fuel are lower than in many other countries. There is an extensive infrastructure for car maintenance and repairs at affordable prices.

Latin America

Mexico, Brazil and to a lesser extent Argentina are the leading countries in Latin America when it comes to the car industry. Colombia, Ecuador and Venezuela produce no more than 100,000 vehicles a year and Chile has no car production at all.

Mexico has applied a very international model by developing close economic integration with the United States and with Europe through trade agreements with the European Union. Automotive products are Mexico's largest exports and many cars driven in the United States and Europe are produced in Mexico.

Mexico and Brazil suffer heavily from the drawbacks of extensive car use. Average journey times have increased in large cities because of widespread automobile ownership and the resultant traffic congestion. Societal development has also contributed through increased distances between home and work brought about by urban sprawl. Hence cars, once a luxury item, have become a quality-of-life problem in larger Latin American cities. Safety is poor compared to international standards, too. The likelihood of dying in a traffic accident is three times higher in Brazil than in Canada, Sweden, Germany or Japan (Bacchieri and Barros, 2011).

Mexico

In 1903, motorcars first arrived in Mexico and in 1910 Mercedes-Benz and Renault established small facilities for the local assembly of vehicles, primarily for the Mexican government. Buick became the first automobile producer to be officially established in Mexico in 1921, followed by Ford in 1925. In 1959, Mexico produced its first fully domestic vehicle, a small truck called the Rural Ramírez, from the Ramírez truck company. Chrysler entered Mexico around 1937. General Motors was the sales leader in Mexico until 2009, when Nissan took top spot.

In the early 1960s, government regulations forced car companies to assemble cars in Mexico using local as well as imported components to promote employment and technological advances. In protest, Mercedes-Benz, Fiat, Citroën, Volvo and Peugeot left the country while General Motors, Ford, Chrysler, Volkswagen, Datsun, Renault and Borgward complied and remained there. The growth of Mexico's economy during the late 1990s stimulated car sales in Mexico and, eventually, most of the departed car makers came back to re-establish assembly facilities.

In Mexico, cheap, affordable and reliable cars are particularly popular, eg the Chevrolet Chevy, known as the Opel Corsa in other parts of the world, first imported from GM's factory in Pamplona, Spain, but later produced in Mexico; and the Volkswagen Sedan, a model name first used for the classic Beetle sold since 1954 and until manufacturing was halted in 2003, and later for the Jetta which is the saloon version of the Golf. Old models, abandoned in many other markets, are popular in Mexico. Like in China, run-out models without the latest technology are successful in

Mexico due to their high reliability and affordability. It has also been a common practice to offer two or three generations of cars in the same range at the same time to offer buyers reliable and cheap, but not really updated, options.

In 2002, an agreement was made between Brazil and Mexico that allows free trade in cars between the countries. For a decade it worked as it was meant to, and to Brazil's advantage, by encouraging carmakers in Mexico to specialize in larger models and those in Brazil to make smaller ones. But Latin America's two biggest economies appear to have different approaches when it comes to trade and industry. Mexico, with its large production and export capacity has become a base from which car makers export cars. This has been made possible under NAFTA and numerous other bilateral trade agreements. Volkswagen makes all its Beetles and Jettas in Mexico; 2.1 million of the 2.6 million vehicles produced in Mexico in 2011 were exported. By contrast, 540,000 of the 3.4 million vehicles manufactured in Brazil in 2011 were exported (*The Economist*, 2012). Around three-quarters of Brazil's car exports go to Argentina, a country with little domestic car production.

Brazil

In Brazil the main aim of public policy has been to push car makers to build local factories to supply Brazil's domestic market. The South American trade union Mercosur has long aspired to balance trade in cars and car parts between the two (*The Economist*, 2012). While Mexico sees its car industry as part of a global supply chain, car making in Brazil has a high local content.

Brazil's government sees the country's domestic market as an asset to be protected, with a somewhat negative view on international trade. Accordingly, imports from China are seen as a threat to the domestic car industry. Industry minister Fernando Pimentel has declared that Brazil has to protect its domestic car industry; but protectionism risks locking in high costs or, as Ricardo Mendes of Prospectiva, a consultancy in Sao Paulo, put it, Brazil has 'a competitiveness problem, not a trade problem' (*The Economist*, 2012).

Although Brazil, with a GDP per inhabitant of US$11,340 for 2012[10] does not seem to be overwhelmingly prosperous, the economic outlook and consumption appetite both speak for the future growth of Brazil. With the sixth largest economy by nominal GDP in the world, the largest economy in Latin America and the second largest in the Western hemisphere, Brazil is a key market for multinational companies. Over time, Brazil has accomplished an average annual GDP growth rate of over 5 per cent. As one of the BRIC (Brazil, Russia, India and China) countries, in future decades Brazil is expected to become one of the five largest economies in the world (Sala-I-Martin *et al*, 2009).

Within the BRIC group, Brazil has improved its position despite its rather protectionist position, although there have been measures taken to liberalize and open up the economy. According to the World Economic Forum, Brazil was the top country in upward evolution of competitiveness in 2009, gaining eight positions, overtaking Russia for the first time, and partially closing the competitiveness gap with India and China.

In the 1950s, Toyota and Volkswagen built factories in Brazil, followed by Ford and Fiat in the 1960s. Brazil is now one of the world's largest car producers with about 3.5 million vehicles (including light vehicles, trucks and buses) produced per year. There are major international car makers and domestic producers such as Troller and Randon, but it was not until the mid-1990s that trade barriers were removed and the Brazilian market was finally opened to imports. In the 1990s, more auto companies set up and opened factories in Brazil, including Nissan, Renault, Peugeot, Citroën, Honda, Hyundai, Mitsubishi, Chrysler and Audi. Currently the most successful genuine Brazilian auto company is Troller, with its T4 and Pantanal models. It sells all over Latin America and Africa.

The luxury Brazilian market was estimated to be worth almost US$12 billion in 2012, according to MCF Consultoria. Interest in luxury brands increased online by 24 per cent over 2011, as Miu Miu, Goyard, Chanel, Lanvin, Jaeger-LeCoultre, Ferrari and Van Clef et Arpels opened their first stores in Brazil. Despite the increased local presence of international luxury brands, the Brazilian consumer is estimated to purchase 80 per cent of luxury products outside of Brazil. On average, an imported product will be 2.5 times more expensive in Brazil than in the United States or France, mainly due to logistics, distribution and people costs impacted by domestic and import taxes. Digital Luxury Group, an international company that creates luxury industry market intelligence, suggests a strong market presence in Brazil to be key for luxury and fashion brands willing to take advantage of the wealthy international clientele. According to Digital Luxury Group's research, interest in luxury items increased by 24 per cent in 2012, led by luxury auto brands. Estimated at US$12 billion (MCF Consultoria and GfK, 2011) the luxury market in Brazil is marked by an increase in consumer interest across all segments. Cars had the greatest growth with 68 per cent suggesting global luxury car brands should expect large market potential in Brazil. Audi, BMW and Mercedes are the three leading auto brands in the study (Bondoux, 2013).

Car culture history in Latin America

While in North America the car early on became a key part of daily life, representing individualism, comfort and the emergence of a modernistic society, the history of car culture is different in Latin America, where the car served as a symbol of distinction, similar to jewellery or fine clothing (Giucci, 2012). The emergence of the car in South America became an essential support for the development of modern individualism. Like in North America, the car inspired and brought changes in popular culture, but the car culture that emerged had some specific characteristics in South America.

Between the first and the second World Wars, both Ford and GM set up assembly and marketing channels in Argentina, and promoted local demand through advertising in magazines, newspapers, on the radio and through car shows. At the time, Argentina lacked a good network of roads so urban areas, in particular around Buenos Aires, were the primary places car owners could go to (Heras, 1985). Argentina's economy was very strong at the time and car density was higher than in any other country expect Germany, Australia and the South African Union (Heras, 1985). Around 1930, US companies were dominating the car business in Argentina (Heras, 1985). The emphasis on the wellbeing aspects of car ownership and driving were strongly emphasized at this stage, as in a Ford ad that stated:

> There are many beautiful places near the city that you and your family are
> not aware of. Buy a Ford and get acquainted with all the neighbourhoods of
> the city and its picturesque environs. Drive yourself. Take the street or road
> that seems the most interesting. If an object or a sight attracts your attention,
> stop. Without violence, without hurry, with complete comfort, with utter calm.
> You are the owner of a Ford. You are in command.
>
> (Giucci, 2012: 76–77)

Soon, the growth of cars emphasized the need for better roads and extensive highway development programmes were carried out in the 1930s. Argentina had 2,000 kilometres of highways in 1932 and 30,000 kilometres 10 years later (Giucci, 2012). Road building was an international trend but it took place in Argentina even earlier than in the United States and Germany. Uruguay followed a similar pattern to Brazil and Argentina with extensive road building programmes, while in Paraguay cars were introduced more gradually and they for a long time shared the roads with horses, donkeys and oxen (Giucci, 2012).

In 1893 the first car came to Sao Paulo; 10 years later, all cars had plates. In 1919, Henry Ford established an assembly plant in Sao Paulo to produce the Model T. In 1925, General Motors started operations in Brazil and the first Chevrolet came off the assembly line.[11]

Africa

Africa – a huge continent with 53 countries and almost a billion inhabitants, often seen as a place ravaged by poverty, famine and war – may not be considered a huge market opportunity by car makers. The numbers tell the same story: Africa does not have a lot of potential to constitute a significant market for car sales in the foreseeable future. The UK economy alone is about 30 per cent larger than that of the entire African continent.

Many African countries lack a network of proper roads and in terms of infrastructure they are several decades behind the countries described above. However, ignoring Africa may be a huge mistake. Six of the 10 fastest-growing economies in the world are now found in Africa. Africa has achieved average economic growth of 5 per cent every year since the turn of the millennium – growth figures that by far exceed those of Western economies – and it wasn't much affected by the financial crisis that hit the Western world in 2008 and 2009. The era of grotesque tyrants running the African continent appear to be over. Most African countries now hold elections of varying degrees of credibility but the tendency is clear. Africa is less poor than we may think. The Seychelles, Botswana, South Africa, Morocco, Tunisia, Reunion-Mayotte and Gabon have mobile phone penetration rates higher than 100 per cent; Africa in total has 644 million mobile phone subscribers.[12]

Notes

1 *Flightglobal Aviation Connected*, 1999, DaimlerChrysler will link headquarters, January 20.

2 *Huffington Post Business*, 2011, 'Number of cars worldwide surpasses 1 billion; can the world handle this many wheels?', August 23.

3 Research by BIPE management consultancy, see Diem, 2013.

4 AXA Survey, 2010; *auto motor & sport*, online survey, 2013.

5 For more scholarly research into the US car history, recommended reading is Berger (2001): a bit old and heavy but very useful. Or read Seiler (2008).

6   According to the US Census Bureau.

7   US 2010 Census data.

8   National Museum of American History, homepage, retrieved July 2013.

9   Australian Bureau of Statistics.

10 Figures from the World Bank, data.worldbank.org.

11 Gmheritagecenter.com, retrieved July 2012.

12 The 2012 African Mobile Factbook.

Automobile brands

More than in any other sector, the brand is at the heart of success in the car industry and, to car buyers, the brand is crucial – attachments to brands are consciously and unconsciously established long before a potential buyer considers purchasing a car for the first time. It is not only car buyers who are essential to how a brand is perceived, but also a complex set of opinions and ideas from other stakeholders too – hence, car makers have every reason to strive to establish attractive and profitable auto brands.

This chapter deals with the role of the auto brand in creating success in the car industry and how strong auto brands might be established and developed. Numerous examples of successful branding strategies are given – and a few that provide insights on how not to do it. Car makers spend enormous amounts on establishing and strengthening their auto brands – figures are difficult to get since branding, by its very nature, is a broad activity that, from a modern marketing perspective, covers a variety of activities including corporate identity, advertising, product design, salespeople training and personnel recruitment. Branding may be perceived as costly – and it is – but car makers are likely to benefit from investing in it. This chapter lays the foundations of a contemporary approach to branding and presents smart solutions to how strong brands are created in the very competitive car industry.

Tough competition puts pressure on car companies to develop business models that are attractive for a multitude of stakeholders, and to profile their brands among the younger audience particularly. It is easier and cheaper to change brand perceptions among younger people – and, as opposed to a few decades ago, older car buyers increasingly buy cars designed for younger car buyers. By cooperating with companies inside and outside the industry car companies have the opportunity to get a stronger foothold in society and to benefit from a good understanding of what is going on in terms of trends

By establishing a fashion store in a shopping centre, a car manufacturer gets a stronger foothold in society and will benefit from having a dialogue with existing and potential customers in a setting different from the dealer environment.
(Anders Parment, 4 August 2009, The Malls at Oriental Plaza, Dongcheng District, Beijing)

and challenges that provide tomorrow's profitable opportunities. A broader approach is necessary for the car industry to stay competitive; this does not only apply at the car maker level but also for retailers and an array of service providers.

The car industry is highly brand-driven and brand perceptions change slowly, probably more so than in most other industries. The physical product – the car – lasts for about two decades and contributes to inertia in making a brand that is appealing. This inertia may also protect brands that make, or are accused of making, poor products; the strength of the Mercedes-Benz brand protected the company when the A Class car tipped over in a road test in 1997, an event that sped up the implementation of Electronic Stability Systems (ESPs) in mass car markets. ESP improves safety significantly.

Brand development is a long-term business: it took Audi two decades of hard work to create a genuine premium brand after the strategy was launched around 1980.[1] By the turn of the millennium Audi had fulfilled its ambition to create a real premium brand – and this was confirmed by its competitors. A way of measuring brand perceptions is to ask representatives of competing brands. While Audi, BMW and Mercedes-Benz consistently referred to the other two in answering this question, other brands show less awareness of their own position: in numerous cases, representatives refer to higher positioned brands but hardly the other way round (see Parment, 2009). For instance, Volvo dealers refer to Audi and BMW as competitors – but there are few references the other way. Volkswagen dealers suggest Audi, Mercedes-Benz and Volvo as competitors; Skoda, Opel, Peugeot and Hyundai dealers refer to Volkswagen and Toyota. To an extent, the comparisons are true but the tendency is nonetheless that most brands would like to be perceived as more attractive and exclusive than they are. This is dangerous for the perception of the brand – brands that interpret their market position in a way different from their target buyer groups are not taken seriously. Brand perceptions vary by country but the point is clear: by not understanding the competition, it is difficult to make use of market opportunities.

Auto brands are very valuable

A range of studies – normally issued yearly – attempt to estimate the value of auto brands, and the results vary across studies. According to Millward Brown's BrandZ Top 100 Most Valuable Global Brands study 2013[2] six auto brands are listed among the 100 most valuable global brands – see Table 6.1. This type of study may give valuable, although not very distinct information about interesting tendencies. In this study, for instance, Toyota and Mercedes increased by 12 and 11 per cent respectively, compared to the year before, while BMW and Honda lost 2 per cent each. Millward Brown suggests Toyota's advance is derived from innovative and class-leading hybrid models that create value for car buyers. No car maker beats Apple, Google and IBM, the three highest valued brands. Ford, Audi, Hyundai and Lexus did not feature in the top 100 list, although Audi managed to increase by 18 per cent.

Although the methods used for ranking can always be questioned – there is no perfect method and very complex models may make it difficult to run the rankings over time – they are important for car makers for two reasons. First, they provide valuable information about changes in the market, about the company and its competitors in the same study – and the data used are normally not paid for or controlled by any company in the industry. Second, it results in media exposure and reactions from a variety of stakeholders:

TABLE 6.1   From Millward Brown's BrandZ Top 100 Most Valuable Global Brands study 2013

Auto Brand	Ranking in top 100	Market value billion $	Brand value % change 2013 vs 2012	Rank change
Toyota	23	24.5	+12	+5
BMW	24	24.0	−2	−1
Mercedes-Benz	43	18.0	+11	+3
Honda	71	12.4	−2	−6
Nissan	86	10.2	+3	−5
Volkswagen	100	8.8	+3	−4

hence, not only the reasons behind changes in brand position and perceptions reflected in the study will matter, but also the reactions to the study results. When a car buyer reads in the newspaper that Mercedes-Benz's brand gained 11 per cent in the last year and climbed in the ranking, it's good for the Mercedes-Benz auto brand.

Strong brands last for a long time

It's a well-known fact that brands are difficult – or impossible – to copy.[3] John Stuart, once chairman of Quaker Oats Ltd, stated: 'If the business were split up, I would take the brands, trademarks and goodwill, and you could have all the bricks and mortar and I would fare better than you' (Dyson *et al*, 1996: 52).

It's interesting to see how long-established brands still enjoy an advantage in the war for customers. German's leading car magazine *auto motor & sport's* 2012 survey on 28 categories in the automobile industry (Hascheck, 2012) provides some interesting results – see Table 6.2 – and cooperating with any of these companies would contribute to making a car maker stronger in terms of competence and reputation, constituting a protection against competition. Companies that are successful in a particular area attract human capital from competitors, benefit from a strong manufacturer brand, media attention and support from politicians. Table 6.2 underlines the importance of building a strong brand – most companies in the list have been around for several decades, maintained their position and enjoyed the benefits of strong brands.

TABLE 6.2 *auto motor & sport's* 2012 survey on leading brands in 28 categories in the car industry

Category	Brand
Tow coupling	Westfalia
Brakes	Brembo
Car hi-fi	Bang & Olufsen
Roof rack	Thule
Car testing	TÜV
Rental car	Sixt
Wipers	Bosch
Car tuning	Brabus
Fuel	Aral
Mail order	Conrad
Repair shops	Bosch
Tools and instruments	Bosch
Spark plugs	Bosch
Exhaust pipes	Eberspächer
Batteries	Bosch
Lamps	Bosch
Suspension	Bilstein

TABLE 6.2 *Continued*

Category	Brand
Rims	BBS
Filters	Bosch
Care products	Sonax
Car banks	Volkswagen
Car exchange	mobile.de
Lubricants	Liqui moly
Car seats	Recaro
Vehicle heaters	Webasto

Pricing and brand strength

In a typical car market with limited car sales taxes, ie the United States, Germany, Spain, the United Kingdom or Italy, relative pricing changes over time, indications of brand attractiveness and how it may change over time. If the price of a Mercedes-Benz was 35 to 40 per cent higher than the average price of a car in the same segment 15 years ago, it may now be 10 to 15 per cent higher, making a Mercedes-Benz an option for a broader audience. If the price of a Peugeot or Ford approaches the segment average, hence moving away from their value-for-money positions, budget brands may be an alternative for many buyers – and a Ford or Peugeot may even compete with a Mercedes-Benz, something that would not happen often a few decades ago. If BMW or Volvo runs heavy discount campaigns, they'll be an option for buyers who never considered buying a premium brand car before.

Understanding the mechanisms that create a brand's pricing in a particular market is crucial to understanding how to survive and achieve success. A price premium reflects a stronger brand: pricing and brand strength largely co-vary over time. But there may be contingency factors that constitute deviations on the strong relationship between brand strength and the market price for a particular brand over time:

- Due to volume pressure from the car maker, particular brands may engage in heavy discounting, which for a while makes the price lower than the brand strength suggests. In the long run, however, lower prices may hurt the brand so oversupplying the market will result in lost brand value.

- In the car maker's home market, a brand tends to be seen as less exclusive than in foreign markets, and market shares are normally higher. This is nothing to worry about: it's normal that locally produced goods are seen as less exotic. A Cadillac in Detroit, a Volvo in Gothenburg or a Mercedes-Benz in Stuttgart are as common as sand in the desert: there are company cars, official cars and employee cars, bought at staff rates, seen all the time and the factories constitute a large part of the local business environment.

- When new very popular models are launched and orderable, there may be a short-term undersupply which is translated into cars sold at list price or, in a few instances, above the list price. However, this does not happen as often as it did in the 1990s when delivery times of 6 to 12 months were common for new models. A popular new model is good for the brand; however, it tends not to influence the brand's price premium as much as the short-term undersupply suggests. And car managers often overstate the role of the new model: a BMW dealer marketing manager was serious when he said that a new model recently launched 'will mark the end of the discount era'. But in less than a year later, 15 per cent discounts were offered again.

Flexible purchase patterns: implications for branding

Over time, we've seen purchase patterns becoming increasingly flexible. Young consumers in particular tend to mix premium, volume and budget brands (Parment, 2011a; 2013a). As Silverstein and Fiske (2003: 50) put it: 'Consumers tend to trade up to the premium product in categories that are important to them but trade down – buying a low-cost brand or private label, or even going without – in categories that are less meaningful to them.' This has far-reaching implications for car makers: purchasing power is more fickle, and a wealthy buyer may purchase a budget car unless the premium car delivers substantially more value, and a higher percentage of buyers would consider a premium brand if it offers something valuable to them.

Premium products must deliver on their promises

When economies or nations reach a certain economic level, a substantial part of discretionary spend may be on luxury goods such as premium cars. However, when purchasing power grows beyond the level necessary for everyday living, it becomes fickle and is subject to a number of factors. Today, consumers have an enormous range of consumption opportunities, supported by extensive advertising and a multitude of product offerings. This gives room for an increasing penetration of premium products – but if they don't live up to buyer expectations, their share in a market could well be very low. Today's customers are flexible and want value for money – hence, strong offers will result in high spending for an industry, a geographical area, or a brand.

The foundation of strong brands

A strong brand draws its advantage from identification, consistency and attractiveness. To achieve these advantages, a company must have a profound knowledge about its history, organizational identity, culture, its strengths and weaknesses, and how it is perceived by different stakeholders. Without this knowledge it's very difficult to put everything together in a consistent and attractive whole and then communicate it to the world around.

High consistency in the communication of the brand is manifested in a shared interpretation of the brand message among buyers, employees and other stakeholders (see Parment, 2009). Here, the customer profile emerges as an indispensable part of the brand communication. Buyers associate the auto brand with a particular brand profile. Accordingly, car makers may not want customers who do not correspond to the brand values since they may represent the brand in an undesirable way. If marketers in the past were going for customers they could reach, a modern marketer will increasingly target customers that are good for the brand image.

Some organizations have an inherent ability to attract employees, customers and other stakeholders. These organizations are good at bringing together and presenting the good sides of the organization and what it stands for in a way that is seen as authentic and attractive by those who are the target of the message. Due to increased transparency and changes in consumer attitudes, marketing and other messages with little or no correspondence with what's really going on are increasingly difficult to get across.

Since a brand reflects customers' and other stakeholders' experiences and impressions, car makers have good reason to put efforts into building a brand that reflects the car maker's competitive advantages. Brands as an outward reflection of the organizational identity go further than the perceived brand image and a falsely interpreted organizational identity may constitute a major impediment in corporate and market communications (Birkigt *et al*, 1992). A clear-cut corporate identity will facilitate corporate and market communications substantially. Brand theorist Kapferer (2004: 82) emphasizes that branding requires a long-term engagement and suggests that identity prevails over image:

> The brand's main concern is to know how it is perceived. Today, marketing considers the notion of identity as the core concept of brand management: before knowing how we are perceived, we must know who we are. Only identity can provide the right framework for ensuring brand consistency and continuity (multi-product, multi-country) and for making capitalization possible.

Strong brands use their strong identity and appeal to connect their brands with a context, eg individuals or a culture. The widespread practice of product placement shares characteristics and motives with using celebrities in marketing – it aims at building a brand indirectly by presenting it in a context that makes it stronger and more targeted towards the desired audience. Mercedes-Benz's fashion week, run twice a year in numerous major capitals, is an example of how an auto brand puts itself into a context: that of metropolitan areas, celebrities, a younger audience and the fashion industry. The main advantage of using such methods – that marketing takes place in an indirect and rather discrete manner – has grown stronger over time, in the light of an increasing information density and message overload.

Strong auto brands are built top-down

Strong brands always build on a consistent realization of a few key ideas, which are implemented throughout the organization. There is always a tension between the integrative top-down perspective, and ideas that are brought forward to make units and divisions closer to the market (Castrogiovanni and Justis, 1998; Coughlan *et al*, 2001; Parment, 2009b). This tricky balance is sometimes referred to as a dilemma of balancing global integration and local responsiveness, a framework assuming that international marketing decisions means tricky trade-offs between adapting to local market conditions on the one hand, and reaching the efficiencies that standardization across countries and regions implies (Grein *et al*, 2001; Haugland, 2010; Parment, 2011a; Roth and Morrison, 1990; Spender and Grevesen, 1999).

Ideas such as, 'We must listen to all our branches', 'We need to adapt to what local offices are used to' or, 'The London approach doesn't work here in Darlington' are commonplace and should be dealt with. However, few successful companies have made local adaptation the overriding branding and control ideology. Giving too much consideration to local initiatives may take a lot of management time and make the organization difficult to control, thus harming the opportunity to implement a strong brand (Nilsson *et al*, 2011). In the worst case, the organization may end up in a situation that is very difficult to control:

> If all local initiatives are encouraged, then the company may become too sprawling; and decentralized, poorly-coordinated actions which lack relevance for the aims of the organization bring dubious benefits. Holding the activities together, developing strategies, and basing the control system on these require someone who is strong enough to generate enthusiasm and a feeling of urgency, of trust, and of faith in the future. Many people perform at their best when being led.
>
> (Nilsson *et al*, 2011: 123)

Like any company, car makers will always benefit from taking the lead in developing the brand. A strong brand is by its very nature created top-down. There are in fact very few examples of companies that have maintained their strengths over time without a strong top-down emphasis. Exceptions may exist with brands that are built and boosted by consumer cultures – for example products made in former East Germany, now promoted as an expression of *Ostalgie* (nostalgia for aspects of life in East Germany) and places, eg Saint Tropez on the French Riviera, San Francisco back in the 1960s or to an extent Berlin in recent years. In these cases, the brand created is not the result of an elaborate city branding strategy but rather of social movements – and the brand perceptions of celebrities may likewise be built through opinions that people in general hold.

For large companies with a strong consumer orientation only top-down approaches are likely to work. Although the share of official and company cars is significant for many auto brands, brands are built in consumer markets and somebody using an official car is likely to relate to the auto brand in a similar way as if the car were bought for private use. In Millward Brown's BrandZ Top 100 Most Valuable Global Brands study 2013, the top 15 list represents very well-known brands with a strong consumer or user orientation: Apple, Google, IBM, McDonald's, Coca-Cola, at&t, Microsoft, Marlboro,

China Mobile, VISA, GE Money Bank, Verizon, Wells Fargo, Amazon and UPS.[4] These brands share the top-down philosophy in building strong brands. Even though many users may get in contact with IBM, Verizon and UPS through their employers' decisions, the brands are strongly emphasized in communication with the users.

This does not mean that the communication is one-sided – in fact, companies rely on their partners, ie retailers and others that are an integrated part of the business model and necessary for the delivery of products and brands. The brand process benefits from feedback opportunities and safe avenues for expressing opinions and concerns of customers, employees and other stakeholders. However, all brand content and brand emphasis must be dealt with in relation to the overall company and brand strategy to make sure that the brand message sent is consistent across all communication channels and over time (Birkigt *et al*, 1992; Parment, 2008).

There may be problems with decentralization and a high degree of freedom for units and departments to create and apply their own principles and strategies in areas related to branding. In fact, car dealers derive many advantages from representing strong auto brands and it's hard to imagine that dealers could reach the same level of success without the support from strong brands, which are partly built by dealers but, where successful, under strong car maker leadership.

Dealer websites – the danger of eliminating local content

A tricky question that often creates controversy is dealer websites. From an overall branding perspective, making the brand appear similar across sites, units and countries may not only facilitate communication, but also save a lot of resources. Consider the case of 175 car dealers – or 225 hotels or 90 supermarkets – representing the same brand. If every unit creates its own website or advertising design, it certainly means a better local adaptation, but from the perspective of the overall brand and also from a cost perspective, a centralized strategy would be more effective. On the other hand, dealers not owned by the factory have several reasons to promote their own identity: they have their own history and strong ties to the local community, and their brand – Mr and Mrs Smith Automobiles – may have been around for many years so they have every reason to promote it. At the end of the day, it's an advantage for the car maker to have committed dealers that are dedicated to their businesses. The benefits of strong local ties will result in more cars sold and contribute to customer satisfaction. However, too often a project leader at the NSC level with little conceptual or real-world experience of the dynamics of global vs local perspectives on brands gets the unwelcome assignment to standardize the websites of the auto brand's dealers in a market. It normally means eliminating or restricting local content – an excellent way of provoking anger among dealers that the brand relies on without getting any advantage other than a slightly easier navigation for customers visiting dealer websites. However, neither NSCs nor dealers want customers to shop around since that is likely to reduce margins, so facilitating easy navigation across dealer sites through a similar structure and appearance does not really make sense.

It's possible to balance the efficiency advantages of a standardized website with generous space for local content about the dealership, its philosophy, its history and its people. Competitive dealers have every right to be proud of their business and promote their local brands – and that's to the benefit of all marketing channel members including the car maker. Strong brands strengthen each other when exposed together – provided that the brands are reasonably consistent and share an underlying idea and philosophy. This is a typical co-branding situation. If car makers and dealers don't want to be displayed together, it's time to move on and look for other business opportunities.

Strong and weak auto brands

Strong brands in general show a higher consistency in their way of dealing with buyers, staff, partners, other stakeholders, and markets in general. Attractive brands normally have a more stable financial situation and are hence likely to provide higher consistency over time in dealer terms and conditions. Dealers have confidence in car makers that make sure that they are sufficiently well off in terms of attractive products, profit opportunities and demands on investment to make the retail business consistently viable. Weak brands, on the other hand, suffer from being competitively disadvantaged and may force their dealers to invest more than they can afford or are committed to – and it's not likely to fundamentally change the inherent problems in the weak brand, since dealer facilities alone are unlikely to be the decisive factor when products lack attractiveness.

In the car industry in particular, strategies to create strong brands must be founded on attractive products. Consistency with brand values and continuity in model policy are basic characteristics of successful brands: Porsche, Mercedes and BMW are good examples in this respect. Consistency ensures that all parts of the brand communication, including products and people representing the brand, move towards a shared goal, rooted in the company identity. Strong auto brands present high consistency between the performance and qualities of the product on the one hand and the brand message on the other hand. When the products offered are clearly differentiated, there will be fewer close substitutes, something that results in less competition and potentially higher margins. Differentiation may be in a variety of dimensions: lifestyle, image, design or functional product characteristics. A Volkswagen Passat and an Audi A5 share the same platform and powertrain but are, like a Volkswagen Golf vs a Seat Leon, perceived as substantially differentiated from each other from an image, design and lifestyle perspective. Older people may well remember that Volkswagen and Audi once were very similar. The Audi 50 and Volkswagen Polo from the mid-1970s were actually identical. And the first Seats produced after Volkswagen bought the Spanish company in the 1980s (a stepwise take-over that began in 1983 and was finalized in 1990) were based on components from other parts of the Volkswagen Group.[5] At the time, Seat design was more similar to that of Volkswagen than it is now. People who remember the time when Audis were poor attempts to add some flavour to high-volume Volkswagen models are fewer and fewer – and it's seldom heard these days that the Porsche 924, introduced in 1976, was not a real Porsche since it used an engine from the Volkswagen LT light truck portfolio. Consistency should also be provided over time; the underpinnings of the brand should not change too often. Strong brands find it easier to provide consistency in all areas that affect communication with customers too.

The advantages are enormous in having a strong brand: a better product, a better customer profile, and better factory support; more resources and commitment; and a more long-term direction for car maker strategies (Parment, 2009). A strong brand creates a natural flow of customers coming to dealers to buy the products and sell on the strength of the brand, thus enjoying more customers buying on brand and not primarily on price. In general, strong brands have a healthier balance between demand and supply. Higher demand means less discounting. Lower discounts and higher product attractiveness result in higher residual values, which is a clear customer advantage through a lower cost of ownership. In addition, as supply and demand largely match, a substantial price premium may be charged.

A strong brand functions as a self-reinforcing wheel-of-fortune through its power to attract distributors and customers who represent the brand in a good way, and a price premium can hence be charged (Aaker, 1991; Kapferer, 1997; Keller, 2003; Wileman and Jary, 1997). In addition, a more restrictive discount philosophy characterizes premium brands, although in recent years there are strong signs this has begun to change.

When brand awareness is low, there is no or little shared sense of brand values, which will create problems for car makers as well as dealers. Hence, communicating not only with target groups – as suggested by traditional marketing wisdom – but also with non-customers is important in making the brand known to a broader audience (Kapferer, 2012). In an explorative study of Ikea and its identity, it was found that marketing channels owned by the company constitute a key part of the communication base:

> An ad presenting the unique features of an organization communicates as much to organizational members as it does to external audiences. Ikeans often discuss the company's ads and use the slogans as a part of their vocabulary in describing the company. Seeing one's company presented in a magazine contributes to the organization's self-view.

> (Salzer, 1994)

Customers are likewise important in this context: the culture and image of a company largely become an essential part of the purchase criteria. An interplay between the brand and its customers thus exists: customers representing values similar to those underpinning the brand are likely to strengthen the brand and the brand is likely to strengthen the image of the user: customer profile constitutes an essential part of the brand image. This is part of the explanation why brand separation at the dealership level may strengthen the brand: the customer's brand identification is stronger in a solus retail environment.

Communicating with non-customers may be particularly important for premium brands. Buyers automatically integrate brand messages, regardless of whether they plan to buy a particular brand or not (Birkigt *et al*, 1992; Duncan and Moriarty, 1997). Also, people not belonging to the target group should be conscious of the brand values. The aim is to build a desire for the product even in those who cannot afford to buy it. Car buyers may not prefer or like the brand, and are hence unlikely to buy it, but if they know its meaning, it will facilitate brand communication and positioning. The brand, hence, will have appeal to a broader audience but be consumed only by the happy few, as Kapferer (2012) puts it.

Regardless of the position in the marketing channel – or elsewhere – those who represent a strong brand are likely to derive a lot of benefits. A strong brand brings certain standards to the job. Selling a premium brand brings more prestige than selling a volume brand, which in general makes the dealership a more attractive employer. A strong brand is able to squeeze suppliers while maintaining high prices at the market end and may enjoy advantages in relation to other stakeholders too.

Strong brands face a different set of supply-demand mechanisms

Strong brands act in a market that in many respects differs from that of weaker brands. With a strong brand and strong products, cars can be built to order, since there is a natural demand and a steady (although not heavy) flow of customers wanting the brand and seeing dealers. For particular models demand may exceed supply – a very desirable but nonetheless rare situation. This represents a clear contrast to the situation of weaker brands, as explained by a UK Vauxhall dealer:

> The Insignia is always going to be a fleet car, it's not a retail car, you don't get a man walking off the street and wanting to buy a new Insignia since you can buy a six-month old car for 30 per cent or 40 per cent less than the original list price. It makes the new car retailing very difficult because they can buy a former rental car at a huge discount.

How can a strong brand and all the advantages it entails come about? Buyers want a lot: high product performance, an attractive price and high quality, and great brands that provide emotional content. The one cannot substitute for the other like in the good old days when buyers were less demanding and there were fewer cars for sale than there were potential buyers. An ugly car that is functional and cheap is very difficult to sell: there are nice and functional cars available at decent prices. An emotionally appealing car that is attractive from a consumer culture perspective is difficult to sell unless it delivers on functional expectations. Hence, value-for-money car makers such as Kia, Hyundai, Skoda, Chevrolet and Dacia work intensively on design and emotional appeal while up-market brands put a lot of effort into reducing build costs. All car makers have to deal with the simultaneous pressure to decrease costs and strengthen the appearance of the brand.

Weak brands – characteristics and implications

In the worst case, a combination of weak products, weak brand management, low product quality and lack of product innovation may be hazardous for the brand. Weak brands are largely weak in the same areas as strong brands are strong. Lack of consistency in marketing and brand management disappoints buyers for a number of reasons: product quality, product characteristics, image problems or general attitudes against the car reduce the customer value of owning and driving the brand. Weak brands lack a clear direction in marketing and branding, also manifest in a lack of consistency across communication channels, eg national advertising being inconsistent with dealer communication. Although signs and physical appearance might be consistent – this is an area that is tightly controlled by car makers – a more thorough analysis of the attitudes may reveal considerable inconsistencies across communication channels. Low consistency may reflect poor communication and strained relations between the car maker and its unhappy dealers. A lack of consistency in dealer network strategies, leading to strained relations between car makers, NSCs and dealers results in a poor brand impression. Dealers see no clear long-term strategy in the car maker's strategies, and so are less willing to invest. Investment in a weak brand dealership is perceived as more risky because of less stable demand and low retained margins. Little agreement on brand definition and content along with low brand awareness are likely to result in image problems. In one case, only three out of 17 Opel dealers were able to suggest a reasonably specific brand content (Parment, 2009).

Weak brands result in a competitive disadvantage with major competitors. Dealers are being stressed and find it difficult to persuade customers since there may be no or few good reasons for the customer to buy the brand. The competitive disadvantage puts pressure on the dealer to offer discounts (which has an adverse impact on residual values), thus, the dealer is likely to sell on price.

Market forces contribute to making life difficult for weak brands: only weak dealers may be available unless very good terms are offered; it's difficult to recruit great staff as they are likely to prefer working for stronger brands; and even advertising agencies and other partners prefer working with strong brands that have a more stable presence in the market and they gain more prestige from working with strong auto brands.

Stuck in the middle – brands with premium aspirations

Like in many other industries, car makers have found that premium brands generate a set of advantages that as an overall package appear very appealing.

Many auto brands, however, lack essential premium qualities, hence aspirations that never translate into real premium brands entail fundamental problems that go back to the lack of inherent product and brand attractiveness. Premium aspiration brands are certainly more desirable than the majority of volume brands, but lack genuine premium qualities; this is a disadvantage for the dealer as the products are not sold on brand or on price, but are stuck in the middle.

When the products lack premium attractiveness but are marketed and sold as genuine premium brands, a mismatch and a range of inconsistencies arise. First, premium showrooms and premium marketing campaigns cost money and are a heavy call on dealer resources, resulting in a competitive price disadvantage. Second, a premium attitude does not fit very well with products that the customer does not perceive as premium. Third, dissatisfied dealers, forced into heavy discounting and under pressure to sell cars have a poor impact on the customer interaction. Fourth, while premium brands are well-known and brand exclusivity could be based on a broad knowledge and awareness of the brand, premium aspiration brands have lower awareness and attractiveness, which makes it more difficult and costly to communicate with the market. It's a well-known truth in marketing that it's cheaper for strong brands to communicate, since they easily activate positive associations among target groups, due to high brand awareness and positive stakeholder attitudes (see, for example Kotler *et al*, 2011). Fifth, and very important from a branding perspective, the mismatch between premium claims in marketing and products lacking premium attractiveness confuses customers. Sixth, the characteristics mentioned above are reflected in low residual values. Strong brands remain more desirable on the used car market and hold their values better. Poor residual values reflect products that are not as desirable as genuine premium brands and are sold neither on price nor on brand – they are sold at highly discounted premium aspirational prices. As residual values are normally based on list prices, premium aspiration brands often appear towards the bottom of rankings of residual values. That's an irreversible effect of giving a lot more discounts than value-for-money brands such as Skoda and Kia or premium brands such as Audi and Porsche. Discounting and residual values can be traced back to basic supply-demand mechanisms – where there is a genuine demand for the product, less discounting is needed.

Lack of dealer profitability is a direct consequence of sales being forced, hence selling efforts tax dealer resources, and there are limited sales numbers and a general lack of attractiveness – brilliant staff and excellent dealers are likely to prefer working for a genuine premium brand, or an attractive volume brand. The entire situation is difficult to deal with. The heavy pressure to sell and discount cars, more significant than for other brands, and the lacking of desirability undermine viability and hurt profitability. Hence, dealers are reluctant to invest: they see no certain economic return on their investment and are less dedicated to the brand.

Which are the premium aspiration brands? Typical recent examples have been Saab, Cadillac, Volvo and Lancia in numerous markets, and Land Rover, Jaguar and Audi in a few. It varies over time and across countries, hence car makers, NSCs and dealers should be aware of the warning signs. And it varies across a brand range too: a Mercedes A Class may be a direct competitor of a Toyota or Volkswagen while a Mercedes S Class is very competitive in the prestige segment and enjoys a price premium over competitors.

How to deal with weak auto brands

We've witnessed large restructuring in car makers' portfolios in the last decades. New brands like Lexus, Infinity and Acura have emerged; traditional brands like Skoda, Bentley and Lancia have been brought to life under a new regime, Daewoo cars were badged Chevrolet for a while and numerous other brands may have been lost forever: will we ever see a new Hummer, Plymouth, Pontiac or Saab again?

An option that is worth considering, although initially painful and expensive, is to remove brands from the portfolio. Brands may be taken up later if new opportunities emerge. Who would have thought that Skoda, with poor cars and a poor reputation in the 1970s and 1980s, would arise again and become very successful? In 2012, 939,000 cars were produced. This is, of course, not only because of the brand but also due to successful integration into the Volkswagen Group portfolio, smart marketing strategies and access to Volkswagen Group dealers.

How could weak brands be turned into attractive brands? Experiences from within and outside the industry provide useful insights for deciding how weak auto brands should be dealt with. The product is essential to success – obviously – but the fact is that in many other industries, extra services provided, guarantees, customer benefits, etc could compensate for a lack in product quality. In many service businesses, information asymmetry leads to a situation where the buyer makes judgements based not on the quality of the core service but on how it is presented, packaged and delivered. In the car industry, premium marketing channels selling non-premium products are not likely to be successful. Mismatching and inconsistencies create problems.

The first thing a car maker must do in this respect is to learn to know its brand and how it should be positioned. This requires an understanding of, and to an extent a dialogue with, the market. Cadillac wanted to capitalize on its strong brand in Europe and planned to sell 50,000 cars in 2006. Towards the end of the year, only a tenth had been sold. Premium prices for badge-engineered European products didn't work, and European buyers were not willing to pay prices close to the European premium SUVs for a US SUV. The Cadillac BLS was built in Saab's factory in Sweden. The plan was to sell the slightly modified Saab 9-3 at 10 per cent higher prices than the (from a European perspective) more mass market Saabs. However, many of the cars were finally sold for prices 30 to 35 per cent under price list. The SUV SRX was finally sold for less than 50 per cent of the original price – what else could be done with the cars after having flooded the marketing channel for three years? Chrysler cars sold under the Lancia brand in Europe may be successful if they also deliver on value for money, but they are unlikely to capitalize on the traditional Lancia brand name.

A key problem with weak brands is often residual values. It may, for instance, be more expensive to own a €40,000 premium aspiration brand than a €55,000 premium brand, since the former loses value much faster, not only as a percentage of the list price but also in absolute numbers. It might be beneficial to take control of the used car market, eg by selling used cars through franchised dealers with certified used vehicle programmes instead of disposing of used cars at auctions and trading them to non-franchised dealers 'to get rid of them efficiently' as is common practice. A car maker may even subsidize its used car operation through its NSCs by offering a used-car warranty with attractive terms.

BMW, now performing excellently in terms of resale values, implemented two smart programmes that definitely contributed to strengthening the brand and its reputation on used cars. BMW has never been a weak brand in terms of used cars, but there were some reputational problems in the 1990s due to quality issues and high costs of ownership. The 7 Series in particular did not perform as well as premium competitors the Mercedes S Class, Lexus LS and Audi A8 in terms of reliability. So BMW decided to start its own road assistance programme in the German market (this was at a time when mobile phones had penetrated the market and most luxury car drivers had one). Instead of walking to an ADAC phone along the road, BMW drivers called BMW directly when there were problems. The result was overwhelming: BMW now appeared as the most reliable luxury car along with Lexus in the ADAC statistics.

Consistency is a key word in successful branding – it should, however, not be interpreted as 'always doing the same' or 'never surprising customers'. A misunderstanding, sometimes supported by brand consultants, is to confuse the advantages of a consistent corporate identity with an overemphasis on standardizing customer treatment, marketing campaigns and marketing communications. Customers do like surprises and flexibility in how they are addressed and treated, but it should be within the realms of a consistent corporate identity (Parment and Söderlund, 2010). In other words, the visible should be consistent and based on a clear identity programme, while the invisible could be adapted to local circumstances, customer needs and opportunities that arise in the market.

Brands with premium aspirations often lack the resources, commitment, patience and dedication necessary to accomplish a real upward stretch and become an established premium brand. Hence, it was a clever move by the European Ford operation in the mid-1990s to cease producing the Scorpio and concentrate on cars without premium ambitions – including those in growing segments such as the MPV S-Max and the minivan Galaxy. Ford is a typical volume brand with cheaper budget brands as well as more exclusive upmarket brands in all the segments it runs.

It has always been difficult for a brand which adheres to the volume brand ideology and logic to achieve upward stretch – but even more so with all the challenges the car industry is facing. Focusing on accomplishing upward stretch, something that Audi successfully did in the 1980s and 1990s, may detract focus from much more pressing and urgent issues. The premium segment is very competitive, and the general tendency among car buyers is to be less interested in premium qualities, at least if they come at a significant cost.

Brands with a broader purpose give brand extension opportunities

Brands with a higher purpose enjoy consumer permission to introduce other relevant products and services – just like Mercedes-Benz engages in a fashion week, Peugeot sells bicycles and BMW sells clothing, there may be an almost infinite range of other opportunities that car companies hitherto haven't discovered or explored. If brand extensions are common in other industries, why would it not work for car companies? Brands with a broader purpose – making life easier, better, simpler – in general terms enjoy greater flexibility when it comes to brand extensions. The best brands are built on an ideal that encompasses not what people buy, but what they buy into. A key question for auto brands is to what extent a higher purpose could be defined and realized in a trustworthy way. And if the auto brands as they are defined today lack the broader purpose that is required, it may be built by introducing products that help consumers improve their lives. Electric cars, eg the BMW i3, or plug-in hybrid cars, eg the Toyota Prius or Volvo V60, give many opportunities to introduce offers that use the cross-fertilization that co-branding with companies in other industries may generate.

Brands that sustain greatness over time connect to a fundamental reality: people want a better life for themselves and for others. For global brands with an ambition to be sustainable, the rising middle classes of Africa, India and Latin America represent not only potentially lucrative markets, but also the opportunity to help people rise from poverty and improve their lives in a broad sense. To young people in particular, meaningfulness is key to attractiveness. Meaningful means making a difference in the life of the customer, which helps the brand create customer enjoyment to stay viable and gain market share. Even premium brands can be meaningfully different through functional and emotional advantages. Functional advantages may be high quality and high reliability – which makes life easier for the car owner; timeless design that doesn't make the product look dated – which translates into higher resale value and less need to exchange the car; or the integration of the newest technology – something that may improve safety and reduce maintenance and operating costs. Emotional advantages may include improved active and passive safety, a stronger lifestyle profile of the car, and owner image advantages created by a car that has a reputation for being more sustainable than others.

BMW

Why do we start with BMW? It's far from the largest car brand in sales numbers! The reason is that BMW is a unique brand, and has caught brand theorists' attention for several decades. In sum, the BMW brand's greatness relies on the combination of the following factors:

- Despite relatively small volumes, BMW has been consistently profitable and enjoyed growth in the last few decades, due to a strong mixture of evolution and revolution in design and concepts. A BMW is always easy to recognize, and it delivers consistently on its brand promises. It does not have to deliver the most spacious or practical car to defend its brand values – but increasingly, over time, BMW has become competitive in terms of function too. The 3 series, introduced in late 2011, inherits the classic BMW brand values while offering a lot of passenger and luggage space – substantially more than earlier 3 series cars – high safety, low emissions, and a smooth ride.

- The strong BMW brand and its appeal have created a sense of uniqueness among marketing channel members, a guarantee of high quality in this very important aspect of building long-term customer relationships.

- The cars are generally good in terms of quality.

- The appeal of BMW is heavily geared towards a brand appeal that goes beyond the car concept. BMW cars were until the 1990s heavily associated with their drive train: a powerful six cylinder petrol engine and rear-wheel drive. BMWs increasingly have four or three cylinder engines; non-petrol driven; and front- or all-wheel drive – and the brand continues to grow.

- BMWs have become cheaper compared to competitors in many markets. Despite heavy discounting it is still seen as a real premium brand. In fact, BMW has applied downward stretch through the introduction of low-range 3 series models, the 1 series, more standard equipment and appealing prices.

To many BMW owners and enthusiasts, a BMW is a rear-wheel drive car with a straight six cylinder engine. By tradition, this powertrain set-up has been very strong in the BMW model portfolio. In the late 1970s, the six cylinder was used in even the smallest BMW (by then the 3 series), as 320 and 323i (e12). Until 1988, there were no 8 or 12 cylinder engines available and diesel engines were not selling much. In 1988, a 12 cylinder was introduced with the new 7 Series (e32). In 1992, BMW introduced eight cylinder engines in the 5 and 7 Series cars. The six cylinder engines remained strong until they were gradually replaced by four cylinder engines, with a first step in 2005 when the 2 litre engine was replaced. Beginning in 2011, all six cylinder petrol engines except the powerful 35i (306–340 PS) were replaced by four cylinders. Since the 1990s, diesel engines have become significant and account for about 80 per cent of sales in some European markets.

All these changes and evolutions have been completed without losing focus on the brand heritage – and without fear of reinterpreting the brand when circumstances change. On Forbes' 2013 list of the World's Most Powerful Brands, BMW is the highest ranked auto brand, listed at nine – some way ahead of premium competitors Mercedes-Benz (16), Audi (32) and Lexus (87). In consumer perception, BMW is even more successful: ranked at five, far ahead of Audi (24), Mercedes-Benz (54), and Lexus (82).[6]

Considering the history of BMW with petrol engines, primarily six cylinders, at the heart of the brand's success, it's impressive how its diesel engines, until recently seen as powerful but not very reliable, have improved. In 2014, BMW will start delivering diesel engines for Toyota cars in Europe. Considering Toyota's great history in terms of product quality, this is a strong indication of great achievements.

BMW has been very successful in many areas of developing cars for the future, eg the self-driving car. However, many legal issues have to be dealt with until the self-driving car can go on sale but staying ahead of the competition in this respect generates numerous advantages for BMW: feedback from the marketplace, building relations with other industries and authorities necessary to develop the self-driving car, image, etc.

Mini

Mini is owned by BMW, and the link between the two brands technology-wise is a lot stronger than most people would believe. In the registration documents of a Mini, BMW is listed as the manufacturer. Despite this, there's a broad gulf between the traditional luxury marque BMW and its funky small-car brand Mini.

Like BMW, Mini is expanding its model range and its less formal and more youthful attitude makes it obvious that Mini can do and say what BMW dares not. A couple of years ago, the rock band Kiss kicked off Mini's new test-drive programme, Mini Rocks the Rivals, at the New York auto show. Three members of Kiss bounced onto the Mini stand followed by McDowell in a curly wig and outrageous black and white Kiss makeup.

Through a distinct brand and a totally different brand heritage, BMW has the chance of using the Mini brand and growing it in a much more discrete way than when the Volkswagen Group helped Seat by providing it with the former Audi A4 or an MPV that is a copy of the Volkswagen Alhambra. That will not happen with Mini.

Mercedes-Benz

One of the strongest auto brands over time is Mercedes-Benz, a brand with a long history that goes back to 1886. Daimler AG is one of the world's most successful automotive companies. The company's founders, Gottlieb Daimler and Carl Benz, made history with the invention of the automobile in 1886. As a pioneer of automotive engineering, Mercedes-Benz has been among the industry leaders in terms of innovative and green technologies as well as car safety – all part of making the car sustainable for the future.

The brand name Mercedes-Benz first appeared in 1926 under Daimler-Benz but traces its origins to Daimler-Motoren-Gesellschaft's 1901 Mercedes and to Karl Benz's 1886 Benz Patent Motorwagen, widely regarded as the very first automobile. Like many other great brands, Mercedes-Benz history has followed a path that includes numerous innovations and a couple of moves that with hindsight appear to be not very clever.

With its divisions Mercedes-Benz Cars, Daimler Trucks, Mercedes-Benz Vans, Daimler Buses and Daimler Financial Services, the Daimler Group is one of the biggest producers of premium cars and the world's biggest manu-facturer of commercial vehicles with a global reach. Daimler Financial Services provides financing, leasing, fleet management, insurance and innovative mobility services. Although commercial Mercedes-Benz vehicles also have a good reputation for building great heavy trucks, the Mercedes-Benz brand never reached the unique position it has had for decades in the car sector.

Mercedes-Benz is the key brand in the Daimler AG Group. Other brands include Smart, Maybach and AMG. More recently the Daimler brand name, which may not be used by the Daimler AG Group, has been used for Jaguar cars, under the ownership of Jaguar Cars, later Ford and since 2008 Tata Motors. Maybach was introduced in 2002 and production stopped in late 2012 due to poor sales – it will be replaced by an S Class with an extra-long wheelbase in 2014. The Maybach was built on the W220 (1998–2005) S Class; only two years after the first Maybach deliveries in 2003 the lower target-market S Class was based on a more modern platform and more up-to-date technical solutions.

AMG, founded in 1967, became a majority-owned division of MB in 1998. AMG is very important for MB in terms of image, as AMG cars are known to be among the fastest and sportiest in the segments in which they operate, something that is very good for MB's not very dynamic image. MB increasingly makes use of this opportunity and the AMG range has exploded in the last decade, now including the Mercedes-Benz A, C, CLS,

CLA, CL, E, G, GL, ML, S, SL, SLK and SLS ranges – seemingly the entire MB portfolio, but there are more ranges and even more on the way; the range is continuously growing.

Although MB has never had a reputation for being a manufacturer of sporty cars, it has the longest history of powerful car models among the premium brands, starting with the 300 SEL 6.3 in the late 1960s (V8, 250 bhp) and the 450 SEL 6.9 (V8, 286 bhp) in the mid-1970s. Audi, BMW and Jaguar – brands with a sportier image – cannot compete with Mercedes-Benz on its range of super-fast cars.

The SLS AMG Coupé Electric Drive (2014), the world's fastest electric car, delivers 552 kW/751 bhp and 1,000 Nm. Audi's competing R8 e-tron is not only less powerful with 380 bhp and 819 Nm, even worse, it will not go on sale. Audi blames expensive batteries. From a brand perspective, this gives Mercedes – and BMW, with a couple of innovative new electric and hybrid cars – i3 and i8 – an image advantage over Audi.[7]

Mercedes-Benz has been very successful in creating new car classes. The A Class (1997) began the premium car era in the compact car segment and the CLS (2004) introduced four door coupés. The S Class and the SL Class were introduced in the 1950s and have defined their classes. The CLA 45 AMG (2013), a compact saloon with 360 bhp from a 2-litre engine, is also innovative through its extremely high output-per-litre engine, and stretches the AMG brand downwards. The SLS, introduced in 2010, was the first MB car constructed in-house by AMG. Through its gull-wing doors and combination of sportiness and comfort, it's a real Grand Tourer and seen as a spiritual successor to the Mercedes-Benz 300SL Gullwing built between 1954 and 1963.

Mercedes-Benz's position in popular culture is beyond doubt: movies, song lyrics, sitcoms and celebrities refer to Mercedes-Benz more often than arguably any other auto brand. For instance, the Mercedes-Benz SL has been very popular among Hollywood celebrities and filmmakers ever since its introduction in 1954. It's now in its seventh generation and has played a role in over 150 movies and television programmes not to mention fame on studio lots and fashionable streets. The long running W107, which was the fourth generation built from 1971 to 1989, is maybe the best-known one, frequently seen as Bob Ewing's car in 'Dallas'. In addition, MB has a strong position as an exclusive brand in everyday conversations: 'You can't pay for a Volkswagen and get a Mercedes-Benz', 'Look, she's got a Mercedes-Benz, she must be successful' or, 'This is the Mercedes-Benz of air conditioning systems', underlining Mercedes-Benz's strong market position.

Increasing competition in the premium segment makes Mercedes-Benz a lot more vulnerable to competitor moves than it used to be; however, it may also result in advantages. It has to be innovative and can't rely on its historic advantages: competition forces the company to defend and broaden its position. And the downside of the Mercedes-Benz image – suggesting arrogance, a car for the newly rich, a symbol of success that is easier to realize than many other symbols, etc – is now less problematic when competing brands like BMW and Audi take over the emblematic role of premium brands. If a few decades ago it was argued that it was inappropriate in many situations to drive a Mercedes-Benz, now its social acceptance has increased and it may even be seen as a more discrete choice than brands like Audi and BMW, which have more of the newcomer and less of the classic premium brand in their brand appearance.

Quality problems, not least extensive corrosion, were significant around the turn of the millennium but appear to be overcome – although it always takes some time to repair any damage to image. A variety of test reports, including car magazines' endurance tests, JD Power's report on owner-reported quality, insurance companies' statistics on powertrain breakdowns and repairs, etc indicate that the quality is, if not excellent, far above the industry average. As long as cars are running they influence the auto brand through the opinions of owners, drivers, car repairers and others, and if quality is poor for a period of time, it may not be seen in statistics on average car duration until 15 to 20 years later.

Mercedes-Benz appears to be well prepared for the future through the very strong diversification that is inherent in the business model. First, there is a very broad range of models from the compact A Class to the unbeatable multitude of luxury cars, eg the numerous S models, the S, the GL, the SLS and the CLS. Second is the broad range of customer segments covered through the variety of cars. While a CLS Shooting Brake, a CLA or a GLA is an eye-catching stylish car, and the S Class a luxury car which, with a long wheel base is the natural choice for many individuals with a chauffeur, the C or E Class cars serve as reliable taxi and transport vehicles over high mileages. Third, geographical diversification is strong. Out of 1.45 million cars sold in 2012, 300,000 were sold in the United States and 358,000 in Asia. Although the main hub is, without doubt, Stuttgart in Germany, there are other production sites in the United States, China, France, Hungary, South Africa, India, Vietnam and Indonesia (Daimler, Mercedes-Benz Cars at a Glance, 2013). From the perspective of risks such as currency fluctuations and political decisions, a high degree of diversification makes the business more sustainable and Mercedes-Benz represents diversification in a variety of respects including production capacity, model portfolio and consumer tastes.

The Volkswagen Group

The Volkswagen Group, parent company of the Audi, Bentley, Bugatti, Lamborghini, Porsche, Seat, Skoda and Volkswagen car marques, Ducati motorcycles, and MAN, Scania and Volkswagen commercial vehicles is head-quartered in Wolfsburg, Germany. In addition to vehicles, the VW Group offers engines and turbo machinery, and related services including financing, leasing and fleet management. As the world's second-largest motor vehicle manufacturer by unit production, it vies with Toyota and General Motors for global car manufacturing leadership. The VW Group operates 100 production facilities across 27 countries and holds a 19.9 per cent non-controlling shareholding in Suzuki along with two joint-ventures in China: FAW-Volkswagen and Shanghai Volkswagen.

If Volkswagen is now a car for the masses, with certain premium ambitions, it was a cheap car that contributed to fast car penetration in many countries during a large part of the 20th century. However, the early part of its history is marred by the company's political connections. Volkswagen was founded in 1937 during the turbulent World War II era and its close connection to the Nazi regime at the time may explain why Volkswagen does not emphasize its early days in marketing communications, although the idea to provide Germans with cars was a proactive idea at the time.

Henry Ford was somewhat earlier occupied by the idea of bringing cars to the US people, and at the time he expressed strong anti-Semitic attitudes, particularly in the book *The International Jew: The world's foremost problem*, which he published in 1920 followed with three other volumes that took an explicit position against the Jews. Ford's books proved to be rather popular, not least in 1930s Germany, and Adolf Hitler awarded Ford a medal. Ford is the only American mentioned in Hitler's book *Mein Kampf*. At the Nuremberg Trials, Baldur von Schirach, head of the Hitler Youth *(Hitler-Jugend)* mentioned that *The International Jew* made a deep impression on him and his friends in their youth and influenced them in becoming anti-Semitic (Ryback, 2008). So the birth and early growth of the Ford Motor Company and Volkswagen shared a deep involvement in anti-Semitism.

At the time there were strong reasons to listen to Henry Ford. In the mid-1920s, a German worker earned a quarter of a US worker's salary and there were 81,000 cars in Germany compared to 15.4 million in the United States. In discussions around 1934, Opel and Daimler-Benz shared the opinion that manufacturing a cheap car for the masses would be too expensive. It was decided that the project overall should be handled by Volkswagen, and Ferdinand Porsche became designer. In July 1936, he brought two prototypes to Hitler's summer house in Obersalzberg. About a month later, Ferdinand Porsche visited Henry Ford in the United States and was soon appointed manager of the Volkswagen factory in Wolfsburg.

In 1945, UK forces succeeded in restarting the war-damaged VW factory in Wolfsburg and the Volkswagen Beetle began to make its mark on the world: 21,549,000 Beetles were produced between 1938 and 2003, superseding the 15 million Ford Model T cars built, in 1908 to 1927. In Europe it was seen as a car for the masses while in the United States, with its existing high car penetration, the Beetle was rather known as a handsome second car. Volkswagen's production grew rapidly in the 1950s and 1960s, and in 1965 it acquired Auto Union, which subsequently produced the first post-war Audi models.

Volkswagen launched a new generation of front-wheel drive vehicles in the 1970s, starting with the K70 (on sale 1970–75) developed by NSU, a company known for the innovative and at the time very modern Ro80 (produced 1967–77). Volkswagen absorbed NSU in 1969 after heavy reliability problems with the Ro80's wankel engine put NSU in financial difficulties. The K70's future was threatened by management concerns that it was too close in size and price to the Audi 100 launched in 1968. This event – plans for the K70 launch were at the last minute deferred, with rumours that Volkswagen staff removed the K70 from NSU's show stand on the eve of a motor show – was the first instance of the Volkswagen Group's problems with cannibalism. While in the late 1960s with the introduction of the K70, Volkswagen appeared to prefer avoiding cannibalism, the attitude has gradually changed over time. Starting in the 1990s, the Volkswagen Group made clear that competition among brands in the VW portfolio would be fruitful and contribute to making products and offers more competitive – an attitude that reflects a modern view on competition. With the introduction of the Passat, Polo and Golf between 1972 and 1974, Volkswagen founded a very successful car range portfolio for the future.

Volkswagen acquired a controlling stake in Seat in 1986, making it the first non-German marque of the company, and acquired control of Skoda in

1994. The three prestige automotive marques Bentley, Lamborghini and Bugatti were acquired in 1998, Scania in 2008 and Ducati, MAN and Porsche in 2012. In 2000, Volkswagen AG, after having gradually raised its equity share, turned Skoda Auto into a wholly owned subsidiary. In 2009, Volkswagen AG bought a 49.9 per cent stake in Porsche AG and became its parent company through further transactions in 2012. Volkswagen AG completed the purchase of 19.9 per cent of Suzuki Motor Corporation's issued shares on 15 January 2010.

The main problem for Volkswagen reflects the advantage the company has had for several decades; actually since the first Beetle was introduced in the 1930s: manufacturer of the people's car that attracts the masses but hardly stands out. If that has been a winning formula for many years, and still is to an extent, it may be a challenge in future with buyers having many interesting opportunities and with a pronounced preference for well-designed cars that are emotionally appealing and make a difference. A 2012 German survey highlights Volkswagen's appeal and intention to upset nobody through its design, great functionality, timeless design and good quality. Among 14,600 survey answers, 0 per cent sees the design as exciting. However, 69 per cent of the respondents suggest that the brand and its design fit well together, only beaten by Porsche with 72 per cent. In a way, the brand and its design seem to be consistent but stuck – it hardly creates emotion and it never provokes.

Volkswagen, with the enormous resources of the Volkswagen Group, is now one of the industry's forerunners in terms of developing efficient powertrains, recyclable cars, electric cars, etc and the strong diversification provided by the broad range of brands that, after a successful integration over the years, makes the VW Group well-prepared for the future.

Audi

Audi, headquartered in Ingolstadt, Germany, is one of a very few examples of real upward stretch, ie transforming a typical middle-of-the-road brand into a very attractive premium one. Ever since Audi became a Volkswagen-owned subsidiary in 1966, the ambition has been to keep the Audi brand distinct from the Volkswagen brand, but it wasn't successful until a more pronounced differentiation was initiated in the early 1980s. In 1964, Volkswagen acquired a 50 per cent holding in the Auto Union business, by then owner of the Audi brand, which included the new factory in Ingolstadt and the trademark rights of the Auto Union. Eighteen months later, Volkswagen bought complete control of Ingolstadt and the Audi brand, and by 1966 was using the spare capacity at the Ingolstadt plant to assemble an additional 60,000 Volkswagen Beetles per year.

In the 1970s Audi largely produced the same cars as Volkswagen but with ambitions to offer an upmarket flair. The two brands were sold together – at the time there were few or no people who suggested they shouldn't – so Audi had to share with Volkswagen the same salespeople and showrooms, where potential customers could compare a Volkswagen Passat with an Audi 80 and notice that they were very similar. Audi was the static brand shadowed by Volkswagen. When in 1976 Audi launched the new, more exclusive five cylinder Audi 100 (the 5000 in the United States – including the following two generations of Audi 100) in 1976 it was made clear that an Audi could be spacious, quiet and comfortable. But the brand lacked the strength and attractiveness of BMW, Mercedes and Jaguar. The Audi brand was weak and associated with static, older people rather than young and dynamic drivers. Mercedes and BMW dominated the premium segment at a time when Audi wasn't selling more cars than Volvo (in 2012, Volvo sold 422,000 cars compared to 1,455,000 for Audi). In the late 1970s, an Audi 100 GL 5E was the choice of those who wanted something more comfortable and inexpensive than a BMW 528i, and considered a Mercedes 230 too dear. The Audi 100 GL 5E, the most upmarket Audi at the time, was positioned between a Volvo 244 GL and a Volvo 264 GLE. At the time, the driving experience was not as emphasized as it became later.

Around 1980, Audi started a campaign to become a leading premium car manufacturer, and it proved more successful than any other attempt in modern auto brand history. The transition from a boring brand of interest to few people, to a brand that has a very strong appeal for dynamic car consumers had begun. In 1980, Audi launched the Audi 200 turbo, a first serious attempt to become a premium player, although it hardly matched the Mercedes new S Class or the BMW 7 series as a luxury car. More important, Audi decided to launch the Audi quattro, the first four-wheel driven high-powered sports car. As a rally car, the quattro was initially regarded as too heavy and complex for rally stages, but this changed when it won three competitions in its debut season, including a maiden victory for Michèle Mouton at the Rally San Remo. Audi went on to win two world rally driver's and two world rally manufacturer's championships.

Shortly after the quattro was launched, Audi introduced the Audi Coupé, which used the same basic body as the quattro, and it became very popular although the five cylinder 136 bhp engine was not really a sporty engine.

The Coupé became a very important image-builder for Audi, and the first Audi car that really appealed to trend-setters and yuppies. Remember: this was the decade of overselling, overspending young people, with the car as an important lifestyle item.

Audi cars quickly moved away from their old image of being conservative. In 1982, Audi launched the all-new 100 model, known for its extremely good aerodynamics and excellent comfort. Mechanical quality did not really match premium customers' expectations, something that improved significantly during the lifecycle of the car. The Audi 100 product range had engines from 75 up to 165 PS and in 1989 the innovative Audi five cylinder diesel engine was introduced in this model.

In 1984 the Audi Coupé had a facelift and was now available with quattro – like all other Audi models. In 1986 the new Audi 80, soon available as a five cylinder Audi 90, put design as a top priority. In 1990, the fourth generation of the Audi 100 was launched, now in every key aspect comparable to Mercedes and BMW. The newcomer had the advantage of being seen as a fresh choice and many Audi owners benefited image-wise from driving an Audi during a period when it was seen as a left-field choice and more innovative and forward-looking than classic luxury brands such as MB and BMW.

The Audi V8, built between 1988 and 1993, was in some aspects a superior product both to Toyota's luxury brand Lexus, which was launched at the same time, and to German competitors. The Audi V8 was the only car in its class to offer four-wheel drive and a fully galvanized body as standard, with a 10-year anti-perforation warranty against corrosion. Although this was a well-built car, it couldn't really match the new Mercedes S Class introduced in 1990 – no surprise, maybe, since the Audi V8 despite all its qualities was based on the Audi 100 platform from 1982.

If the Audi 100 C4 made Audi a real premium competitor in the business car segment, the Audi A8, launched in 1994, made Audi a serious competitor to Mercedes and BMW in the luxury car segment. The Audi A8 was the first car with an integrated aluminium body, the Audi Space Frame, something that made it a dynamic luxury car. The 1994 Space Frame saved weight and improved torsional rigidity compared to a conventional steel frame. The disadvantage of the aluminium frame was that it was very expensive to repair and required a specialized body shop, hence insurance premiums were high.

BMW and Jaguar finally had a serious competitor! The new A8 that was launched in 2010 further strengthened Audi's position as a leading premium manufacturer. Since the mid-1990s, Audi's model range has been very strong, and it has improved continuously. '*Die Konkurrenz schläft nicht*' is a German expression that catches what the automotive industry looks like ever since: regardless of how successful you are, competitors always try to beat you. Many new models have been launched since the 1990s – the TT, the R8, the A5, the S5, the RS5, the A7, the S6, the RS7, the Q3, Q5 and Q7 to name a few – and the model expansion continues to strengthen the Audi brand, broadening the client base and increasing sales volume: Audi aims to overtake BMW in terms of the number of cars sold worldwide no later than 2020. An expanding model range is necessary to stay ahead of the competition – competitors are launching new products and new sub-segments every year.

An important part of the Audi brand's upward stretch is the reorientation of marketing channel strategies that was emphasized around 2000. In many markets, the dealers didn't achieve the premium qualities of its competitors at the time. In most cases the Audi dealer was also a dealer of other Volkswagen Group brands and, in some cases, eg in Australia, brands from other manufacturer groups as well. The premium car customer is assumed to differ from those buying Volkswagen, Skoda and Seat in terms of expectations and demands; as a Mercedes dealer in one of Sydney's socio-economically flourishing areas says:

> Our customers are used to a high level, they would normally not travel on an airplane in economy class, or stay in motels or caravan parks, they'll be staying in five-star hotels, they will be travelling probably business class or maybe first class when they fly, and they get used to a certain level of service, and when you don't provide that, the environment that they had expected, it stands out.

Hence, even though the car market is largely product-driven, dealer quality is definitely crucial in completing a premium brand experience. As a German factory-owned BMW dealer puts it:

> At the end of the day, a Volkswagen Polo customer is very different from an Audi A8 customer. I don't understand why Audi with its strong product range didn't do this earlier. Audi had to make the decision to separate the dealer networks to be able to serve the Audi clients in the way they wanted to be served.

A couple of years later, around 2002 to 2005, Mercedes, BMW and Audi all referred to each other as 'the premium competitors'. Many others – including Lexus, Jaguar and Volvo, and more exclusive Citroën, Alfa Romeo and Jaguar models – wanted to be in the premium brand segment, but those setting the tone didn't mention these brands. Audi had completed its journey from being a boring, conservative brand producing mechanically robust, but rust-sensitive cars, to being one of the world's leading premium auto brands.[8]

Like its competitors BMW and MB, Audi has had quality problems and evidence suggests that being a forerunner in terms of technology often implies having to deal with problems that new technologies entail when implemented in real-world situations, like everyday use of a car. Several tests run by consumer organizations suggest a Skoda to be a better pick than cars from the upper end of the VW Group like Audi – simply because new technologies are first implemented in the exclusive auto brands.

Audi cars had severe rust problems in the 1970s and early 1980s and the rust protection was below industry average at the time – the resulting problems were limited in many parts of the United States where rust is not much of a problem while European countries experienced heavy corrosion. Cars in States close to salt water like California and Hawaii experienced problems related to poor paint quality. Since the mid-1980s, Audi has galvanized cars to prevent rusting and was the first mass-market auto brand to do so, following introduction of the process by Porsche in the mid-1970s. The full-body zinc coating has proved to be very effective in preventing rust and was initially used heavily in Audi advertising – however, other auto brands, eg Peugeot, Renault and Volvo, have provided a similar high level of rust protection and the initial competitive advantage has become less important. This is similar to Volvo's excellent safety standards, which don't stand out as much as they did when competitors lagged on safety issues.

A tragic event in the Audi brand history is the incidents of sudden unintended acceleration, primarily reported in the United States by Audi 5000 drivers, linked to six deaths and 700 accidents. This was a major reason why Audi sales fell after a series of recalls from 1982 to 1987 of Audi 5000 models. A lawsuit filed in 1987 by more than 7,000 Audi 5000 owners (still not settled!) contributed to enormous image problems. Although several investigations suggested driver error, specifically pedal misapplication, Audi's US sales fell from 74,061 in 1985 to between 12,000 and 13,000 cars a year in the early 1990s. Resale values fell and made Audi a very expensive car to own – at least for new car buyers. The Audi 5000 became the 100 (200 for the upmarket models) and increased warranty protection was implemented – at the turn of the millennium sales had recovered to mid-1980s levels and since then Audi has gained solid ground – in 2012, 139,310 Audi cars were sold in the United States. Toyota had a similar period of problems due to unintended acceleration in 2010. Floor mat incursion under the accelerator pedal, referred to as Sticking Accelerator Pedal by Toyota, was suggested as a likely explanation and Toyota recalled about 9 million vehicles in the United States, Europe and China.

Audi manufactures vehicles in seven plants around the world, some of which are shared with other VW Group marques although many sub-assemblies such as engines and transmissions are manufactured within other Volkswagen Group plants. In addition to the two main assembly plants in Ingolstadt and Neckarsulm, vehicles are produced in Belgium, Hungary, Spain, Slovakia, China, India, Indonesia and (from 2016) in Mexico. Build quality appears to be high across the world – there have been limited discussions on reduced quality in factories run in foreign factories, while MB had severe problems with the first ML generation built in the United States in the 1990s and Japanese cars built in Europe have also been accused of having lower build quality than cars built in Japan.

Having a leading position – and bold ambitions that put a lot of pressure on the Audi organization, partners and staff – Audi plans to be the world's leading car premium brand with the highest sales numbers. That's not very easy given the strong competition. What should Audi do to protect and develop its position in the future? One danger is the risk that the brand becomes too perfectionist and hence lacks the liveliness of successful brands in other industries. The Audi brand reflects German perfectionism and, in recent years, the design – which generally has a strong appeal – has been criticized for being too conservative with new models looking too similar to their predecessors. A senior Audi manager replied to this criticism in a discussion in 2012: 'Not anymore – if you buy an A1, you can now get the roof and the pillars in a different colour than the rest of the car.' It doesn't make a huge difference when Renault, Ford, Mercedes, Citroën, Volvo and many other brands are far more innovative and less conservative when it comes to new design features. When it was announced in June 2013 that Audi will swap development chiefs for a second time in less than a year, it was extensively reported in the business and other press that Audi may be losing momentum. *Der Spiegel, auto motor & sport*, Reuters and other very influential media channels reported this; and a senior VW group executive said in an interview that Audi has become a follower of technology trends too often set by luxury-market leader BMW and is too dependent on China. Independent industry expert Ferdinand Dudenhofer, head of the CAR think tank at the University of Duisburg-Essen, Germany, said: 'Audi doesn't uncover new market segments and too often borrows VW group technology... Their sales slogan doesn't meet the requirements.' A spokesman for parent VW declined to comment and Audi did not return calls seeking comment. *auto motor & sport* has emphasized the image implications of Audi's decision to cancel the Audi R8 E-tron at the same time as MB is putting its SLS AMG Coupé Electric Drive on sale. Audi stopped the electric A1 hatchback, while BMW is launching the i3 electric vehicle that sports a lightweight carbon-fibre skeleton. Dudenhofer says the i3's arrival throws Audi further behind its main competitor on an alternative powertrain technology that may drive future growth and end the brand's pioneering role in lightweight construction, noting Audi in 1994 launched the A8 with a body fully made of aluminium. In addition, numerous car journalists not only criticize Audi's design for being too conservative but also the driving experience as lacking liveliness.

Seat

Seat is a good example of how the Volkswagen Group is exploiting the advantages of badge engineering – a concept that emerged in the United States as the Big Three were using different badges for the same car, with slight modifications.

The Seat Mii is the same car as the Volkswagen Up! – and it is very obvious, which is an interesting change from the strategy applied by the Volkswagen Group for several decades: extensive investment was made in differentiating products, and trying to convince journalists, car testers and potential buyers that the brands within the group are different. With the new smallest model sold in the group, it's different. Volkswagen's Up! city car, part of the Volkswagen Group New Small Family (NSF) series, has led the way for a very obvious application of badge engineering. Within just weeks of the Up!'s debut at the 2011 Frankfurt Motor Show, Skoda announced its new Citigo and Seat its Mii. All are powered by the same three cylinder petrol and diesel engines. In addition to the production models, VW has used its Up! platform to demonstrate several concepts, including the GT, Cross Up! and Buggy Up! so the NSF range will grow intra- and inter-brand. Production of the NSF started in December 2011 in Bratislava, Slovakia, and the Spanish Seat, the German Volkswagen or the Czech Skoda are all manufactured in the same plant. Again, an example of how branding – 'the visible' – and product development and engineering – 'the invisible' – become detached. But this time the visible is not as differentiated as it could have been.

In the compact segment, there is little doubt that the Golf is a very good car, but the image of German perfectionism is not everybody's cup of tea so there is a market for other choices. The Seat Leon, introduced in 2012 as the second car after the Golf based on the new MQB platform, has been marketed heavily on the fact that it's the first car in its class with optional full-LED headlamps combined with a full beam assistant. LED headlamps certainly offer advantages: improved illumination with a near-daylight colour temperature, low energy consumption and an extended life, but very few buyers in this very competitive segment are likely to see LED headlamps as adding a lot of value compared to xenon headlamps – in fact, on a worldwide basis, only a few per cent of cars in the Golf segment are equipped with the optional xenon headlights so it's unlikely that full LED will make any difference. The strength of the Leon rather lies in the combination of German Volkswagen Group engineering and Spanish flair. It's assembled in Spain but built with just about the same parts as the Volkswagen Golf. It lacks the oddness of the old Leon, which was designed based on Seat's former slogan *'Auto Emoción'*, which was strongly emphasized in 2002 to 2005. For instance, the rear door handle was hidden á la Alfa Romeo 156 (not a big surprise since Walter de Silva was involved in the design of both).

As opposed to many other marques, Seat's brand heritage is not very clear. Ever since the company was founded in 1950, Seat cars have been built under licence, badge engineered, or shared platforms with the Volkswagen Group since it took over in the 1990s. This heritage is still strong. For instance, the Seat Alhambra is a slightly cheaper but not significantly different version of the Volkswagen Sharan; and they are built in the same factory. Hence, it's normally sold on price since the Volkswagen will have a higher resale value (Fersainz, 2013). The 2012 Leon is based on the new slogan 'Enjoyneering' – a mixture of German engineering and functionality on the one hand, and Spanish emotions on the other. A smart way of broadening the base of attractiveness for the Seat brand and making it more fit for the future – as a much smaller brand with a substantially weaker brand heritage than Volkswagen, Seat can move in wilder circles without taking the risk of destroying market opportunities and the brand heritage.

Porsche

Porsche is without doubt one of the strongest brands in car industry history and its brand heritage, linked to the 911 introduced in 1963, provides an attractiveness that has been used to broaden the model range. In the 1970s, Porsche decided to replace the mid-engine, targa-topped, two-seat roadster 914 and the classic 911 with the front-engine 2+2 seaters 924 and 928. However, the demand for the 911 remained strong and many enthusiasts wanted the classic 911 car rather than the more comfortable 924 and 928 models. The 924 was developed significantly with the 944 (1982) and 968 (1992) models but never gained full acceptance as a Porsche that could match the 911. The 928 was also refined but never reached significant sales numbers.

The 911 – developed into entire new models but with a consistent design built on earlier generations – remained the cornerstone of Porsche's product portfolio. However, it would have been difficult for Porsche to survive without the SUV Cayenne, which builds on the Volkswagen Touareg, introduced in late 2002. The Cayenne, now in its second generation, constitutes more than half of all Porsche sales with 77,800 sold in 2012 compared to 26,200 911s, 11,700 Caymans and Boxsters and 27,300 Panameras. It's no surprise that Porsche will introduce the smaller Macan SUV in 2014 – it's likely to be successful in terms of sales numbers. However, there are also challenges that come with the introduction of a lower-range car.

Approaching the mass market means a new breed of customers will have to be dealt with. The Macan may mean a revolution for Porsche's dealers when car buyers who have been looking for a Mercedes-Benz GLK, a BMW X3, a Volvo XC60 or an Audi Q5 get the opportunity to buy an entry-level Porsche. If not dealt with carefully, there is a risk that the emerging client base, eager to get a Porsche for their limited budgets, pay less attention to traditional Porsche brand values, hence diluting them. When a Porsche is seen as less unique and more mass market, there is a risk that the brand loses attractiveness. There have been similar challenges in Porsche's history, like with the 924, the Boxster and to an extent with the Cayenne (which is certainly a very sporty SUV, that inherent Porsche value, at least in its second generation launched in 2011).

On the other hand, Porsche may have no choice but to broaden its model portfolio to reach a critical mass of volume to be able to invest in product development, and to ensure marketing channels are fit for the future. Evidence from other German premium brands, and Mercedes-Benz in particular, makes clear that it's possible to combine mass-market products with very exclusive models. While the A and B Class cars are mass-market products, the SL has kept its position as a leading luxury roadster over its six generations. It can't really be argued that the S Class has lost attractiveness following Mercedes-Benz's ever growing supply of cheaper, mass-market products.

General Motors

General Motors led global vehicle sales for 77 consecutive years from 1931 to 2007 and is now fighting with Toyota and the Volkswagen Group on sales volume leadership. GM produces vehicles in 37 countries under 11 brands, including Chevrolet, Buick, GMC, Cadillac, Baojun, Holden, Isuzu, Jie Fang, Opel, Vauxhall and Wuling and each brand has its own challenges and history.

General Motors has made many brand portfolio reorganizations, something that has contributed to less focus on the individual brands and their brand heritage. The list of discontinued brands is extensive and includes well-known and influential brands such as Oldsmobile, Pontiac, Daewoo, Saturn, Hummer and Saab. Chevrolet, for instance, is a brand with a long heritage and strong position among Americans in particular. In 2005, General Motors relaunched the Chevrolet brand in Europe, using Korean cars that had previously been sold as Daewoos. At the same time, substantial effort is being made to strengthen the position of the sports cars: the Chevrolet Camaro and Corvette. Considering General Motor's extensive portfolio of brands, why use the same brand for everything from cheap Korean budget cars to luxury sports cars? The 432 PS eight cylinder Camaro sells for €39,990 in Germany – a bargain, but maybe an indication that Chevrolet doesn't make use of its brand heritage when it also sells the €8,990 Spark and the €10,990 Aevo under the same brand. Like in a supermarket, all prices end with '990'!

What happened with Saab, the Swedish brand, partly owned by General Motors since 1989 and acquired in 2000? A key explanation for its failure is the lack of integration of Saab into the GM corporation. When Saab, one of the companies that Sweden was very proud of, became a subsidiary of the world's largest car maker, it offered resistance and didn't want to use General Motors parts into its cars – and General Motors did not make use of Saab's traditionally strong innovativeness, which slowed down substantially. Needless to say, it's unlikely Saab, which had been making substantial losses since the 1980s, would survive on its own – Porsche has stated it wouldn't have survived without the introduction of the Cayenne in 2002, so it's unlikely the less profitable and generally weaker Saab brand would.

In 2002, a German Saab dealer complained that it was extremely difficult to sell the 9-5 with a Subaru 3 litre diesel engine with no automatic gearbox available. Integrated GPS or xenon headlights were not even offered as options – while the German premium brands offered all these features in attractive packages. In 2000 and beyond the plan in Germany was to sell 20,000 cars a year but sales never reached more than 6,000. New cars that had been stockpiled in Germany for two or three years were sold in Sweden 'with full warranty at highly discounted prices' – a strong indication of the lack of success for Saab.

In Europe, Cadillac was launched on a broader basis in 2005. The plan was to sell 50,000 cars in the first year, but only 5,000 cars were sold. In 2008, Swedish GM dealers – which made large contributions to newspapers' advertising income at the time as they were widely promoting heavily discounted cars – had 2005 Cadillac SRX cars in stock and they were sold for less than half the original price: SEK 199,900.

Through General Motor's acquisition, Saab had become part of the GM badge engineering empire – something that worked better in the United States than in Europe. The 9-2X (based on the Subaru Impreza) and the Saab 9-7X (based on the Chevrolet Trailblazer) were introduced in the United States in 2005. Both models were a commercial failure and were discontinued after a few years' production. General Motors also delayed the 9-3 wagon, the all-wheel drive 9-3X and the new 9-5 and announced a planned shift of production away from Saab's historic home in Trollhättan to Opel's factory in German Rüsselsheim. In the end, the Trollhättan factory started producing the Cadillac BLS, another example of badge engineering. Initially planned to be sold at a significant price premium over the Saab 9-3 on which it was based, sales became very difficult to achieve – if a European wanted a Cadillac, he or she wouldn't go for a modified Saab but rather for a US-built six or eight cylinder model – and discounts of around 30 per cent on the initial list price were soon announced as sales were nothing but a catastrophe.

The BLS was a Saab 9-3 upgraded with Cadillac attributes, a chassis for a smoother ride and noise reduction measures. The car lost a bit of its sporty road performance, but did not gain much in comfort. Buyers did not support the redesigned Saab 9-3 and the planned price premium did not materialize. Cars remained in dealer stocks for a year or two and were sold with large discounts. The company and official car markets are significant in this segment and few employers would accept a Cadillac, partly for image reasons, but primarily for fear of very low residual values.

Badge engineering has worked rather well in the United States for volume brands, but it hardly works for premium brands. The late history of Saab illustrates a number of problems related to lacklustre management, overuse of badge engineering in contexts when a car buyer and car culture perspective suggests it wouldn't work, small manufacturing volumes and difficulties in integrating a small subsidiary into a large corporation.

Volvo

Volvo is an interesting brand, for many reasons. Since the early 1980s it struggled to gain a genuine premium brand position. Although there were some signs it succeeded at times – it even managed to beat German competitors in Germany's prestigious motor magazine *auto motor & sport*, first with the 2001 XC70, which was found more convincing than the Audi Allroad, and secondly with the 2008 V70 3.2 which beat the Audi A6 3.2 – Volvo always had problems in consistently delivering excellent products, high quality and environmentally-friendly cars with a strong emotional appeal. The emphasis on Scandinavian design and a buyer profile that differentiated it from the German competition was an advantage made good use of in some markets, eg the United States, but on a global basis it has not been exploited enough to make the company sustainably profitable.

Back in the 1980s, Volvo was very strong in the United States and it looked like it would manage to become one of the most attractive premium brands. However, Volvo never established a profile and position that is both premium and Scandinavian, or whatever is 'Volvo-ish', at the same time. The premium qualities of Audi, BMW, Mercedes-Benz and Lexus – great build quality, sophisticated suspension set-up, powerful and smooth engines and an edge in design – were reached at times but hardly in a convincing way. If Volvo could not succeed in the premium dimension, it had to deliver in another dimension. And there were at least two opportunities. First, the Scandinavian design advantage: it was characterized by simplicity, user-friendliness, minimalism and functionality, a fresh and modern alternative to German perfectionism. In the late 1980s, Volvo had extensive teams that were appointed to make the cars attractive to women buyers and users, something that certainly contributed to the user-friendly Scandinavia-influenced driving and user experience. Second, the customer profile and being an alternative to primarily German premium cars, which were seen by some buyers as to a certain extent representing arrogance and a newly-rich attitude. Volvo never managed to build on its advantages and the company has ended up in a difficult situation with profitability problems and is stuck with relatively modest sales of around 400,000 cars a year.

Partnerships are common sense among car makers, but Volvo doesn't have a major partner at the moment, something that is rather rare in the industry. The costs of developing new car models are huge and it may be difficult to succeed without an opportunity to spread R&D and product development costs on either high volumes or through high margins. Jaguar Land Rover, another brand without tight partnerships with other car makers, has success-fully grown by standing on its own, investing heavily in new products, and modernizing two classic auto brands in a number of respects (safety, technology, fuel efficiency, quality, etc), thus drawing upon the advantages of an established brand with a position that makes it stand out in the premium segment.

Safety has always been at the heart of Volvo's brand. The laminated glass windscreen in 1944, the three-point front seat safety belt in 1959, the lambda and three-way catalyst in 1977, the first three-point seat belt for the middle rear seat in 1990, a child safety cushion integrated in the middle armrest in 1990, the Side Impact Protection System that channelled the force of a side impact away from the doors and into the safety cage in 1991, a head-protecting airbag deploying upwards from the door in 1998, the Pedestrian Detection with full auto-brake in 2010 and the City Safety System in 2011 are all sig-nificant innovations in Volvo's history. Competitors have caught up and the safety advantage is smaller than it used to be, but Volvo is still innovative and the industry – and car users – should be thankful to Volvo for all its life-saving innovations. The Volvo V40 (2012) that comes with a pedestrian airbag was declared by Euro NCAP to be the safest car it had ever assessed. When auto motor & sport run the first test of the new Mercedes-Benz 2014 S Class, it was compared to four cars, all seen as 'best in class': Porsche Panamera (road performance), comfort and build quality (Volkswagen Phaeton), power-train and infotainment (BMW 7 Series), and safety (Volvo V40).

In emerging markets with great market potential, eg China, Volvo could be an attractive brand but buyers in these countries tend to prefer tradi-tional luxury brands over 'cooler', minimalistic, less well-known ones. Audi, BMW and Mercedes have put a lot of effort into being successful in China and it's difficult for Volvo, with less resources (Geely has announced that Volvo has to survive on its own) to catch up. BMW will have 25 models in 2015, Audi and Mercedes show similar numbers. Not an easy situation for Volvo and it's difficult to see how it could compete in a market where people with less money look for value for money and richer people like to demonstrate their success by buying a luxury auto brand.

Jaguar and Range Rover

Jaguar and Range Rover have an interesting history in terms of company ownership. Jaguar and Rover Automotive is a British car maker with a deep British heritage, headquartered in Coventry, United Kingdom. Jaguar Cars and Land Rover were first united under a single entity by Ford Motor Company in 2002. Ford acquired Jaguar Cars in 1989 and Land Rover from BMW in 2000. In 2006 Ford purchased the Rover brand name from BMW. This reunited the Rover and Land Rover brands for the first time since the Rover group was broken up by BMW in 2000, and also brought Jaguar into the same stable position as Rover/Land Rover more than 15 years after it was spun off from the former British Leyland owner in 1984.

Since 2008, Jaguar and Land Rover is a wholly owned subsidiary of Tata Motors of India, a subsidiary of the large Tata Group. The two traditional brands Jaguar and Land Rover, both acquired by Tata Group for £1.15 billion, may be even more well-known under the brands Jaguar and Range Rover, both undergoing heavy product development since the Tata takeover took place. Interestingly, they are not seen as Indian cars but as very British.

The Range Rover car range, introduced in its third generation in 2002 based on BMW parts (BMW owned Rover and Land Rover until 2000) was extended by the Range Rover Sport that was launched at the Detroit Motor Show in 2005 into the market for four-wheel drive SUVs – or Chelsea Tractors as they are often called in the United Kingdom. It took on the crowd of German challengers such as the BMW X5, the Mercedes ML, the Audi Q7 and the Porsche Cayenne. In the initial branding, Victoria Beckham and Daniel Craig were running the Range Rover Sport, hence securing the car's anchorage in popular culture.

Later, a product offensive took place and with the Evoque (2012), a new Range Rover (2012), the Range Rover Sport (2013), and plans for a new super-luxury stretch Range Rover, the Tata Group-owned company appears prepared for the future in very competitive segments. Being different from the German premium brands, and now offering great product performance and a brand that stands out, is promising for the future. When German competitors reach very high sales numbers, that's an opportunity for brands like Volvo, Jaguar and Range Rover since they are perceived as different and unique.

Hyundai and Kia

It is not really fair to discuss the sister brands Kia and Hyundai together, but their history and development are linked tightly so it's difficult to talk about one of them without considering the other.

The history of Kia started in 1944 when the Kyongseong Precision Industry was set up. In 1961 Kia founded the Korean automotive industry with the construction of a three-wheeled motorcycle and a mini-truck. In 1973, the company went public and Kia built the first Korean petrol engine. One year later the first Kia car, the Brisa model, was launched, whose pick-up version was the first Korean car export. From 1979 to 1981, the Peugeot 604 and Fiat 132 models were built for the Korean market under licence and in 1983 a licence manufacturing agreement was made with Mazda – a history not dissimilar to that of Seat.

In 1992 and 1993 there was expansion in the United States and Germany, respectively. Cars were built not only for Europe but also in it: the Kia Sportage was built between 1995 and 1998 by Karmann in Osnabrück. In 1998 Kia was acquired by the Hyundai Group, now named Hyundai Kia Automotive Group. Through setting up marketing intelligence and product development in Europe in 2007, Kia and Hyundai cars are developed for the European market at the centre in Rüsselsheim, Germany. Vehicles are produced in 15 plants in 10 countries.

Recently Kia and Hyundai have developed specific design features and Hyundai in particular has a distinguished design profile. High quality and good engineering combined with attractive pricing and appealing design have made the brands successful – but as with other brands such as Skoda that are somewhere between a budget brand and a volume brand, there is a risk that higher prices will make potential buyers take a look at other brands. And tough competition may force brands like Ford, Opel, Skoda and Peugeot to deliver as much value for money as Kia and Hyundai.

What about the future? As announced in 2013 by German global design chief of Hyundai and Kia, Peter Schreyer, the two sister brands need greater differentiation in market positioning and in segmentation. Based on the same platform and technical layout, Schreyer says the two brands could be more differentiated 'so that the cars actually serve a different purpose. Maybe one is roomier and one is sleeker and flatter, for example' (Greimel, 2013). By announcing that the upcoming shift will be a 'dramatic evolution' of the two sister brands, expectations are high. The Volkswagen Group knows how challenging it is to separate sister brands in relation to car buyers

– but that is likely to be necessary to fully exploit the market opportunities of the high-quality and well-engineered Korean brands. Separating the brands at the dealership level, at least in metro areas, may be a necessary step to reach this goal.

Ford

Henry Ford was a skilled mechanic, and he made various attempts to design and build cars until the Ford Motor Company was founded in 1903. The company produced and sold 1,700 cars in the first 15 months. The pace of progress was significant: in 1905, 300 employees produced 25 cars per day. In 1908, the Model T was launched, known as the first affordable automobile that began to put middle-class Americans on wheels. In 1927, Henry Ford watched the 15 millionth Model T roll off the assembly line in Michigan.

Through factory innovations, Ford could double workers' salaries, shorten working hours and introduce three shifts, and the price of the car dropped from $950 at the introduction of the Model T to $290 at the end. With higher wages and lower prices Ford employees could buy the cars they produced – if not a bonus at least a strong incentive and source of gratification.

The profitable company could invest in new products and Henry Ford was now a wealthy man. There soon followed the Model A, with 4,849,000 cars produced between 1927 and 1931. Between 1932 and 1936, the Model B, Model 18, Model 40 and Model 48, which were all completely new developments, were introduced and proved to be very successful. The Model 18, with its flathead V8 engine, was particularly popular and contributed to making large engines part of US car culture.

In 1943, Henry Ford took over after his son died, and became CEO again until he retired in 1945; then grandson Henry Ford II ran Ford for a couple of years. It was not until 1960 that Ford had its first president from outside the family: Robert McNamara, who would later make a name for himself as US Secretary of Defense.

The fascination of Germany and its engineering capacity wasn't limited to Henry Ford. When the United States was building its interstate network:

> American engineers and politicians flocked to Germany to see the marvellous
> new super-highways in operation. Visitors drove the concrete roads and, if
> time permitted, chief engineer Fritz Todt took them on a zeppelin overview of

the national network. Back in the United States, they debated whether Hitler was building the highways *(Reichsautobahnen)* for economic purposes, as he claimed, or for military reasons, as visitors feared. The reaction of US Rep. Wilburn Cartwright of Oklahoma, chairman of the House Committee on Roads, was typical. After touring the Autobahn in 1938, he said: 'When I think of super-highways, I think of Germany, for, regardless of what we think of him as a man, we must give Fuhrer Hitler credit for building a system of super-highways in his country which are second to none in the world today'.

(Weingroff, 2000)

Ford continued to be a major player during the post-World War II era with a strong market presence in all major markets. Beginning in the early 1980s, Ford introduced several highly successful vehicles around the world including attempts to introduce World Cars: the third generation Escort (1980–1986) was built in the United Kingdom, Spain, Brazil and Germany, and the fourth generation (1986–1990) was in addition produced in Argentina and Venezuela, something that emphasized the strong success of Ford in South America. The Sierra (1982) was very successful in Europe and marked another change in design from the conservative 1970s models such as the Escort, Granada, Consul and Taurus, a move completed with the Scorpio (1985) that replaced the Granada. The Scorpio was successful in its first years, but lost competitiveness during its extended lifecycle due to quality problems and major improvements in competitors' portfolios. A low price was not reason enough for car buyers to choose the Scorpio, and after the second facelift (1994) the car received a lot of negative attention for its design.

Ford's decision in Europe to discontinue the Scorpio saloon in 1998 and turn its focus to growing segments proved a good move: the S-Max and the Galaxy have been great successes. Ford was one of the first brands to announce that it will not go for the premium segments but rather provide value-for-money products for a broad range of customers.

Premium aspiration brands – a difficult position

Not going for a premium position is a very clever strategy for companies that have little likelihood of success in becoming genuine premium brands. In many industries there are companies that try to create a premium brand, and sometimes claim that they have done so, but unfortunately neither their customers nor others such as journalists agree. To accomplish a real premium brand, all characteristics of premium brands must be present and be internally consistent. But that's an option that will lose attractiveness as the traditional premium values will put car makers in a very competitive segment where it's difficult to win. Established premium brands have an advantage over those who try, in a number of respects. Marketing channels are designed for reaching the premium segment in terms of dealer location, showroom design, facilities standards, dealer training etc, and it will always take time to build a brand that reflects these real qualities.

If the market doesn't agree, it's not possible to state that the brand is a premium one. Premium brands are more profitable and give more prestige to everybody involved, in any area related to the business. Selling Miele dish washers adds some prestige to the occupation compared to selling cheap dish washers; having a degree from Harvard University gives a certain element of prestige, as does living in Kensington, London, having a summerhouse in Sotogrande or spending the London weekend at Sofitel St James' hotel. Most people like the idea of working for an attractive employer, living in a nice and progressive area, and driving a nice car. People like premium brands – it's where the design, the innovations, the comfortable life and the creative people are. And even in anti-United States or anti-consumerism movements there are hierarchies and brands that are more desirable and wanted by many people (Kotler *et al*, 2011).

Many companies fail even though their attempts to create a premium brand are serious. It can be counterproductive if corporate management over-estimates the 'premiumness' of the brand and makes decisions that irritate dealers and customers. To live the brand and make it consistent all the way from the customer's first contact to delivery and after-sales, the brand owner must make sure that each step in the customer process, and every channel that communicates the brand, sends a consistent brand message.

Peugeot has managed a turnaround quality-wise within the volume segment. Being a producer of mediocre cars in the 1980s, Peugeot has accomplished great improvements in terms of quality: it is one of the auto brands with superior rust protection, and the powertrains are known to be very reliable. The design, too, has improved and if the Peugeot 407 went a bit too far with the bizarre front, the exterior as well as the interior design of Peugeots now offers a distinct and sober feeling, without being too staid or traditional. Pricing is good, too, which makes it a strong competitor to budget brands, a position it shares with Renault. And like Ford, these French brands want to accomplish some premium qualities but don't present themselves as premium.

Everybody wants to go upmarket – excessive competition in the premium segments

We've learnt over the years that brands must have a strong profile and be positioned differently from other brands, which often meant differentiating the brand from the volume brands and turning them into premium brands. But the premium brand segment has become very crowded. Car makers, dealers and customers share the tendency to strive for higher society, something that explains a lot of the changes and rising standards in automobile marketing channels, eg why car makers improve the standards of dealer showrooms and processes. There may be many other dimensions to define a strong or attractive brand than its 'premiumness'. In fact, it's a solid dimension but appears to reduce the industry's innovativeness.

A number of advantages associated with upmarket segments explain why car makers strive for making their brands more premium: higher profitability and a more prestigious image create and underpin a wheel-of-fortune (Parment, 2009; Silverstein and Fiske, 2003) and attractive brands are positively correlated with higher margins and profits (Wileman and Jary, 1997). As many car makers have shared the ambition to go upmarket in recent years, it may even put some general pressure on car makers to go upmarket to protect their position relative to competitors.

Car makers often refer to upmarket brands in defining their competitors. Studies reveal a substantially higher satisfaction for premium dealers compared to their volume counterparts, and this is also largely reflected in dealer satisfaction surveys. It has been argued that many middle-market consumers want to trade up from volume brands to premium brands (Silverstein and Fiske, 2003). Car makers and dealers try to make use of the industry's maturity and customers' search for strong brands by putting a lot of effort into going upmarket. For example, Opel executives a couple of years ago communicated the intention to 'recapture the design leadership' through making 'all new cars sporty and emotional', based on the new styling priorities: 'sexy, sexy, sexy'.[9] In fact, Opel delivers on both product quality and appealing design, but it remains one of GM's main concerns because of image problems.

The future of premium brands

Traditional industry wisdom – and established knowledge about how upward stretch can be accomplished – suggests that a real premium brand can only be created if all aspects of the offer and how it is communicated reflect premium qualities and are internally consistent (Parment, 2008; see also Kapferer, 2012). But given the situation in the industry at hand, the option to 'go premium' is likely to lose attractiveness as the traditional premium values will bring car makers to a very competitive segment where it's difficult to win. Established premium brands have an advantage over those who try, in a number of respects:

- It will always take time to build a brand that reflects real premium qualities, and creating a solid premium offer in the car industry requires a lot of resources and attention paid to strategic issues as well as details.

- Marketing channels are designed to reach the premium segment in terms of dealer location, showroom design, facilities standards, dealer training, etc.

- The higher prestige involved in working for a premium brand gives an advantage in terms of how great it is perceived to work there – hence, more qualified and premium-minded staff are likely to prefer working for the established premium brands.

On the other hand, newcomers may benefit from existing players being too content and satisfied, hence lacking the motivation to always become better, more customer-focused and more competitive. In terms of attracting staff, it may be an advantage to be seen as a fresh brand that is up and coming.

Where has Mondeo Man gone? Premium brands going mass market

If sales representatives two decades ago were happy to be driving a Ford Mondeo, a Chevrolet Malibu, an Opel Vectra or, even better, a Volkswagen Passat, a wide array of options now exist for sales reps since new cars have become cheaper since the 1990s. In addition, premium brands with high volume targets are increasingly approaching the mass market by lowering prices as well as by introducing less exclusive models. 'Premium is an attitude, not a size' is a statement often heard from premium car brands when the risk of going mass market is discussed, but there is little doubt that the combination of lower prices, higher volumes and less exclusive models make the premium brands less exclusive. However, given the challenges that auto brands face, the strategy to go mass market may prove to be the only reasonable way forward when the existence of the car is questioned, there is less interest in the car as a status symbol, there are high taxes, sustainability concerns, etc.

Company cars, sales rep cars and official cars are – with a few exceptions for top management – normally subject to strict limitations. The user may choose from a number of brands but not all, and there may be restrictions on the price of the car, the powertrain and factory options, to secure low emissions and high residuals. A key difference compared to a couple of years ago is that there is a lot more choice now. If two decades ago a Ford Mondeo or a basic Volkswagen Passat were on the list of permitted choices, it's now possible to select a BMW 3 Series, an Audi A4 or a fully loaded Opel/Vauxhall Insignia.

In Europe in particular, premium brands are going for the mass market. A comparison with the United States is interesting in this respect. The lowest spec Mercedes E Class car in the United States is the E350 with 302 bhp – in Europe it's the E200 CDI with 136 hp. The CLS starts with 250 CDI, 204 bhp, in Europe and in the United States the 550 with 402 bhp. The Volvo S60 starts with the 250 bhp T5 in the United States – in Europe with the 115 bhp D2.

Sweden is an interesting example of how local market conditions provide opportunities to gain market share. Tax authorities charge official car beneficiaries with low taxes on a basic spec car, but high taxes if the price of the car exceeds around SEK 334,000 (c. €38,000) for 2013; the threshold is adjusted for inflation. With the limited size of the market (c. 250,000 new cars sold in a year), 25 per cent VAT and a three-year warranty against damage included in the car price, along with heated seats and a more powerful heating system for Scandinavian winters included in all cars except a few budget models, prices could not be expected to be low. But heavy competition has forced premium car makers to move into the market below the tax threshold. A 2014 Mercedes E220 CDI with full LED lights, navigation and Park Assist, a BMW 328i Touring or a BMW 520d Touring, or an Audi A6 2.0 TDI Avant all come with a lot of extras and are available for SEK 330,000 or less. No premium car maker would like to end up in such a situation – but they'll have no choice when their competitors go for the mass market.

Buyers now expect to buy premium cars at attractive prices, and social acceptance has increased, or in other words, few people now turn their heads when they see a Caddy ATS, a BMW 114d or a Mercedes-Benz B200. At the same time as there is excessive competition in the premium segment, premium brands are going mass market. Something has changed with regard to the exclusiveness of premium brands and the profile of their buyers. When price premiums for premium auto brands are low, it gives employers an incentive to offer premium cars to their employees. As a dealer marketing manager put it: 'In the 1990s or around the turn of the millennium, if a medical rep would turn up at a health centre in a BMW, it was seen as inappropriate; now they're all driving Audis, BMWs and Mercedes-Benz. How come? I guess offering a great car is part of making the company an attractive employer.'

The traditional logic suggests premium products have two basic characteristics: being expensive and rare. As suggested by brand theorist Kapferer, price is a barrier for the mass market: 'BMW concerns only a minority of people: the happy few who are able or want to pay for its highly priced cars' (Kapferer, 2012: 18). But premium auto brands take market share and price premiums are going down. Even if the European market currently shows the strongest tendency to heavily discount premium brands, it will certainly reach other continents too, maybe with the exception of markets with very high taxes on luxury cars (eg Thailand, Norway and Australia).

To create a healthy balance between a focus on cost and on brand, it is important to consider what is relevant from the customer's point of view. A good dealer for a particular brand may not be a good dealer for another. For volume brands, a premium brand attitude may make customers feel uncomfortable while the lack of a premium attitude is likely to be perceived as a disadvantage from the premium customer's point of view. In general terms, raising the standards of retail facilities to a level not corresponding to the perceived image of the brand may not only make customers feel uncomfortable, but may also result in a competitive disadvantage for the dealer: direct competitors have lower requirements on facilities. This is not a problem in cases of downward stretch: a Porsche Macan buyer is likely to be happy with and even impressed by the exclusive showrooms and premium attitude of the dealership.

But premium brands that go mass market will face other problems: Porsche Macan buyers are inherently different from traditional 911 buyers. Porsche took one big step with the introduction of the Cayenne in 2003, a vehicle that was much cheaper, much more practical and much more mass market than other Porsche models offered at the time. The Macan is a further step in this direction, and it may be difficult to create a customer approach that appeals to the buyer of a low spec Macan and a Porsche 911 GT3 at the same time. Audi, BMW and Mercedes have long had the same problem: their A3 1.4, 114i and A140 cars are basically direct competitors of a Volkswagen Golf and a Toyota Arius – hence, the customer profile is very different from that of an A8, 6 series or GL buyer.

Again, we're back to the discussion on costs vs 'premiumness' or volume vs margin – while the marketing department works with strengthening the brand, improving margins and making sure all customer-facing areas reflect the soul of the brand, the sales manager – at the car maker, NSC or dealer level – will be busy coming up with creative ways of maintaining and increasing sales volume without destroying the attractiveness of the brand that has been built over several decades.

Beyond premium brands? Emerging values and consumer attitudes

For a number of years and since the late 1980s particularly, the characteristics of premium brands have been a guiding star for many car makers in their attempts to create successful product and market strategies. The advantages of premium brands are well-known – however, it's getting increasingly tight in the premium segment and success depends heavily upon product strategies and consumer brand perceptions.

The success of premium brands, eg BMW, Audi and Lexus, is convincing and many other car makers have tried to reach the same level of success. The driving forces are strong: premium brands enjoy substantial price premiums, something that increases margins not only for car makers but also for downstream marketing channel partners. Premium brands can hand pick their dealers since dealers often want to go upmarket. Customers are happy when they buy a premium brand and don't hesitate to pay rather high prices for maintenance and repairs. However, although supply-demand patterns for existing premium brands are convincing, it is unlikely that the premium segment will expand and flourish for ever. Given changes in the market and a more pronounced desire for value for money, buyers are likely to be less willing to pay for items and features that don't add value.

The next generation of car buyers will most likely buy cars that are sustainable, affordable, practical and convenient – but also deliver on design and emotional appeal. Hence, one may question whether the price premium of established premium brands can be maintained or if they will erode. When volume and even budget brands build appealing cars of good quality for a much lower price, and Baby Boomers get older and finally leave the market, it will be a great chance for brands that charge substantial price premiums but also deliver a substantially higher (emotional or functional) value. When high margins are invested in product development, unique combinations of convenience, sustainability, comfort and road performance will be greatly appreciated by future buyers. Premium brands will have to consider changes in the market, and among young buyers in particular, to be able to adjust.

Beyond 'premiumness' there is an opportunity for brands that aren't mainstream or traditional premium brands. There will always be a significant number of buyers who want something different. Saab was known for having architects, doctors, engineers, industrial designers, IT people and journalists as clients. They didn't want a mainstream premium brand that might be associated with newly-rich people who want to brag. The customer profile of Saab was a great asset but not enough to save the company. Beyond 'premiumness' there is a chance for companies like Jaguar, Volvo, Porsche and Alfa Romeo. They aren't mainstream, and they aren't cheap to own, but they have a coolness that appeals to a significant number of people – not to everybody, and that's the point of not being mainstream.

Another opportunity is to launch new brands, something that seldom happens in the car industry. Since the launch of Lexus and Infinity in 1989, and Tesla in 2003, few new brands have emerged and the car industry has experienced a reduction in the number of brands available. But why not launch new brands? As long as there is a strong car maker group in the background, the risks are limited. Just like Insignia, 1 Series and CLA are new names within the portfolio of an existing car maker, there may be a great chance of success for existing car manufacturers to launch new brands without a brand heritage – something that may hinder immediate success but also give opportunities to build the brand from scratch.

The auto brand portfolio

A portfolio approach is increasingly applied at the manufacturer and retail levels when it comes to auto brands – in both cases, a significant consolidation has taken place in recent years and all but a few car makers now rely on their portfolios rather than individual brands to stay viable and successful. Suzuki and Mazda are the only major car manufacturers that only use one brand – and BMW and Daimler/Mercedes-Benz still have the major part of their business coming from their core brands. The tendency is clear –

increasingly, car manufacturers merge and add sub-brands, as with BMW now complemented with Mini and Rolls-Royce, Renault with Dacia, Nissan with Infiniti, and Toyota with Lexus and Daihatsu.

Brand portfolios provide great opportunities to derive scale advantages in manufacturing while at the same time operating brands that have a different profile, hence reaching a broader variety of customer segments, price levels, lifestyles and images. The enormous values that brands represent make clear that what car manufacturers want when they acquire a brand may not be product and manufacturing knowledge and expertise, but rather the auto brand and its heritage, something that in the best case gives access to millions of buyers, lower marketing costs through automatic demand and free media exposure, easy recruitment of qualified employees and thousands of qualified dealers wanting to sell the products.

Notes

1 See case study on Audi's branding in Kotler *et al* (2011), Chapter 8.

2 BrandZ Top 100 Most Valuable Global Brands 2013, WPP: Millward Brown.

3 This is extensively discussed in the branding literature, see for example Dyson *et al* (1996), Kapferer (1997), Kay (1993) and King (1984).

4 BrandZ Top 100 Most Valuable Global Brands 2013, WPP: Millward Brown.

5 This practice is still applied for one of the Seat models: the Exeo, launched in 2008, is based on the Audi A4 B7 that was replaced a few months before the Exeo was introduced; the Volkswagen Group moved the factory equipment to Seat's plant in Martorell. Production of the Exeo ended in 2013 and the model has not been very successful – it never reached more than 23,000 cars produced in a year.

6 http://www.forbes.com/powerful-brands/list/, retrieved 6 July 2013.

7 See also chronicle with Bernd Ostmann, chief editor of German *auto motor & sport*, **14**, 2013, p 164.

8 Sources for the historical exposition: Parment (2009) *Automobile Marketing Distribution Strategies for Competiveness*, VDM Verlag; Interviews with premium car dealers in Germany 2002, various issues of *auto motor & sport*; Phillipp G Rosengarten and Christoph B Stürmer (2005) *Premium Power: Das Geheimnis des Erfolgs von Mercedes-Benz, BMW, Mercedes und Audi, 2. erweiterte und aktualisierte Aufgabe*, London: Wiley & Sons; *AutoBild*, 28 2010; Test Audi A8 4.2 FSI '*Limousine mit dezenter Eleganz*', *Motorbranchen*, various issues (1998–2002); Cremer and Schwartz, 2013.

9 *Automotive News*, 7 April 2003.

07 Sustainable business models

Car buyers will take advantage of increased market transparency and there appear to be few other ways to create sustainable profitability than to keep costs under strict control or deliver customer value through superior functionality or an emotional appeal reflected in a strong auto brand. Key to creating a business model that is sustainable is marketing intelligence. However, marketing intelligence is reactive: a problem at hand is defined and a research process is launched, with data collection, customer clinics, project and board meetings and, finally, a new product offer or approach is made – by which time the competitive situation has changed and again, reactive methods are applied to adjust the solution to the new market situation.

Car managers need to understand this problem along with influences on buyer behaviour such as demographic and geographic changes, consumer environmental concerns, popular culture, etc. This chapter provides tools and examples that illustrate how consumers and their attitudes are influenced by what happens in the environment and how these things can be used to develop more sustainable business models.

Many car makers place a very strong emphasis on sales and marketing. Afraid of being competitively disadvantaged, some major car makers spend 10 to 15 per cent of the car's retail price on marketing and advertising. Interestingly, there are other business models – extensively applied in other industries – that are more focused on product performance and customer value. When will car companies try a different business model? In this chapter, the obstacles that need to overcome are identified and discussed. It seems like the industry as a whole is so afraid of competitive disadvantages that nobody has the courage to do something different – a herd mentality that might reduce the industry's innovativeness and overall attraction to customers, staff, policymakers and other stakeholders.

Key dimensions of the business model are product portfolio and pricing. At the car maker level, established groups have broadened their brand and model portfolios – Toyota and Volkswagen are great examples here. Volkswagen offers cars from the €8,000 Up! to the €100,000+ Phaeton under its own brand, in addition to Skoda, Seat, Audi, Porsche or even Lamborghini and Bugatti. It's all about getting the balance right in making use of shared technologies to save costs while making sure cars of different brands have a unique profile. This is a very complex matter as it involves car maker strategies, marketing channels, branding decisions and complicated trade-offs between long-term brand building on the one hand and short-term profit maximization on the other. The shift in market power that is going on with an increasing share of purchasing power in BRIC countries and emerging economies emphasizes another important dimension in creating a sustainable business model that makes use of global market opportunities.

Sustainability – an absolute requirement in the future

There is, without doubt, a strong and growing demand for mobility in our world, something that makes serious ecological problems topical. Products and services flood into an increasing number of markets, and companies apply creative approaches to find new ways of persuading consumers to buy their products. A paradox lies in the benefit companies, their owners and employees derive from ever-increasing consumption – something that creates serious sustainability problems. Research has suggested a number of measures down the road to achieve sustainability: green product development (Ritzén, 2000), green marketing (Belz, 2001), changes in consumption patterns (Solér, 1996) and green accounting (Gray and Bebbington, 2001). There is a lot of knowledge about what needs to be done, and there are plenty of ideas about how a sustainable future could be achieved. However, there is a risk that the growth in population, mileage covered and consumption worldwide will eliminate the effects of all business, consumer and political attempts to reach sustainability.

There is little doubt that a company that succeeds in creating real sustainability will have an advantage in relation to buyers and other stakeholders in the future. And sustainability is largely related to design. Consider the BMW electric car i3 and the hybrid sports car i8; the great design these cars represent is a solution (or part of one) for sustainability concerns and at the same time a great achievement in integrating environmentally friendly cars and mobility needs.

State regulation and the industry's attitude

A core characteristic of a sustainable industry is its ability to adapt to new circumstances and see state regulation as a support, not a problem. Modern history shows many examples of how state regulation can improve not only society but also an industry's way of relating to society and its different stakeholders. When smoking bans were introduced in various countries (the first was in California in the late 1980s) a lot of concerns were raised about the adverse impact on restaurants, bars, etc. A few years after the ban was introduced few complained, and hardly anybody wanted smoking back – including smokers. In addition, restaurants did not experience any drop in demand but rather the opposite. Few people miss the days when smoking was allowed in trains, planes, theatres etc.

In the 1970s and 1980s most countries introduced laws on using seat belts, first in the front seats and later for back seat passengers. People in their early 40s can remember that 'My parents were very safety-oriented, but in the back seat of the car, we were playing, my brother lay on the floor while I was hiding' or, 'My parents were smoking all the time, they opened the windows, something that didn't really help since all the smoke was blown on us, and of course we didn't have safety belts since we were sitting in the back.' There is no debate now on the benefits of seat belts.

When catalytic converters were introduced in Europe in the mid-1980s, BMW made (again) a very smart move. There were a lot of complaints and worries about the effect of emissions reduction – and many car buyers argued loudly against the idea of reducing engine power while fuel consumption and maintenance would increase substantially. A limited set of regulations to reduce emissions were introduced in a few European countries (Switzerland and Sweden) in 1975, which reduced the engine's power substantially – for instance, the Mercedes 280 went from 160 to 140 bhp, and the 280 E with fuel injection from 185 to 156 bhp. Fuel consumption increased and car enthusiasts were negative – why would politicians want to infringe on their territory? History repeated itself in 1985 when catalytic converters were introduced in Europe (California had introduced them in the mid-1970s). The Mercedes 560 had 240 bhp instead of 300 and the Volvo 760 turbo 156 bhp instead of 182. Less power and higher fuel consumption weren't the only drawbacks – people worried about durability: there were concerns the catalytic converter would only last 60 to 80,000 kilometres (that was true in the case of some Ford models – apart from that, many converters from the 1980s are still in use and they aren't too expensive to replace) and the effectiveness of catalytic converters was questioned. In this climate, BMW introduced the new BMW 325i in 1986 with 171 bhp – a significant upgrade from the 323i with 143 bhp (only available without converter). The version with a catalytic converter had 170 bhp – it was a new construction and it turned the assumptions about converters destroying power upside-down. If buyers couldn't give up 30 or 50 horsepower for the sake of the environment, they could give up one!

An Australian professor involved in the development of catalytic converters tells how, contrary to popular belief, measurements showed no emissions when the converter was connected to the exhaust pipe: 'They thought the measuring instrument was broken, since there was no indication of emissions at all, but in actual fact, we were all impressed by the non-existing emissions. They could not even be measured with the instruments we used at the time.'[1] Today, nobody wants a world without catalytic converters.

Avoid focusing too much on customer satisfaction

'Our main focus for 2013 will be customer satisfaction! If we reach higher CSI scores, we'll get everything else. All our priorities for the next year will be based on reaching higher customer satisfaction.' This was said by the CEO of a large dealer group in a top management training session in September 2012.

A key challenge for many auto brands is, no matter how counterintuitive it may sound, an overemphasis on customer satisfaction. There are a number of potentially grave problems associated with measuring customer satisfaction. First of all, and maybe most important, it irritates customers. A premium car buyer called the dealership when the sixth survey in a year arrived and yelled at the salesperson: 'I've told you five times that I'm happy, what's the problem?' It's a sign of poor cooperation in the marketing channel when six surveys arrive in a year. The first survey was a purchase survey, the second a delivery survey – both are tools for the NSC to check whether the sales process and the delivery of the car, respectively, followed the car maker's guidelines. The third was an image survey from the car maker, to track progress in how buyers experience the brand. The fourth was sent by the repair shop to measure customer satisfaction from the first inspection. The fifth and sixth surveys were identical – both measuring the overall experience of the first year with the new car. But why two identical surveys? One comes from the NSC and is used to judge the performance of the dealership; the results are very important to the dealer, so it decided to send an identical survey in advance to see what would come up in the forthcoming NSC evaluation. There is a significant likelihood that the result will be slightly different in the last one. How come?

Surveys in general are time-consuming to fill in – and why should a customer, who paid, say, US$50,000 for a new car, spend his or her valuable time on filling in numerous surveys with detailed questions about the car? In 2011, before an initiative was taken to make the questionnaire easier to complete, a Volvo buyer was asked to fill in eight pages of detailed questions, eg on the ranking of the Volvo from 0 to 10 compared to two other products the car buyer considered buying. The quality of the results was far from satisfactory – how can an average car buyer give a detailed appraisal and comparison of hundreds of characteristics of a car that at best was test-driven for 25 minutes?

Research proves that in customer surveys, satisfied customers are over-represented (Söderlund, 1998) and customers who don't complain evince a higher likelihood of changing provider (Fornell and Didow, 1980; Fornell and Wernerfelt, 1987; Peterson and Wilson, 1992). In addition, a customer tends to state a higher level of satisfaction in a face-to-face situation with the interviewer compared to a survey study (LeVois et al, 1981; Parment and Söderlund, 2010; Sudman, 1967). Survey studies tend to activate customers' critical thinking – and critical views are found to be more specific and thought-through than positive criticism (Ofir and Simonson, 2001).

A major problem with surveys is that customers uncover problems when they fill them in. Assume you have spent a weekend in a great spahotel in the countryside. You're very happy and your friends are a little envious since they've been working all weekend. When they ask you about it, satisfaction tends to go up: they generally raise questions with a positive orientation: 'How was the spa?', 'What about the dinner?', 'I've heard the views are awesome – did you like it?' etc. When you get the survey, there are 128 detailed questions with a negative orientation: 'Did the cleanliness of the room live up to your expectations?', 'Were all the TV channels you expected offered?', 'Did you get information on how to connect to the Wi-Fi by code?', 'How long did you have to wait in reception?' It would be surprising if you don't identify a couple of things that didn't live up to your high expectations, since you paid a lot of money to go there.

The same experience will be true of car buyers. The fact that asking too much and too often irritates customers and reduces customer satisfaction is proven in several studies. Does this mean customer satisfaction should not be measured at all? No, but it should be in reasonable balance with the customer's engagement. Let's take an insurance company as an example:

- A potential customer is invited to fill in a survey on the first time he or she visits the website. Don't!

- An existing customer contacts the call centre to ask for a four-digit code for log in purposes. 'We'll track your call for training purposes' and, 'You'll get 10 per cent discount on your boat insurance if you buy a fire extinguisher' are played in the background while the customer is waiting. After the 20-second call is ended (it's a very easy issue to solve) a telemarketing company calls the customer to ask questions about the service provided. Don't! And by the way, only a very small percentage of the customers will have a boat (and those that do tend to have facility managers that take care of such things).

- A loyal client contacts the call centre and raises a specific technical question on an insured machine. The client is important for the insurance company in terms of lifetime value and the customer's feedback, both in the discussion with the technician and the evaluation of how useful the information was, is important. Sending a survey makes sense.

- A client has a fire at his house and the process of identifying the condition of the property is difficult. Restoration takes a couple of months and includes dealing with decisions that have an affective dimension. A relatively extensive evaluation makes sense.

Asking too much and too often is costly, can give rise to uncertainty and doesn't deal with the problem that only existing customers give feedback. For product development purposes, marketing research has limitations since it normally means asking customers who are within existing categories. It may be useful for incremental developments, but to come up with something that is really innovative it's crucial to have the courage and competence to think beyond existing categories. Companies that have succeeded in this respect – Amazon, Benetton, Body Shop, Club Med, Dell, FedEx, Ikea, Sony, Swatch and Virgin to mention a few – have applied a market-driving approach. In other words, if they had listened intensively to existing buyers within defined markets, their innovative approaches might never have come about. Paying too much attention to customers' ideas may even reduce innovation and result in failure in the market, as has been proven in studies (see Christensen and Bower, 1996). Businesses in general should therefore think about the opportunity to look beyond the ongoing discussion in their industry regarding buyer preferences and desired product features.[2]

Measuring customer satisfaction and the match between pre- and post-purchase expectations and experiences has a number of well-known advantages. It may be used internally as a vehicle to measure the performance of marketing channel members in general and dealers in particular, even at salesperson level, and it puts pressure on dealers and employees to perform – it's a proactive measure since people know their performance is going to be measured. It can also be used for marketing purposes: high CSI figures give general confidence in the brand and convince buyers that they've made the right purchase decision. From a general market standpoint, it's likely to improve quality as customers can compare figures – nowhere as easily as in the case of hotel bookings. All hotels on Trip Advisor, booking.com, hotels.com etc are user ranked.

However, considering these characteristics and advantages, measuring customer satisfaction must be done carefully, for a number of reasons:

- Even though questions may be thought-through and well-formulated, there is a strong spill-over effect across questions. Opinions about the salesperson will be influenced by the location and opening hours of the dealership: if they are attractive, the buyer will have a more positive attitude towards the salesperson. Responses are strongly influenced by external factors, too. Conditions like the weather, if it's a workday or weekend, time of day, etc have an impact. In addition, extensive surveys are less likely to be answered and the answers get shorter the later they come in the survey form.[3]

- Moreover, it's proven that the more questions are raised, the lower the customer satisfaction. The reason is simple: questionnaires are often extensive and have a negative orientation since they are run to measure quality. Hence, the more a buyer answers the questions, the more negative experiences will be discovered. A buyer may not have thought about the function of the radio, the power of the headlights, the condition of workshops, or the wind noise of the car – but the survey raises questions about these, or other areas, and the buyer may identify negative aspects.

- As the car is a very emotional item – and expensive, too, for most people – buyers cannot be expected to answer surveys in a strictly rational manner. Things that irritate buyers will be manifested in survey answers.

- Customers have very different expectations. It's like hotels. It's possible to divide hotel evaluations on booking sites based on the family situation of hotel guests who have answered a survey. But it's not possible to divide hotel evaluations based on the expectations of the hotel guests. One guest at a four star all-inclusive resort in Greece may be on his or her first vacation abroad – another guest may be an experienced business traveller with gold and platinum cards in the Marriott, Hilton or Radisson. The former guest may be overwhelmed by the breakfast buffet or flowers in the room upon arrival – the latter blasé about the benefits that experienced business travellers get. The very same customer treatment (in reality, it varies with customer response and many other factors) may result in very different evaluations. The same holds in the car industry: a Chevy or Kia customer in general has lower expectations than the Audi or Caddy customer. Complaints on wind noise over 100 mph would not come up for budget brands but could do so for premium car buyers.

- Customer satisfaction is measured at a particular point in time and the results give limited information about how things could improve. In general terms, customer satisfaction gets lower as time passes and the memories of the purchase situation become blurred (Parment and Söderlund, 2010).

- It can rise to uncertainty – a buyer has paid an awful lot of money for a very expensive and attractive car (or other product), and the seller and others want to track every single part of the purchase experience. 'What's wrong? I'm happy with the car, why do you have to ask me all the time?'

- Focusing heavily on CSI measurement results in conformity – all car makers identify similar reasons for customer satisfaction (or its lack) and implement similar measures. This gives room for new entrants in the industry that apply a different approach! Apple shook the computer world – and later the world beyond computers – with innovative products that leading companies in the industry didn't even think about.

Major international companies like Apple, Microsoft, Coca-Cola, IBM, Google, Intel, McDonald's, General Electric, BMW and Cisco use surveys to a limited extent, and less than many other less successful companies. They know they're good and don't need to track consumer perceptions all the time. They use other methods for tracking what consumers think, eg indicators of business performance (margins, product mix, demand patterns), automatic feedback from websites, product support, scanners in store, etc and selections of customers for focus groups and experiments. There is no general best way of doing it, and different companies work differently with these issues. But over-use of customer surveys appears to create more disadvantages than advantages, although it is difficult to convince the CRM department about this – to them, more data is an advantage. But more data also means the company's customers have to spend more time on something that is likely to lower their satisfaction.

Satisfaction, in general terms, means that somebody is, in a rational way, satisfied with the performance of a product or service delivered. But there are other emotional states that may make more sense from the perspective of an auto manufacturer wanting to strengthen its brand. What about happiness, excitement, surprise and attractiveness? These words have a positive connotation and suggest 'energizing', while satisfaction certainly has a positive connotation but also suggests a reduction in the level of energy (Parment and Söderlund, 2010).

The assumption that emotional expressions of car ownership generate a different result than traditional customer satisfaction measures has been proven in a study by AutoIndex[4] on buyer satisfaction vs buyer loyalty vs buyer pleasure (see Table 7.1). The study came up with some interesting findings. Satisfaction was defined as satisfaction with the brand; loyalty as the extent to which the car owner would recommend the brand to others; pleasure as the level of pleasure the car gives in everyday life.

TABLE 7.1   Buyer satisfaction, buyer loyalty, and buyer pleasure may give very different results in asking car owners

Satisfaction	Loyalty	Pleasure
Subaru	Lexus	Mini
Lexus	Subaru	Lexus
Mini	BMW	Subaru
BMW	Mini	Honda

TABLE 7.1   *Continued*

Satisfaction	Loyalty	Pleasure
Mercedes	Mercedes	BMW
Honda	Toyota	Mercedes
Audi	Honda	Mazda
Hyundai	Audi	Mitsubishi
Toyota	Volvo	Saab
Skoda	Mazda	Citroën
Saab	Volkswagen	Volvo
Nissan	Mitsubishi	Audi
Mazda	Skoda	Skoda
Suzuki	Kia	Toyota
Volvo	Nissan	Suzuki
Fiat	Citroën	Volkswagen
Kia	Hyundai	Hyundai
Mitsubishi	Suzuki	Nissan
Volkswagen	Ford	Fiat
Renault	Peugeot	Peugeot
Citroën	Seat	Kia
Seat	Opel	Opel
Opel	Renault	Renault
Ford	Fiat	Ford
Peugeot	Saab	Seat
Chevrolet	Chevrolet	Chevrolet

Again, there is a strong overlap between the three categories, which should be no surprise. But the result is nonetheless interesting. The most striking example is Saab, a General Motors brand that closed down sales in 2012. Saab owners are above average in terms of the pleasure the car gives, they are slightly more satisfied than average but they are not loyal since it's unclear whether it will be possible to buy Saabs in the future (most likely not!)

It is crucial that car makers and dealers understand these problems with customer satisfaction surveys as they attempt to develop their competitiveness for the future. Some brands have a 'precision' look – eg Audi – so even though quality is good, design is appealing, etc there is a risk that the perfectionism and avant-gardism associated with the Audi brand, which is appealing to many car buyers today, will have less appeal to the next generation of buyers.

Status issues

Many dealerships have problems that go back to management, history and social hierarchies: for instance selling is seen as a more prestigious job than working in the after-sales area. Some measures have been taken to reduce this problem. But the after sales-business is more profitable than sales – even if the questionable practice of charging market prices for transactions between departments is applied by many dealerships – so why is the status of the former lower? First of all, without car sales there will be no demand for after-sales; on the other hand, if after-sales doesn't work well, loyalty will go down. Second, increasing competition in after-sales may reduce their profitability advantage. Third, it's not really correct to state that after-sales is more profitable than selling if market pricing is used internally: charging market prices for in-house transactions tends to move profits from the car sales department to the after-sales department.[5]

Dealerships may apply desperate strategies to promote after-salespeople. A Swedish Volvo dealer printed visiting cards with a salesman in a tie on one side, and a mechanic in an overall on the other. First of all, because of the way they dress and the salesman being much more comfortable being photographed, the visiting card didn't really give the impression of a level playing field among salespeople and mechanics. Second, is it really smart to inform a potential client that she or he will have to see a mechanic soon? If it is a person you'll not see often, then there would be no need to advertise him at this stage.

The idea of having a 'personal service technician' – a common practice – may be questioned. Contacts and discussions with clients take a lot of time, and there is a risk that a person who is more qualified socially will be perceived as doing a better job as a personal service technician than somebody who is not very

A strong brand will increase the attractiveness of all positions in the car company. For instance, selling cars to buyers on Bond Street in central London will add prestige to the job of car salesman. (Anders Parment, 2 July 2013, Bond Street, London)

sociable but a great car mechanic. In the long run, this development is not good for the reputation of the mechanic. On the other hand, a mechanic may have an advantage when it comes to selling additional services to the client through better mechanical knowledge and a customer will hardly question a mechanic's advice. This sales opportunity, however, is heavily underutilized.

By creating a strong auto brand, the attractiveness of all positions within the organization, and among partners, gets stronger. As a Sydney Mercedes-Benz dealer operating in an area with high socioeconomic standards said: 'Traditionally, a car salesman was not an occupation that was viewed very highly, but I think there is a difference if you say to someone "I'm a car salesman", or if you say "I'm a MB sales person." The product brings certain standards to the occupation.' This will also apply to mechanics, or any other position.

Successful marketing communications

The phrase 'The medium is the message', coined by Marshall McLuhan, is often referred to but may now be questioned. It could be argued that the message is now the medium because of several contemporaneous developments, including: the advent of social media, the rapid and wide dissemination of information, and the emergence and development of CRM systems.

It's getting increasingly difficult to get through with marketing communications. There are more industries that engage in advertising than ever before, and people are tired of companies persistently attempting to communicate. Combining traditional and emerging channels, like in this Open University ad, while referring to real experiences of customers (students) appears to be a proactive, clever and efficient way of communicating. This ad calls for interactivity, is published in a traditional channel and makes use of users' desire to share their experiences of the Open University. (Anders Parment, 2 July 2013, Oxford Street, London)

Traditional media still have authority, and the more digital media is used the more difficult it may be to get through unless one is very innovative. The car industry, however, is not known for its fast transition into the new. Social media opinions can be harsh and the best way of dealing with adverse messages may not be to sanitize them, but to respond appropriately and use the opinions to improve products and communications.

Thanks to computerized CRM systems, it's now possible to approach customers as individuals, not demographics. Salespeople who can instantly access a customer's buying history and preferences can respond more personally. Communication can be more individualized. A customer spending an average amount of money over time might receive a personalized thank you, while a higher-spending customer might receive an invitation to a special event. The data-driven ability to understand and respond to customers individually crosses most categories. For instance, insurers have often focused more on acquiring new customers than on introducing more products to existing customers. With the ability to quickly analyse data, insurers can anticipate when a home insurance customer may be ready for additional products.

One-stop shopping – a competitive advantage in transparent markets?

A key strategic dimension of after-sales is the development of one-stop shopping vs car buyers looking around to find the best deal. It's hard to say which is more likely or stronger, and will vary with customer profile, brand strength, competition in different areas, etc.

One-stop shopping means the dealership (or another company) provides the car owner with everything he or she needs for car ownership: finance, insurance, tyre storage, spot repair, car wash, rental car, etc – the needs may vary among brands, customer segments and geographical areas. Shopping around means that the buyer will look for the best deal for every single aspect of owning and maintaining a car. Where are brake pads cheapest and where can I get the cheapest insurance? The industry's response is to offer bundled products, for example the roadside assistance offered with most new cars could last for a further 18 months after an inspection in the authorized repair shop.

Internet auction websites that offer reduced prices for car repairs are a threat to existing actors in the industry. German car magazine *AutoBild* tried a website called MyHammer.de and found that a repair of a Mercedes-Benz 190 E would cost €1,684 in the local Mercedes-Benz workshop, €1,086 in a unauthorized repair shop and €751 in a bid provided by the MyHammer.de website. The bidder, an authorized Nissan dealer, says it's a good way to use its free capacity (Rosin, 2012).

In offering one-stop shopping it is most likely that, as in any well-functioning market, different strategic options may be successful. Companies – dealers or others – that take care of all aspects of car ownership, including finance, insurance, inspection scheduling, risk taking for resale value, damage to paintwork, etc may derive competitive advantages from their business models if they provide excellent service, make life easy, reduce risks for the car owner, and create a great package at a reasonable price. By spreading the risks over many customers, services of great significance for the customer but little cost and risk for the provider might be offered.

In a market where customers expect fast service and low prices, increased transparency makes it hard to charge high prices. It is, for most auto brands, difficult to add value that justifies very high prices for maintenance and repairs. It's not like restaurants where people may be willing to pay more for location, the social setting, interior design or, of course, great service and tasty, locally produced, nice looking food. There are several reasons for this development. First, services that come with car ownership are low-involvement products. Second, the legal protection for authorized dealers has been reduced and, particularly in the European Union, authorities have opened up servicing to competition. Third, there is more legal protection for private buyers, something that to an extent spills over to B2B buyers.

The Market Court in Sweden operates under the competitive legislation framework set by the European Union. Two judgements recently emphasized how difficult it is for car makers to gain an advantage in the market by attempting to create protection from competition, thus reducing the impact of market mechanisms.

Korean car maker Kia offered a seven-year warranty in Sweden, conditioned by inspections and repairs being done at authorized Kia dealers. The Market Court, however, gave a thumbs down to this rule and forced Kia to offer the warranty without any restrictions on car owners that inspect and repair their cars through companies not authorized by Kia. The case was brought by suppliers of spare parts (eg Bosch and free-standing repair shops) whose market was undermined by the Kia warranty since they ran the risk of not having a market for their products in the first seven years of a Kia car's lifecycle.

In a similar manner, Mercedes introduced a very generous 30-year warranty against corrosion in 2004, at least in part in response to extensive rust problems in the 1990s and beyond. The warranty is only valid if the car is inspected according to the inspection scheme at an authorized repair shop. While a substantial number of cars are still inspected at the authorized repair shop at seven years of age, it is unlikely that cars, with the exception of very expensive ones, will still be inspected by authorized dealers after 30 years. As it seems, Mercedes-Benz legally get away with not delivering on the warranty unless the car is inspected at an authorized repair shop.

With the introduction of the new Mazda 6 in early 2013, Mazda has announced a 10-year warranty in several markets for cars that are inspected in Mazda repair shops or by other qualified repair shops. In addition, spare parts used have to be of original Mazda quality or better. This openness to free-standing repair shops is a result of increased consumer protection, not generosity per se towards competitors of the original workshops.

Greater transparency and market forces make it more difficult to sell services that are expensive but don't add substantially more value than cheaper competing services. Another reason is changes in buyer attitudes and behaviour. At the same time as buyers have become more proactive, cars have become more complex and difficult to repair or maintain. Unauthorized repair shops may not have the competence or skills required to carry out all types of repairs – or they are large, multi-brand operations with high marketing costs. Since the authorized repair shop is the natural choice for new car buyers, the unauthorized have to engage heavily in marketing to reach car buyers. On the other hand, fewer manufacturer groups and more cooperation among car makers makes clear that in many instances, supported by competition laws, it may be easier to run a multi-franchised workshop in the future. If the gearbox, satellite navigation system, air conditioning system and headlights for a range of brands are produced in the same factory, lengthy training for each auto brand may not be necessary.

All this doesn't mean it makes no sense to take a car to an authorized repair shop. Around the turn of the millennium, price competition on new cars was fierce but other parts of the dealer's business – repairs, maintenance, finance, etc – were often highly profitable. This is unlikely to happen again. What transparency does to this industry is striking: it gives large actors an advantage through the way car buyers and users talk about them on websites and gives greater access to profound knowledge about product choices and experiences for buyers.

Reducing the impact of transparency – product bundling

If we look at other industries, managing the client relationship is key to success. Retailers with a good customer base, great locations and a lot of market power in relation to their suppliers can use that power to lower procurement costs while building a strong brand and gaining high margins from their retail businesses. This to an extent happens with weak or medium auto brands sold in multi-franchised retail environments.

What can the manufacturer do to take advantage of this difficult situation? Product bundling may be the solution: if the car buyer signs up for car insurance, the first year's tyre storage will be free. If the car is inspected once a year at the authorized workshop, one year's free roadside assistance will be included. Taking out car finance means discounts on fuel or inspections – in this way, the relationship between the dealer and the client gets stronger and more multi-faceted, and the car owner has fewer reasons to look elsewhere for a better deal.

Small-scale or large-scale advantages

Companies in all industries, markets and situations show a strong tendency to become narrow-minded and myopic.[6] This also applies to car dealers and, in order to stay viable and develop the business, it's very important to identify the strengths of the business and how they can be developed for the future. There is, in general terms, a risk that small operations will close down while big, international retail groups will grow. Economies of scale are extensive; this applies not only at the car maker level but also increasingly to insurance, finance, retailing, repairs and other areas.

It is not only large operations that have the opportunity to develop competitive advantages – small-scale operations might derive a variety of benefits: direct customer relationships; an overlap of professional and social networks with anchorage in local society; the repair shop is more flexible on administration and working hours; trade-in cars could be dealt with in a more flexible way; and used cars could be sold based on an individual rather than a principles-based approach. (Anders Parment, 1 March 2009, 34th Street, New York)

However, customers get tired of standardized solutions – this is an opportunity for small-scale operations – and operating on a small scale certainly has some advantages. Customers are different – an underexplored and often over-looked profit opportunity. There are customers who prefer small, family-run dealerships while others prefer to be anonymous clients of larger operations. Some customers prefer multi-franchised operations while others prefer the exclusive profile and strong product knowledge of solus dealers. Some customers love dealing with local entrepreneurs, while others enjoy the solid manufacturer support from a dealership owned by a car maker.

In retailing, small-scale advantages are derived from more direct customer relationships. An overlap of professional and social networks means a car salesperson or other dealer employee is also part of local society; the repair shop can be more flexible with administration and working hours; trade-in cars can be dealt with in a more flexible way; and used cars can be sold on an individual basis. There are disadvantages, though, mirroring the advantages of large-scale operations. A large repair shop could have specialists for transmission issues, fuel injection systems, spot repairs, electronics, etc. Used cars could be dealt with on a 'principles' basis, meaning potential 'lemons' could be dealt with more efficiently. And the risk that the dealer gets emotionally connected to a used car is lower.

So there are plenty of arguments on both sides. A Sydney multi-franchised dealer selling almost 20 brands praises the efficiency advantages of its multi-franchised repair shop; rural German dealers say their clients come from the big cities to enjoy 'being somebody, not just a number in the system'. At the same time, some clients may prefer being a number in the system to dealing with a local business where the client contact is less anonymous.

Methods for dealing with high customer demands while keeping costs down

Every business has to deal with a simultaneous pressure to reduce costs while keeping customers happy. A computer may be bought from a zealous salesperson working in a very lean organization on the basis of the lowest bid, with a poor service level as a consequence. A hotel may outsource any activity to low-cost providers while working intensively with customer relationship management. A car maker, in cooperation with its NSCs, may outsource roadside assistance, the customer call centre and key sales activities to third-party providers while spending enormous amounts of money on building customer relationships.

One way of dealing with this pressure is to create a dichotomy between apparent and non-apparent areas and activities through putting activities that do not directly involve customer contacts into one category – cost-efficiency; and the customer-facing activities into another – image and appearance. Categorizing activities based on whether they involve direct customer interaction or not has important implications for how the activities should be performed to accomplish efficiency and customer satisfaction simultaneously. In principle, activities involving customer interaction should be carried out with the goal of communicating values and delivering a brand-specific experience while activities not involving customer interaction should aim at being as efficient as possible. If this issue is managed well, a certain degree of purposeful brand communication and low-cost distribution could be accomplished simultaneously. The main emphasis may vary according to brand and whether cost-efficiency or brand considerations are the primary goal of the distribution strategy.

What does the customer see? Brand separation to sharpen the brand image

An implication of the simultaneous emphasis on costs and brands is the search for synergies in non-customer-facing areas. The platform strategies in car manufacturing mirror this dichotomy between what is seen and what is not. At the retail level, brand separation has a similar effect. Sharpening the image of different brands through separated showrooms while saving money in back-office functions is, at least in theory, a smart strategy. However, it is crucial to make sure that the attitudes conveyed through the unseen areas such as dealer communication do not contradict the intended brand values.

The impact of the non-apparent on attitudes conveyed

Measures to control the brand appearance throughout the marketing channel are normally extensive, and they may create attitudes that promote or contradict the brand image conveyed. There is a hidden dimension to branding which is essential to the understanding of how competitive advantages are created and maintained. Also, areas that are not apparent to the customer strongly influence his or her perception (Birkigt et al, 1992; Parment, 2008). That is, people pay attention to the invisible parts of the communication. To create a genuine brand image, a firm should not be a functionalistic entity to which some elements of brand image are added: the brand image must be based on a consistent focus on the brand content along with smooth and harmonious relations in all areas of the business. For example, poor relations between car makers and dealers are likely to spill over to the customer's experience and thus undermine the brand experience. An unhappy dealer may not present himself, the products and the brand/s he represents in the best manner, since there is no genuine commitment to and identification with the brand. Although corporate identity programmes may be well implemented, harmful attitudes will have a strong negative impact on perceptions of the brand.

Successful dealer business models

There are two primary factors that determine whether a dealership will stay viable and profitable over time: the brands represented and the terms offered by the car maker. Market forces largely make sure that over time, great dealers get great brands to sell and vice versa. Hence, a weak brand has to compensate for lack of attractiveness by offering great terms.

The quality of the dealer network is in general terms not as decisive as the product but is still crucial to customer satisfaction, market coverage, sales figures and the extent to which the car maker gets the desired customer profile – it's crucial for an auto brand to get the desired customers, not just (as has been the traditional approach in marketing) to get lots of customers. In the UK, for instance, Skoda's great dealer network has contributed to making some of the press as well as customers choose Skodas over Volkswagen cars. According to *Auto Express*: 'The [Volkswagen] Up! is almost identical to the Citigo, but is slightly more expensive and lacks the assurance of Skoda's award-winning dealer network'.[7]

After investigating close to 100 car dealerships in different countries, a pattern emerges: successful dealers are proactive and take opportunities that competitors don't take. A proactive, entrepreneurial attitude and running the dealership based on a mixture of principles, closeness to the market and gut feeling are all key.

Finding the relevant service level

In the past, marketing wisdom suggested, more or less, giving the customer whatever he or she wanted and always aiming to over-deliver – that was, it was argued, the basis of making customers satisfied. Things have changed, though, and customers are now more aware and informed and they use all sorts of tools to make good deals. It is becoming increasingly difficult to over-deliver – how can a company over-deliver when the customer satisfaction figures are good and expectations higher than ever? It's still just about possible to over-deliver but the more companies try to do so, the higher expectations become. For instance, German buyers of the Volvo V60 D6 plug-in hybrid get membership in the Ambassador's Programme. If there is a problem with the car Volvo pays for upmarket hotel stays (up to €200 a night) and a Business Class flight back home. If this becomes the norm, what next?

Incentive systems

The extent to which people are influenced by financial incentives varies substantially across industries. A group of professions that stands out includes salespeople, brokers and insurance advisers (who are, in fact, salespeople). They are strongly driven by incentives and their behaviour could actually be controlled by applying bonuses, performance-based remuneration and other benefits. A common practice in car finance in some markets is to offer car salespeople a free overseas trip with a stay in a luxury hotel for five days or a week if sales targets are reached. It might be called a 'sales conference' but there aren't any substantial seminars or speeches. This type of benefit is frowned upon by tax authorities, so it's not really sustainable. It shows, however, the creativity that comes out of two truly incentive-driven professions working together: car finance salespeople and car salespeople.

Three factors suggest this behaviour is less likely in the future. First, increasing market transparency makes it easier for buyers to compare financial offers, and undertaking comparisons is getting more common. Second, CSR policies and sustainability ambitions will make top management of dealers, and large dealer groups in particular, more aware of this type of practice, which may mean non-salary remuneration for salespeople at the cost of dealership profitability. Third, regulation by authorities increasingly targets the finance sector and may make some schemes difficult to run. In the short run, incentives are always a good way to boost sales and market share, but may harm sustainability from a social and financial perspective.

Internally and externally consistent incentive systems

Many dealerships apply incentive systems that lead to salespeople boosting short-term sales. The only criterion in many cases is volume; measures to improve customer retention, secure quality during the purchase process, stimulate sales of additional services that might contribute to showroom traffic and future demand are not considered.

Car makers have long implemented margin systems that incentivize dealers to work with the purchase process, salespeople training, product demonstration etc. The problem essentially is, however, that many dealers have not translated the way they are being evaluated and rewarded by car makers into their business models and internal incentive systems. Staying profitable is easier when the incentive structure of an organization, ie the dealer in this case, reflects how the business earns its money, ie to a high extent from the car maker. If the car maker has developed a more sophisticated incentive system to move away from a short-term sales volume orientation, there is little reason for the dealer not to implement a similar approach to internal incentives. The only reason it doesn't happen is inertia or lack of understanding and a negative attitude towards car makers and their attempts to control dealers. The latter might be understandable, but in general terms, car makers are emphasizing the right things in developing margin systems. And dealers have a certain degree of freedom in applying the ideas in their local markets.

Securing quality: workshop issues

In recent years the quality of services provided by car dealers has improved significantly. Nice showrooms, clean toilets and other aspects of facility standards have improved significantly, and customers are treated much better. Policies for good customer treatment are common and the impression a customer will get when visiting a car dealer is generally good.

However, when it comes to the quality of the services provided in workshops, there is still room for improvement. German *auto motor & sport* has run 1,200 workshop tests since 1984. Workshops have been judged on the percentage of pre-prepared faults repaired, how the customer is approached, waiting time, pricing, proper invoices, etc. In 2004, 66 per cent of the faults were repaired, in 2013 62 per cent.[8] Regardless of the explanations provided by the dealerships, a customer paying typically €150–200 an hour could expect this result to be close to 100 per cent – a mechanic strictly following the rules would reach 100 per cent or occasionally slightly less (everyone can have a poor day). Aeroplane mechanics repairing 62 per cent of faults would get fired immediately! Excuses such as, 'The manager was sick' or, 'Unfortunately, you came during our busy period' don't really help workshop customers.

One could always argue that pre-prepared faults do not reflect the real conditions of a typical fleet of cars. For instance, the spare wheel is very seldom used – in many cases not during the entire life of a car – so the risk a customer will discover air pressure not being checked is minimal. Nonetheless, it's included in the inspection schedule and it may constitute a danger if the owner has to put the spare wheel on the car, or an accident occurs because of low tyre pressure.

Authorized vs unauthorized workshops

Until around the turn of the millennium – this varies significantly across countries – the competition from unauthorized workshops was limited for newer cars (up to five to seven years of age) and authorized workshops could charge high prices, compensating for the low margins on new cars. Later, and in EU countries when the Block Exemption changed in 2002, unauthorized workshops gained power, merged, consolidated and offered free-standing smaller workshops the opportunity, for a fee, to become franchisees. High costs for branding, marketing and business development for unauthorized workshops on the one hand, and more competitive offers from authorized workshops on the other, have decreased the price gap between authorized and unauthorized workshops.[9] In *auto motor & sport's* 2013 test, the free-standing ATU workshop was actually found to be more expensive than the authorized Kia workshops, and free-standing workshops performed worse than the average authorized workshops for all the brands in the magazine's test: Audi, BMW, Kia, Opel and Skoda.

Authorized workshops have several advantages over unauthorized workshops. Costs for mechanic training and technical support – which may have a similar price tag as for unauthorized workshops due to legislation – may be high, but are still part of a broader business relationship with the car maker. Warranty repairs may contribute to overall profitability – although workshops would not agree because of extensive administrative costs and discounts given to the NSC/car maker for warranty repairs. Customer workshop visits mean a visit to the dealership, hence products and services can be marketed – the customer may wait for the car while it's in the workshop and meanwhile inspect or test drive a new car. One-stop shopping means an advantage to the buyer and according to our data, a significant proportion of buyers – about two-thirds – are willing to pay more for the higher service level offered. Last, but not least, product bundling means car buyers buy more services from the dealership. For instance, the yearly inspection at an authorized workshop may result in 12 months' free roadside assistance, or discounts on insurance. Financing the car at the dealership may give free or discounted tyre storage, etc.

The car industry: a great place to work?

Generation Y individuals will change jobs more often and have a more positive attitude towards starting a new venture. Their career strategies are more focused on self-realization and staying competitive in the labour market than on a commitment to one firm, which was a strong preference among Baby Boomers (individuals born in the 1940s and 1950s) and also a significant part of Generation X (born in the 1960s and 1970s) (Parment, 2011a). A manufacturer CEO said: 'From the customer's point of view, one of the key points in retailing is to always have standard processes. So when the customer goes to a dealership, any dealership, they get handled properly, every time.' By putting this argument, it's also said that principles and customer processes secure high quality at the dealership level. That's only part of the truth – dealers also need great people who can deal with clients in a professional manner, create a great culture and warm atmosphere, be business-minded and, when it's appropriate, go the extra mile to meet and exceed customer expectations.

The car industry has therefore to put a lot of effort into being a great place to work. Following the decreasing attractiveness of cars over time, extensively discussed in this book, and the progress many other industries have achieved in being attractive to great talent, it's pressing that car companies work harder to make sure they attract the best. It will be an absolute necessity to have employees with a strong interest in societal developments, politics, popular culture, buyer behaviour and emerging technologies. Reactive individuals who long for 'the good old days' are something that car makers, NSCs and dealers can ill afford.

Translating good ideas into action: a difficult path

In a broad sense, there are a lot of things that car makers and retailers should reconsider in order to stay competitive. For instance, the industry's strong focus on customer satisfaction has a number of drawbacks: it irritates customers when companies ask them too much and too often, it is costly, it gives biased market feedback, it makes customers notice deficits they hadn't thought about until they filled in the survey, and it gives car dealers and salesmen an impression of not believing in what they are selling. Moreover, satisfaction is not something that creates sales these days – while happy, engaged and excited customers would. Unfortunately, many car makers are stuck in strategies that effectively eliminate those desirable emotional states to get through to customers. A number of misapprehensions about how customers think and act will be put forward, for instance: 'Don't push the customer too hard, you will turn them off' – something that is contrary to research and industry evidence. Good salespeople know how to treat customers and when it's time to put some pressure on them to make a purchase decision.

Notes

1 Interviewed at the Fachhochschule Vorarlberg, Dornbirn.

2 See Jaworski *et al*, 2000; Kumar *et al*, 2000 and their arguments against a traditional market orientation approach. They instead suggest companies should be driving markets.

3 Galesic and Bosjnak, 2009; see also Söderlund, 1998. For a more general discussion on problems related to survey construction, see Biemer and Lyberg, 2003; Groves, 1987; Lyberg *et al*, 1997.

4 AutoIndex is Sweden's leading annual car owner/ship survey run by Vi Bilägare.

5 There is rich evidence from the industry on this, although there is a lack of knowledge about transfer pricing in many car dealerships. Numerous management accounting cases and exercises dealing with transfer pricing problems in car dealerships are available; see for example Nilsson *et al* (2011); Anthony and Govindarajan (2013).

6 When we collected empirical data for Nilsson *et al* (2011) across a broad range of industries, a clear pattern emerged: public sector representatives were discussing the pros and cons of their business models while for-profit companies consistently argued for the solutions they had decided on and implemented.

7 *Auto Express*, Special Issue, No 1275, 2013, p 53.

8 *auto motor & sport* Spezial, Wie gut sind Deutschlands Werkstätten, No 13/2013, 27 June.

9 *auto motor & sport* Spezial, Wie gut sind Deutschlands Werkstätten, No 13/2013, 27 June.

The car in the future

The strong criticism of the automotive industry for its lack of interest in 'green strategies', ie strategies that put sustainability, environmental concerns, etc as a top priority in the short as well as the long run, could be assumed to turn the attention of car makers and the car retail trade towards green issues. Increasingly, consumers ask for sustainable solutions and the negative image of cars in this respect means it will take a lot of effort from the car industry to gain a reputation of caring about the environment. This might be a huge business opportunity in the future. This chapter presents a number of smart, effective and sustainable ways to deal with current and future challenges and how the car can have a major role in the emerging society. For green strategies to succeed, they must be implemented all the way from car maker product strategies to the attitudes that customers encounter when they enter a showroom, as evidence from other industries shows. But it must not be the traditional car maker-controlled marketing channel that comes up with the most attractive green solution. Different scenarios about how consumers and the world around will respond are presented and the dialogue among stakeholders with an interest in the car and its future is painted in broad strokes.

Mobility in the future: sustainable and individual mobility

Understanding mobility and how to deal with traffic represent a great challenge for the development of future vehicles. Urbanization is likely to continue – studies on the preferences of young people in particular support such an assumption (Parment and Brorström, 2013), and there are few countries where urbanization is not manifest in the distribution of citizens.

There are numerous cities around the world with around 20 million or more inhabitants – Tokyo, Mexico City, New York, Seoul, Mumbai, Sao Paulo, Manila, Jakarta, Delhi and Shanghai – and traffic congestion and pollution are a problem. Improved fuel efficiency, start-stop systems and tougher emissions legislation all help – but traffic levels are increasing and pollution and congestion will be a serious problem in the foreseeable future. This is not only an issue for metro areas, but the challenges will be much tougher in big cities.

In Sao Paulo in Brazil, people are on average in traffic jams 27 days a year, and in Mexico City people travel on average two hours to work and two hours back home. Similar patterns emerge in metropolitan areas all over the world, and the implications are challenging: more people will live in city centres, which will increase crowding and the cost of living; parking will get more expensive and hence car sharing will become more attractive.

Improved technologies for sharing cars

Improved technologies for booking and sharing cars, particularly with smart phones, mean we'll see more car sharing in the future. Given other trends, eg less interest in owning a car and less focus on the car as a status symbol, there are signs that the interest in car sharing will increase. Each vehicle in a car-sharing scheme on average replaces eight privately owned cars and eliminates the need for nine parking places (Diem, 2013).

The mobility of the future demands a balance between global requirements and individual needs. There is great demand for new solutions for sustainable and individual mobility. Climate change, limited resources and growing urbanization strengthen many people's awareness of their social responsibility and their desire to organize their lives in a sustainable manner. A new consciousness about the premise of individual mobility will follow – and for young individuals it will be integrated into their way of thinking. Changes to infrastructure, limited space and environmental pollution necessitate new mobility solutions.

Dealers have to take an active part in shaping mobility for the future

In recent years there has been industry consolidation and centralization of fleet car sales, eg company cars, official cars, rental cars and pool cars, mostly bought from manufacturers and NSCs. For dealers this has meant that they are less involved and to the extent that they deliver cars they enjoy lower margins than they used to. Dealers can certainly buy these cars after the leasing contract runs out and make money from selling newish former fleet cars. However, even this business is threatened: some rental companies offer consumers a hand in specifying a new car and then sell it to them when the six- or nine-month rental period ends. Considering the enormous discounts that rental car companies enjoy, it may be a profitable option for the rental car company as well as the buyer. Car makers have the opportunity not to agree to rental car companies reselling cars this way but, given that there is oversupply in the market, do car manufacturers really want to stay out of the rental car business when rental car companies come up with innovative ideas? On the other hand, car makers have to make sure their dealers are profitable – if not, good dealers are likely to hand back the contract and start selling a brand that makes them more money.

Large multi-franchise dealer groups in particular have the opportunity to create their own initiatives, eg starting a multi-site car sharing business which, like rental car companies, doesn't guarantee a particular brand but access to cars of a particular size. Cars could then be bought from car makers or spot markets at high discounts. When car sharing grows, which is likely, the dealer derives first-mover advantages, such as having access to the best locations; having a large client base that may be used for other purposes, eg selling cars; market and negotiation power through being a large operator in the sharing business, etc.

Rental car companies have another advantage over national dealers (though not international dealerships): they can offer car sharing as a complement to their existing business model, thus increasing their market and negotiation power, and offer clients access to cars all over the world. That is, the sharing business is integrated with thousands of car rental sites in different countries. A good offer can be made to a client who lives in more than one place, eg in Zürich half of the year and in Sydney the other half, or a client whose need for a car varies over the course of a year: no need in the spring, a large car in the summer and occasional (car sharing) during the rest of the year.

When, in mature Western markets, younger people hear others, in particular celebrities, journalists, new venturists and politicians say, 'I don't have a car', 'I borrow my wife's/husband's when there is a need to', 'I have a Yaris Hybrid' etc, it helps the idea of car sharing and pooling gain a strong foothold in the market. Influential people are important to track since they have a strong influence on how larger groups of consumers will behave.

Technology integration

There is a challenge in loading cars with new technology and making it last. There is a high risk that buyers spend money on solutions that are dated a few years after the car was bought. 'I already pay my phone operator on a monthly basis to get internet access, navigation, music downloads... why should I pay for all this a second time?' The Mercedes A Class, introduced in 2012, proudly claims to 'put wheels on your iPhone'. However, assuming a car lasts for 15 to 20 years, there is little evidence the iPhone will remain a dominant design in years to come.

The self-driving car

The self-driving car will soon become a reality; in fact it already exists, but is only driven in tests on roads with limited complexity, eg on highways and race circuits. How it would work in urban settings is yet to be dealt with, and currently authorities don't allow self-driving cars. Through sensors, radars mounted in the bumpers, and cameras that work with a highly detailed GPS system, self-driving cars can steer, accelerate, brake, merge from slip roads and park. Urban driving, however, is very complex and it is unlikely there will be self-driving cars that can deal with all types of traffic situations before 2025.

Although the self-driving car may sound like a danger to traffic safety, it generates a number of advantages that taken together can contribute to creating a future where the car has a good reputation:

- Fewer traffic collisions – the autonomous system has higher reliability and lower reaction times than humans.
- Increased roadway capacity through improved ability to manage traffic flows.
- Lower emissions and improved fuel efficiency as a result of better traffic flows, less congestion and smoother journeys.
- Shorter distances between cars and higher speeds may be allowed so travel times will be shorter.
- The self-driving cars works even with impaired drivers.

It's unlikely that authorities will allow individuals without a driving licence to travel alone in self-driving cars in the near future, so the following advantages may not materialize until later:

- Alleviation of parking scarcity, as cars could drop off passengers, park far away where space is not scarce, and return as needed to pick up passengers.

- Reduction in the need for traffic police and vehicle insurance.

- Reduction of physical road signage: autonomous cars could receive necessary communication electronically – physical signs will be required as long as there are human drivers on roads.

Alternative fuels

There has been intensive debate over existing fuels – primarily petrol and diesel but also ethanol, extensively used in South America and to a more limited extent in North America and Scandinavia. There are arguments for and against different fuels. Diesel cars consume about 25 per cent less fuel than petrol cars, and CO_2 emissions are about 20 per cent lower (diesel has a slightly higher emission quota per litre); but diesel vehicles emit nitrogen dioxide. A London-based campaign group (Clean Air in London[1]) has produced a report, based on access to environmental information from 41,000 sections of road, which concludes that London has the highest NO_2 of all European capitals, and that diesel vehicles are 30 times more polluting than petrol ones. The effects of different fuels, however, are unclear and many research reports on the matter are based on assumptions that might be questioned.

By linking emissions to vehicle weight, there is a strong incentive to make safe and spacious vehicles that are environmentally friendly. However, the incentive to make cars lighter is thwarted by unintended consequences of environmental moves, as illustrated by Hyundai's strategy to meet emissions requirements in Sweden. Here, the heavier the car, the higher the CO_2 emissions allowed in defining a car as environmentally friendly; such a car brings tax benefits to the owner. Hence, to add weight, the i30 Business Eco now comes with a full-sized spare wheel, double boot floor and rear electric windows – and as a result the buyer enjoys a reduction in the yearly car tax.

Biofuels and bioethanol

Biofuels include fuels derived from biomass conversion, solid biomass, liquid fuels and various biogases. As they are derived from biological carbon fixation, they are based on renewable sources. Biofuels have gained increased public and scientific attention, driven by the search for renewability, the fear of oil price hikes, and a greater need for energy security. However, it has been widely questioned as to what extent biofuels address global warming concerns.

Bioethanol is an alcohol made by fermentation, mostly from carbohydrates produced in sugar or starch crops such as corn or sugarcane. Cellulosic biomass, derived from non-food sources such as trees and grasses, is also being developed as a feedstock for the production of ethanol. In the United States to some extent and even more in Brazil, bioethanol is used to reduce vehicle emissions. Cars that could be run on bioethanol can also be found in Germany or Sweden, but their percentage of the vehicle stock is low. In Europe, biodiesel is the most common biofuel. Biodiesel is usually used as an additive to reduce levels of particulates, carbon monoxide and hydrocarbons from diesel-powered vehicles. The International Energy Agency has a goal for biofuels to meet more than a quarter of world demand for transport fuels by 2050 to reduce dependence on petroleum and coal.

Discussions on the implications of a transition to biofuels are extensive and, as it is a complex matter, many types of arguments can be put forward. The main criticism is to do with the 'food or fuel' choice – the raw material used for bioethanol could be used for food by the many millions of people around the world without enough to eat. Critics argue, however, that it's populist to argue that by not using biofuel for cars, Africa's food problems could be solved. There is, as argued by critics, a complex set of mechanisms including corruption, war, lack of training and lack of democracy that must be solved.

Another criticism concerns the energy consumed in producing bioethanol. What's the point in transporting bioethanol from Brazil to northern Europe if doing so creates emissions that neutralize the vehicle emission advantage (Haschek, 2013)? A solution suggested by biofuel proponents is to use only raw material that can't be used for food. There are numerous reports and books written on alternative fuels and they are often based on strong preferences for one specific solution.

Electric cars

Numerous makers of electric cars have gone bankrupt. It's not a lack of good ideas; rather it's a combination of an immature industry, buyers who for good reasons are hesitant to buy an expensive car from a start-up company, and a lack of the financial muscle necessary to make investments in new technology that pay off after a couple of years.

Market penetration of electric cars is conditioned by the development of infrastructure. Danish-Israeli Better Place, bankrupt in May 2013, launched a business concept that would eliminate the problems associated with extensive charging times. A key challenge of the electric car – the lack of driving range – would be solved by the switchable battery launched by Better Place. However, for the advantage to materialize, an infrastructure with great market coverage has to be available. Assume a family go on holiday in the summer, travelling from Florida to Michigan or from the Netherlands to Spain, with a fully loaded car, at highway speeds and with extensive use of air conditioning. The journey cannot be undertaken unless there are battery switching stations and/or recharging points at a distance of 100 kms or less throughout the itinerary.

Beijing is one of the most populous cities in the world. With 21 million citizens and more than 5 million cars (2011; up from 2.1 million cars in 2004), traffic congestion and air pollution are severe problems. Electric cars could be part of a solution. Authorities plan 500,000 electric vehicles in 2015 and 5 million in 2020. But it will be difficult to produce such high volumes of electric cars, and buyers prefer hybrid cars, so the goal seems unrealistic (Hellmann, 2013). Obviously, the financial stimulus may be insufficient, and even though ownership and running costs are lower than for petrol or diesel cars, other purchase criteria such as car price (the higher price of an electric car would pay off after a couple of years), reliability, service network, etc count.

It's doubtful whether electric cars provide any significant improvement for the environment, particularly in countries like China where coal-fired power stations are the main means of generating the electricity necessary to run an electric car. In addition, resources needed to build and recycle an electric car are very significant so it may take many years until the sustainability calculation is positive.

Electric cars – a success in the oil country Norway

Norway, the rich Scandinavian oil country known for its fjords, black metal bands and A-ha (number one in the United Kingdom and in the United States in 1985!) could be expected to have access to more oil per capita (they are only 5 million inhabitants) than any other country north of the Gulf countries. Nonetheless, it has been very successful in implementing policies that stimulate the sale of electric cars. By June 2013, about 5,000 British-built Nissan Leaf cars had been sold in Norway, far better than the second best country, the UK, with close to 2,000 cars sold.

Car makers that offer electric cars – eg Nissan, Mitsubishi, Peugeot and Tesla – see the development in Norway as an indication of future market potential. However, public subsidies in Norway are about US$8,000 per car, a sum many nations can't afford. The car is not an attractive option for larger groups if market mechanisms determine demand – but through extensive state subsidiaries, free parking, free car tolls etc, sales can be boosted.

Future purchase criteria – the broader picture

A key question in the design of cars for the future should be what buyers, particularly younger buyers, will expect and want from cars. An interesting debate is going on in Germany on the lack of speed limits on some of the country's autobahns. A key part of German automobile culture is the opportunity to drive as fast as one wants. Thanks to high car standards, great lane discipline and drivers experienced in driving fast, the number of accidents is amongst the lowest in the world, despite the fact that it is not uncommon to be overtaken by a Volkswagen Passat or a Mercedes C Class driving at 220 km/h, loaded with kids and luggage for two weeks' holiday.

Winfried Hermann represents the Green Party (Bündnis 90/Die Grünen) and is an advocate of a general speed limit on the autobahn. The arguments Hermann puts forward largely represent what speed limit advocates suggest:[2]

- One person's freedom should not harm others and increase the risk of others. A speed limit would improve safety and make traffic flow more adapted to experienced as well as less experienced drivers. Speed limits – which may be dynamic with telematics techniques – create a better and more harmonic traffic flow.

- Less driver stress and increased safety: the number of accidents would decrease.

- Lower fuel consumption and fewer emissions, something that will improve earth quality for future generations. A 120 km/h speed limit would reduce emissions by 3.3 million tons CO_2 a year in Germany; as a comparison, rail cargo produces in total 2.4 million tons a year.

- The noise created by car traffic will decrease (120 km/h results in half the noise level compared to 160 km/h).

- A speed limit would make cars more fuel-efficient per se: downsizing would be encouraged. A car with a maximum speed of 160 km/h consumes one-third less fuel compared to a car with a 225 km/h speed limit.
- Germany is the only country in the Western world with no speed limit – does it really make sense?

Dr Andreas Scheuer belongs to CSU, the Christian Democrats, and is parliamentary state secretary at the Federal Ministry of Transport, Building and Urban Development and is coordinator for freight, transport and logistics. He sets out the following arguments against a general speed limit:

- German autobahns are very safe compared to other countries, and only 6.5 per cent of the accidents in Germany take place on highways although 30 per cent of the traffic is carried there. Most accidents on the autobahns happen at less than 130 km/h.
- Through dynamic speed limits, the number of accidents could be reduced further.
- High traffic density makes it increasingly difficult to drive very fast.
- Cars are getting safer.
- Through improved fuel efficiency and emission reductions, cars are getting more environmentally-friendly and hence a sustainable level of traffic could be reached.

Which argument will win in the long run? It is unlikely that young car buyers prefer the joy of driving fast to saving the environment for future generations. And it's indisputable that the trend towards more sustainable use of the car will continue.

Notes

1 Clean Air in London: www.cleanairinlondon.org/category/presentations, retrieved June 2013.

2 See *Auto Strassenverkehr*, No 8, 14 March 2012, pp 32–33: 'Pro und contra tempolimit': Winfried Hermann and Andreas Scheuer argue about speed limits.

REFERENCES

Aaker, D A (1991) *Managing Brand Equity: Capitalizing on the value of a brand name*, The Free Press, New York

Adams, T (2004) *I Huvudet på John McEnroe*, Norstedts, Stockholm

Ahlklo, J (2004) Hur allting blev design In Design Vad är det?, in (eds) M Malmstedt, K Ohlsson and U Rigstam, *Kulturmagasinet* Helsingborgs Museiförening, Helsingborg, pp 5–23

Alderson, W (1957) *Marketing Behaviour and Executive Action: A functionalistic approach to marketing theory*, Irwin Inc, Homewood, Ill

Altschuler, G C and Blumin, S M (2009) *The G I Bill: A new deal for veterans*, Oxford University Press, New York

Anthony, R N and Govindarajan, V (2013) *Management Control Systems*, 13th edn, Mac Graw Hill, New York

Aperia, T and Back, R (2004) *Brand Relations Management: Bridging the gap between brand promise and brand delivery*, Liber/Copenhagen Business School Press, Malmo

Bacchieri, G and Barros, A J D (2011) Traffic accidents in Brazil from 1998 to 2010: Many changes and few effects, *Revista de Saúde Pública*, **45** (5)

Baker, W E and Sinkula, J M (2007) Does market orientation facilitate balanced innovation programs? An organizational learning perspective, *The Journal of Product Innovation Management*, **24**, pp 316–34

Batra, R, Ramaswamy, V, Alden, D L, Steenkamp, J-B E M and Ramachander, S (2000) Effects of brand local and nonlocal origin on consumer attitudes in developing countries, *Journal of Consumer Psychology*, **9** (2), pp 83–95

Belz, F M (2001) *Integratives Öko-Marketing, Erfolgreiche Vermarktung von ökologischen*, Produkten und Leistungen Gabler, Wiesbaden

Bennett, R C and Cooper, R G (1981) The misuse of marketing: An American tragedy, *Business Horizons*, **24** (November–December), pp 51–61

Berger, M L (2001) *The Automobile in American History and Culture: A reference guide*, Greenwood Publishing, Chicago, Ill

Berry, B J L *et al* (1988) *Market Centers and Retail Location: Theory and applications*, Prentice Hall, New Jersey

Berthon, P, Hulbert, J M and Pitt, L F (1999) To Serve or to Create? ... Toward Customers and Innovation, *California Management Review*, **42** (Fall), pp 37–58

Biemer, P P and Lyberg, L E (2003) *Introduction to Survey Methodology*, Wiley Series in Survey Methodology, Wiley, New York

Bienkowski, W, Brada, J and Radlo, M-J (eds) (2006) *Reaganomics Goes Global. What can the EU, Russia and transition countries learn from the USA?*, Palgrave Macmillan, New York

Birkigt, K, Stadler, M M and Funck, H J (1992) *Corporate Identity, Grundlagen, Funktionen, Fallbeispiele*, Verlag Moderne Industrie, Landsberg/Lech

Bodisch, G R (2009) Economic effects of state bans on direct manufacturer sales to car buyers, Economic Analysis Group Competition Advocacy Paper, Antitrust Division, US Department of Justice, Washington, DC

Bondoux, F (2013) Luxury auto brands lead share of online search in Brazil, 9 April, Digital Luxury Group

Bound, J and Turner, S E (2002) Going to War and Going to College: Did World War II and the G I Bill Increase educational attainment for returning veterans?, *Journal of Labor Economics*, University of Chicago Press, **20** (4), pp 781–815

Bourdieu, P (1977a) Cultural reproduction and social reproduction, in (eds) J Karabel and A H Halsey, *Power and Ideology in Education*, Oxford University Press, New York

Bourdieu, P (1977b) *Reproduction in Education, Society, Culture*, Sage, Beverly Hills, CA

Bowersox, D J, Smykay, E W and La Londe, B J (1961) *Physical Distribution Management; Logistics problems of the firm*, Macmillan, New York

Bucklin, L P (1966) *A Theory of Distribution Channel Structure*, IBER Special Publications, New York

Bucklin, L P (1967) Postponement, speculation and structure of distribution channels, in (ed) B Blen, *The Marketing Channel: A conceptual viewpoint*, Wiley, New York

Buzzavo, L and Volpato, G (2001) *Car Distribution in Europe: Between vertical agreements and customer satisfaction*, Cockeas Research Network, Brussels

Castrogiovanni, G and Justis, R (1998) Franchising configurations and transitions, *Journal of Consumer Marketing*, **15** (2), pp 170–90

Christensen, C M and Bower, J L (1996) Customer power, strategic investment, and the failure of leading firms, *Strategic Management Journal*, **17** (3), pp 197–218

CIA World Factbook (2012) Central Intelligence Agency, Skyhorse Publishing, Washington, DC

Ciferri, L (2002) Building to order could save 99 Euros a car, *Automotive News Europe*, June, p 3

Cohen, M M (1994) Forgotten audiences in the passion pits: Drive-in theatres and changing spectator practices in post-war America, *Film History*, **6** (4), pp 470–86

Coughlan, A, Andersson, E, Stern, L and El-Ansary, A (2001) *Marketing Channels*, 6th edn, Prentice Hall, Upper Saddle River, NJ

Cremer, A and Schwartz, J (2013) VW's Audi swaps R&D chiefs as criticism grows: source, Reuters, US edition, 20 June

Cutler, S J (1977) Aging and voluntary association participation, *Journal of Gerontology*, **32**, 470–79

Dargay, J, Gately, D and Sommer, M (2007) *Vehicle Ownership and Income Growth, Worldwide: 1960–2030*, Department of Economics, New York University

Davis, B, Dutzik, T and Baxandall, P (2012) *Transportation and the New Generation: Why young people are driving less and what it means for transportation policy*, Frontier Group, US Pirg Education Foundation, Washington, DC

Dettmer, H William (1998) *Breaking the Constraints to World-Class Performance*, ASQ Quality Press, Milwaukee, WI

Diem, W (2013) Decline of car culture under scrutiny in France, *Wards Auto Europe*, 11 June

Dobers, P and Strannegård, L (2005) Design, lifestyles and sustainability aesthetic consumption in a world of abundance, *Business Strategy and the Environment*, **14**, pp 324–36

Duncan, T and Moriarty, S E (1997) *Driving Brand Value: Using integrated marketing to drive stakeholder relationships*, McGraw-Hill, New York

Dyson, P, Farr, A and Hollis, N S (1996) Understanding, measuring and using brand equity, *Journal of Advertising Research*, **36** (6), pp 9–21

Elenkov, D S (1997) Strategic uncertainty and environmental scanning: The case for institutional influences on scanning behavior, *Strategic Management Journal*, **18** (4), pp 287–302

EMCC (European Monitoring Centre on Change) (2004) *Trends and Drivers of Change in the European Automotive Industry: Mapping report*, European Foundation for the Improvement of Living and Working Conditions, Dublin

Evans, M M, Foxall, G and Jamal, A (2009) *Consumer Behaviour*, 2nd edn, Wiley, New York

Fahey, L (1981) Environmental scanning and forecasting in strategic planning – The state of the art, *Long Range Planning*, **14** (1), pp 32–39

Fahey, L and King, W R (1977) Environmental scanning for corporate planning, *Business Horizons*, August

Featherstone, M (1991) *Postmodernism and Consumer Culture*, Sage, London

Featherstone, M (2003) The body in consumer culture, in (eds) D B Clarke, M A Doel and M L Housiaux, *The Consumption Reader*, Routledge, New York, pp 164–67

Feathersone, M (2007) *Consumer Culture and Postmodernism*, Sage, London

Ferlie, E, Ashburner, L, Fitzgerald, L and Pettigrew, A (1996) *The New Public Management in Action*, Oxford University Press, Oxford

Fersainz, R (2013) El gran misterio de Seat En busca del último 600, *Auto Bild España*, **397**, pp 42–47

Flew, T (2002) Broadcasting and the social contract, in (ed) M Raboy, *Global Media Policy in the New Millennium*, University of Luton Press, Luton, pp 113–29

Fornell, C and Didow, N M (1980) Economic constraints on consumer complaining behavior, *Advances in Consumer Research*, 7, pp 318–23

Fornell, C and Wernerfelt, B (1987) Defensive marketing strategy by customer complaint management: A theoretical analysis, *Journal of Marketing Research*, 24 (4), pp 337–46

Foxall, G R and Goldsmith, R E (1989) Personality and consumer research: Another look, *Journal of Marketing Research*, 30, pp 111–25

Freeman, M A and Bordia, P (2001) Assessing alternative models of individualism and collectivism: A confirmatory factor analysis, *European Journal of Personality*, 15 (2), pp 105–21

Friedberg, A (2002) Urban mobility and cinematic visuality: the screens of Los Angeles – endless cinema or private telematics, *Journal of Visual Culture*, 1 (2), pp 183–204

Galesic, M and Bosjnak, M (2009) Effects of questionnaire length on participation and indicators of response quality in a web survey, *Public Opinion Quarterly*, 73 (2), pp 349–60

Garrie, C (2012) *Turning Green: How American car culture is influenced by advertising campaigns that market the appeal of sustainable transportation by targeting diverse demographic sectors. Case study: the Chevy Volt – legacy of the past or the ride of the future?*, University of California

Giucci, G (2012) *The Cultural Life of the Automobile: Roads to modernity*, University of Texas Press

Glenn, C A and Stuart, M L B (2009) *The GI Bill: A new deal for veterans*, Free Press, New York

Goldsmith, M, Ulrich, D and Rampersad, H K (2009) *Authentic Personal Branding: A new blueprint for building and aligning a powerful leadership brand*, Information Age Publishing, Greenwich

Govers, G and Go, F (2009) *Place Branding Glocal: Virtual and physical identities, constructed, imagined and experienced*, Palgrave MacMillan, New York

Gray, R and Bebbington, J (2001) *Accounting for the Environment*, 2nd edn, Sage, London

Greenberg, B, Watts, L S, Greenwald, R A, Reavley, G G, Alice, L, Beekman, S, Bucki, C, Ciabattari, M, Stoner, J C, Paino, T D, Mercier, L, Hunt, A, Hollaran, P C and Cohen, N (2008) *Social History of the United States*, ABC-CLIO, New York

Greenberg, M (2000) Branding cities: A social history of the urban lifestyle magazine, *Urban Affairs Review*, 36 (2), pp 228–63

Greimel, H (2013) Refining the Hyundai-Kia brand plan: Schreyer's vision – Look at function, not just design, *Automotive News*, 8 April

Grein, A F, Craig, C S and Takada, H (2001) Integration and responsiveness: Marketing strategies of Japanese and European automobile manufacturers, *Journal of International Marketing*, 9 (2), pp 19–50

Groves, R M (1987) Survey research as a methodology without a unifying theory, *Public Opinion Quarterly*, **51**, pp 156–72

Hambrick, D C (2006) Environmental scanning and organizational strategy, *Strategic Management Journal*, **3** (2), pp 159–74

Harquail, C (2006) Symbolizing identity: When brand icons become organizational icons, *Academy of Management Proceedings*, August, H1–H6

Hascheck, S (2012) Marken-Zeichen Best Brand Leserwahl 2012, *auto motor & sport*, **7**, pp 131–33

Haschek, B (2013) Ist biosprit nun gut oder schlecht?, *auto motor and sport*, **2**, pp 140–41

Haugland, S A (2010) The integration-responsiveness framework and subsidiary management: A commentary, *Journal of Business Research*, **63** (1), pp 94–96

Hellmann, N (2013) Wenig elektrofahrzeuge auf Chinas strassen, *Neue Züriche Zeirung, Wirtschaft*, 6 May, 103, p 20

Helmers, H O (1974) *Two Studies in Automobile Franchising*, Michigan Business Studies, Ann Arbor, MI

Heras, R G (1985) *Automotores norteamericanos, caminos y modernización urbana en la Argentina, 1918–1959*, Buenos Aires: Libros de Hispanoamérica

Hill, R (1970) *Family Development in Three Generations*, Schenkman Publishing, Cambridge, MA

Hoffmeister, M and Huneberg, R (1998) *Multi-Franchising – Developments and impact on sales channel management of automobile manufacturers*, Paper 1/98, International Car Distribution Programme, Chadwick

Holmes, J H and Crocker, K E (1987) Predispositions and the comparative effectiveness of rational, emotional and discrepant appeals for both high involvement and low involvement products, *Journal of the Academy of Marketing Science*, **15** (1), pp 27–35

Holt, D B (1997) Post-structuralist lifestyle analysis: Conceptualizing the social patterning of consumption in postmodernity, *Journal of Consumer Research*, **23**, pp 326–50

Holt, D B (2004) *How Brands Become Icons: The principles of cultural branding*, Harvard Business School Press, Cambridge MA

Homburg, C, Koschate, N and Hoyer, W D (2005) Do satisfied customers really pay more? A study of the relationship between customer satisfaction and willingness to pay, *Journal of Marketing*, **69**, pp 84–96

Hood, C (1995) The 'New Public Management' in the 1980s: Variations on a theme, *Accounting, Organisation and Society*, **20** (2/3), pp 93–109

Jackson, K T (1985) *Crabgrass Frontier: The suburbanization of the United States*, Oxford University Press, Oxford

Jain, S C (1984) Environmental scanning in US corporations, *Long Range Planning*, **17** (2), pp 117–28

Jaworski, B, Kohli, A K and Sahay, A (2000) Market-driven versus driving markets, *Journal of the Academy of Marketing Science*, **28** (1) pp 45–54

Jenkins, S (2006) *Thatcher and Sons: A revolution in three acts*, Allen Lane, London

Kadatz, H J (1977) *Peter Behrens – Architekt, Grafiker und Formgestalter 1868–1940*, Maler, Leipzig

Kapferer, J-N (1997) *Strategic Brand Management. Creating and sustaining brand equity long term*, 2nd edn, Kogan Page, London

Kapferer, J-N (2004) *The New Strategic Brand Management*, Kogan Page, London

Kapferer, J-N (2012) *The New Strategic Brand Management: Advanced insights and strategic thinking*, Kogan Page, London

Kay, J (1993) *Foundations of Corporate Success: How business strategies add value*, Oxford University Press, New York

Keller, K L (2003) *Strategic Brand Management: Building, measuring, and managing brand equity*, 2nd edn, Prentice Hall, Upper Saddle River, NJ

King, S (1984) *Developing New Brands*, 2nd edn, JWT, New York

Klaffke, M and Parment, A (2011) Herausforderungen und handlingsansätze für das personalmanagement von millennials, in (ed) M Klaffke, *BestPractice-Ansätze*, Gabler, Wiesbaden

Klein, N (2000) *No Logo: Taking aim at the brand bullies*, Fourth Estate, London

Kotler, P and Armstrong, L (2009) *Principles of Marketing*, 13th edn, Global edition, Pearson, London

Kotler, P and Armstrong, L (2013) *Principles of Marketing*, 15th edn, Prentice Hall, Maidenhead

Kotler, P, Armstrong, L and Parment, A (2011) *Principles of Marketing*, Swedish edition, Pearson, London

Kotler, P, Rackham, N and Krishnaswamy, S (2006) Ending the war between sales and marketing, *Harvard Business Review*, July–August

Kuhnimhof, T, Wirtz, M and Manz, W (2011) *Lower Incomes, More Students, Decrease of Car Travel by Men, More Multimodality: Decomposing young Germans' altered car use patterns*, Institute of Transport Studies, Karlsruhe

Kumar, N, Scheer, L and Kotler, P (2000) From market-driven to market driving, *European Management Journal*, 18 (2), pp 129–42

Lenz, R T and Engledow, J L (1986) Environmental analysis: The applicability of current theory, *Strategic Management Journal*, 7 (4), pp 329–46

Leonard, D and Rayport, J F (1997) Spark innovation through empathic design, *Harvard Business Review*, 75 (6), pp 102–13

Levitt, T (1960) Marketing myopia, *Journal of Marketing*, 38 (4) pp 45–56

LeVois, M, Nguyen, T D and Attkisson, C (1981) Artifact in client satisfaction assessment: Experience in community mental health settings, *Evaluation and Program Planning*, 4, April, pp 139–50

Litman, T (2012) *The Future Isn't What it Used to Be: Changing trends and their implications for transport planning*, Victoria Transport Policy Institute, Australia

LMC Automotive (2013) *Automotive Production Forecast*, www.lmc-auto.com, retrieved September 2013

Löfgren, O and Willim, R (eds) (2005) *Magic, Culture and the New Economy*, Berg Publishers, London

Loshin, D (2003) *Business Intelligence: The savvy manager's guide*, The Savvy Manager's Guides, Morgan Kaufmann, Berlin

Lutz, C and Fernandez, A L (2010) *Carjacked: The culture of the automobile and its effect on our lives*, Palgrave MacMillan, New York

Lyberg, L, Biemer, P, Collins, M, de Leeuw, E, Dippo, C, Schwarz, N and Trewin, D (1997) *Survey Measurement and Process Quality*, Wiley, New York

Lynn, G S, Morone, J G and Paulson, A S (1996) Marketing and discontinuous innovation: The probe and learn process, *California Management Review*, 38 (3), pp 8–37

MacDougall, E B and Campbell, C J (1995) *Rural Massachusetts: A statistical overview*, Center for Rural Massachusetts, Boston, MA

Mannheim, K (1952/1927) The problem of generations, in (ed) P Kecskemeti, *Essays on the Sociology of Knowledge*, pp 276–320, Oxford University Press, New York

Mathews, R (2013) Detroit bankrupt: To see Detroit's decline, look at 40 years of Federal policy, Polycymic.com, 18 July

Mau, B (ed) (2000) *Life Style*, Phaidon, New York

MCF Consultoria and GfK (2011) reported in Luxury auto brands lead share of online search in Brazil, *Luxury Society*, 2013

Meredith, G and Schewe, C (1994) The power of cohorts, *American Demographics*, 16 (12), pp 22–31

Merritt, P (1998) *Gendered Mobility: A study of women's and men's relations to automobility in Sweden*, Dept for Interdisciplinary Studies of the Human Condition, Goteborg

Moilanen, T and Rainisto, S (2009) *How to Brand Nations, Cities and Destinations: A planning book for place branding*, Palgrave MacMillan, New York

Morgan, N, Pritchard, A and Pride, R (2002) *Destination Branding: Creating the unique destination proposition*, Butterworth-Heinemann, Oxford

Motavalli, J (2013) Driving in America may have peaked in 2004, *New York Times*, Automobiles, 29 July

Neff, J (2010) Is digital revolution driving decline in US car culture? Shift toward fewer young drivers could have repercussions for all marketers, *Ad Age*, 31 May

Nilsson, F, Olve, N-G and Parment, A (2011) *Controlling for Competitiveness*, Copenhagen Business School Press, Copenhagen

Niskanen, W A (1988) *Reaganomics: An insider's account of the policies and the people*, Oxford University Press, Oxford

Ofir, C and Simonson, I (2001) In search of negative customer feedback: The effect of expecting to evaluate on satisfaction evaluations, *Journal of Marketing Research*, 38, May, pp 170–82

Ortiz, S R (2013) *Beyond the Bonus March and GI Bill: How veteran politics shaped the New Deal era*, Yale University Press, Cambridge, MA

Park, H-J, Rabolt, N J and Jeon, K S (2008) Purchasing global luxury brands among young Korean consumers, *Journal of Fashion Marketing and Management*, **12** (2), pp 244–59

Parment, A (2008) Distribution strategies for volume and premium brands in highly competitive consumer markets, *Journal of Retailing and Consumer Services*, **15**, pp 250–65

Parment, A (2009) Automobile Marketing Distribution Strategies for Competitiveness: An analysis of four distribution configurations, VDM Verlag, Berlin

Parment, A (2010) *Det här måste du också veta om marknads föring*, Wiesbaden: Springer

Parment, A (2011a) *Generation Y in Consumer and Labour Markets*, Routledge, London

Parment, A (2011b) The Car Dealership – A Great Workplace for the Next Generation? Speech for Nordic Automotive Dealerships, Visby, 15 June

Parment, A (2013) Generation Y vs Baby Boomers: Shopping behaviour, buyer involvement and implications for retailing, *Journal of Retailing and Consumer Services*, **20** (2), pp 189–99

Parment, A (2013b) *Generation Y: Mitarbeiter der Zukunft Hotivieren, integrieren, führen*, Wiesbaden: Springer

Parment, A and Brorström, S (2013) Constituents of Place Attractiveness among Generation Y Citizens, Place Management and Place Branding Conference, Manchester Metropolitan University, 14–15 February

Parment, A and Dyhre, A (2009) *Sustainable Employer Branding, Guidelines, Worktools and Best Practices*, Samfundslitteratur, Oslo

Parment, A and Söderlund, M (2010) *Det här Måste du Också veta om Marknadsföring*, Liber, Malmö

Peppers, D, Rogers, M and Dorf, B (1999) Is your company ready for one-to-one marketing?, *Harvard Business Review*, Jan–Feb, pp 151–60

Peterson, R A and Wilson, W R (1992) Measuring customer satisfaction: Fact and artifact, *Journal of the Academy of Marketing Science*, **20** (1), pp 61–71

Porter, M (1980) *Competitive Strategy: Techniques for analysing industries and competitors*, Free Press, New York

Porter, M (1990) *The Competitive Advantage of Nations*, Free Press, New York

Pratten, C F (1987) Mrs Thatcher's economic legacy, in (eds) K Minogue and M Biddiss, *Thatcherism: Personality and politics*, pp 72–94, Macmillan, Basingstoke

Purkiss, J and Royston-Lee, D (2009) *Brand You: Turn your unique talents into a winning formula*, Artesian Publishing, London

Quick, B (2012) Car salesmen: Still sexist, still stupid, *CNN Money Fortune*, 12 February

Rafaeli, A and Pratt, M G (1993) Tailored meanings: On the meaning and impact of organizational dress, *Academy of Management Review*, **18** (1), pp 32–55

Rafer, M R (1997) *Dealer-Manufacturer Relationships in the UK Motor Industry*, Research Paper 6/97, International Car Distribution Programme, Chadwick

Rainisto, S (2009) *Place Marketing and Branding: Success factors and best practices*, LAP Lambert Academic Publishing, London

Rentz, J O, Reynolds, F D and Stout, R G (1983) Analyzing changing consumption patterns with cohort analysis, *Journal of Marketing Research*, February, pp 12–20

Rieger, B (2013) *The People's Car: A global history of the Volkswagen Beetle*, Harvard University Press, Cambridge, MA

Rifkin, J (2000) *The Age of Access: The new culture of hypercapitalism, where all of life is a paid-for experience*, Penguin Putnam, New York

Rigby, D K, Reichheld, F F and Schefter, P (2002) Avoid the four perils of CRM, *Harvard Business Review*, Feb, pp 101–18

Ritzén, S (2000) Integrating Environmental Aspects into Product Development Proactive Measures, doctoral thesis TRITA-MMK, 2000:6 KTH – Royal Institute of Technology Department of Machine Design: Stockholm

Rogler, L H (2002) Historical generations and psychology: The case of the Great Depression and World War II, *The American Psychologist*, **57** (12), 1013–23

Rogler, L H and Cooney, R S (1984) *Puerto Rican Families in New York City: Intergenerational processes*, Waterfront Press, Maplewood, NJ

Rosengarten, P G and Stürmer, C B (2005) *Premium Power: Das Geheimnis des Erfolgs von Mercedes-Benz, BMW, Porsche und Audi*, Wiley & Sons

Rosin, F (2012) Was taugt die Werkstatt aus der Auktion?, *AutoBild Klassik*, 4, pp 134–5

Roth, K and Morrison, A J (1990) An empirical analysis of the integration-responsiveness framework in global industries, *Journal of International Business Studies*, **21**, 541–64

Rotschild, M L (1979) Advertising strategies for high and low involvement situations, in (eds) J Maloney and B Silverman, *Attitude Research Plays for High Stakes*, pp 74–93, American Marketing Association, Chicago, IL

Ryback, T W (2008) *Hitler's Private Library: The books that shaped his life*, p 69, Knopf, New York

Ryder, N B (1965) The cohort as a concept in the study of social change, *American Sociological Review*, **30** (6), pp 843–61

Sala-I-Martin, X, Blanke, J, Drzeniek Hanouz, M, Geiger, T and Mia, I (2009) The Global Competitiveness Index (2009–2010): Contributing to long-term prosperity amid the global economic crisis, *The Global Competitiveness Report*, World Economic Forum, Geneva

Salzer, M (1994) Identity Across Borders – A study of the Ikea world, Doctoral dissertation, Department of Management and Economics, Linköping University

Salzer-Mörling, M and Strannegård, L (2004) Silence of the brands, *European Journal of Marketing*, 38 (1/2), pp 224–38

Sandqvist, K (1997) *The Appeal of Automobiles: Human desires and the proliferation of cars*, Environmental Strategies Research Group and Stockholm Institute of Education, Report 1997:21

Scherer, F M (1996) *Industry Structure, Strategy, and Public Policy*, HarperCollins College Publishers, Harvard, MA

Schewe, C D, Debevec, K, Madden, T J, Diamond, W D, Parment, A and Murph, A (2013) If you've seen one, you've seen them all! Are young Millennials the same worldwide?, *Journal of International Consumer Marketing*, 25 (1), pp 3–15

Schimmack, U, Oishi, S and Diener, E (2005) Individualism: A valid and important dimension of cultural differences between nations, *Personality and Social Psychology Review*, 9 (1), pp 17–31

Schindehutte, M, Morris, M M and Kocak, A (2008) Understanding market-driving behavior: The role of entrepreneurship, *Journal of Small Business Management*, 48 (1), pp 4–26

Schmitt, A and Simonson, B H (1997) *Marketing Aesthetics: The strategic management of brands, identity and image*, Free Press, New York

Schroeder, J E (2002) *Visual Consumption: Interpretative marketing studies*, Routledge, London

Scott, R E (2011) *Heading South. US-Mexico trade and job displacement after NAFTA*, EPI Briefing Paper, No 308

Seiler, C (2008) *Republic of Drivers: A cultural history of automobility in America*, University of Chicago Press, Chicago, IL

Silverstein, M J and Fiske, N (2003) Luxury for the masses, *Harvard Business Review*, April, pp 48–57

Sivak, M and Schoettle, B (2011) *Recent Changes in the Age Composition of Drivers in 15 Countries*, University of Michigan Transportation Research Institute, Chicago, IL

Skidelsky, R (ed) (1988) *Thatcherism*, Chatto and Windus, London

Snyder, J (2011) No new cars, but that didn't stop US automakers and dealers during WWII, *Automotive News*, October 31st

Söderlund, M (1998) Customer satisfaction and its consequences on customer behaviour revisited. The impact of different levels of satisfaction on word-of-mouth, feedback to the supplier and loyalty, *International Journal of Service Industry Management*, 9 (2), pp 169–88

Söderlund, M and Rosengren, S (2010) The happy versus unhappy service worker in the service encounter: Assessing the impact on customer satisfaction, *Journal of Retailing and Consumer Services*, 17 (2), pp 161–69

Solér, C (1996) Ecologically friendly buying – theoretical implications of a phenomenological perspective, *Scandinavian Journal of Management*, **12** (3), pp 275–89

Southerton, D (2012) Consumption, *British Sociological Association Online*, Sage, London

Spender, J D and Grevesen, W (1999) The multinational enterprise as a loosely coupled system: The global integration-local responsiveness dilemma, *Managerial Finance*, **25** (2), pp 63–84

Spillane, M (2000) *Branding Yourself: How to look, sound and behave your way to success*, Sidgwick and Jackson, London

Stocker, F (2012) Manager im Ruhestand treiben Hauspreise Luxus-Neubauprojekte in den Innenstädten verteuern zunehmend auch Wohnraum in der Umgebung, *Die Welt Finanzen*, p 17

Stubbart, C (1982) Are environmental scanning units effective?, *Long Range Planning*, **15** (3), pp 139–45

Sudman, S (1967) *Reducing the Cost of Surveys*, Aldine, Chicago, IL

Tauber, E M (1974) How market research discourages major innovations, *Business Horizons*, June, pp 22–26

The Economist (2012) Two ways to make a car, 10 March

Thomas, P S (1980) Environmental scanning: The state of the art, *Long Range Planning*, **13** (1), pp 20–28

Triandis, H C (1993) Collectivism and individualism as cultural syndromes, *Cross-Cultural Research*, **27** (3–4), pp 155–80

Vickers, A, Bavister, S and Smith, J (2008) *Personal Impact: What it takes to make a difference*, Prentice Hall Life, Harlow

Vinen, R (2009) *Thatcher's Britain: The politics and social upheaval of the 1980s*, Simon and Schuster, London

Weingroff, R F (2000) The genie in the bottle: The interstate system and urban problems, 1939–1957, *Public Roads*, **64** (2)

Whiteman, J (ed) (2000) *Fulfilling the Promise: What future for franchised car distribution?*, International Car Distribution Programme, Chadwick

Wileman, A and Jary, M (1997) *Retail Power Plays: From trading to brand leadership*, London: MacMillan Business, New York

Wilson, J S and Blumenthal, I (2008) *Managing Brand You: Seven steps to creating your most successful self*, American Management Association, New York

Winter, S G and Szulanski, G (2001) Replication as strategy, *Organization Science*, **12** (6), pp 730–43

Wittreich, W J (1962) Misunderstanding the retailer, *Harvard Business Review*, **40**, May–June pp 147–59

Wood, E M (1991) *The Pristine Culture of Capitalism: A historical essay on old regimes and modern states*, Verso, London

World Bank (2009) *Figures from the World Bank*, data.worldbank.org

Yasai-Ardekani, M and Nystrom, P C (1996) Designs for environmental scanning systems: tests of a contingency theory, *Management Science*, **42** (2), pp 187–204

Zhou, L and Hui, M K (2003) Symbolic value of foreign products in the People's Republic of China, *Journal of International Marketing*, **11** (2), pp 36–58

Zimmerman, M (1990) *Heidegger's Confrontation with Modernity*, Indiana University Press, Bloomington, IN

INDEX

NB: page numbers in *italic* indicate figures

CPSIA information can be obtained at www.ICGtesting.com
Printed in the USA
BVOW04s0325161213

338870BV00011B/3/P